SOCIOLOGICAL PARADIGMS AND HUMAN RESOURCES

*In memory of my father
an excellent teacher*

Sociological Paradigms and Human Resources

An African context

KEN N. KAMOCHE
City University of Hong Kong and
University of Birmingham, UK

Routledge
Taylor & Francis Group

LONDON AND NEW YORK

First published 2000 by Ashgate Publishing

Reissued 2019 by Routledge
2 Park Square, Milton Park, Abingdon, Oxon, OXl 4 4RN
52 Vanderbilt Avenue, New York, NY 10017

Routledge is an imprint of the Taylor & Francis Group, an informa business

Publisher's Note
The publisher has gone to great lengths to ensure the quality of this reprint but points out that some imperfections in the original copies may be apparent.

Disclaimer
The publisher has made every effort to trace copyright holders and welcomes correspondence from those they have been unable to contact.

A Library of Congress record exists under LC control number:

ISBN 13: 978-1-138-71702-2 (hbk)
ISBN 13: 978-1-138-71701-5 (pbk)
ISBN 13: 978-1-315-19673-2 (ebk)

Contents

List of Figures

List of Tables

Acknowledgements

This book would never have seen the light of day were it not for the guidance and support of many people. Regrettably, it is impossible to mention them all by name. My first debt of gratitude is to the managers in Nairobi who participated in the interviews and the employees for their generosity. I am grateful to the staff and fellows at Templeton College, Oxford University for their support and guidance, in particular Nick Woodward, John Purcell and Rosemary Stewart. Rod Martin and the late Dan Gowler deserve special acknowledgement for their excellent supervision. Arthur Marsh, Rom Harre, Lord McCarthy and Gavin Williams made a significant contribution with their comments and suggestions on various sections of the earlier thesis. I would also like to thank Peter Blunt, Tony Watson and Jid Kamoche. I owe all my family a special "thank you" for their continued support, patience and understanding. I am also grateful to the editorial staff at Ashgate. I would like to acknowledge with thanks the financial support from the Rhodes Trust, St Catherine's College, Templeton College, Oxford University and the Africa Educational Trust.

Finally, I wish to thank the following for permission to reproduce copyright material: Ashgate for Figs 1.1 and 3.1, from G. Burrell and G. Morgan's (B/M) (1979) *Paradigms of Sociological Analysis;* Elsevier Science for Fig 1 and excerpts from K. Kamoche's (1997) "Managing human resources in Africa: Strategic, organizational and epistemological issues", in *International Business Review,* vol.6, no.5, pp. 537-558; Plenum Publishing for excerpts from K. Kamoche's (1995) "Rhetoric, ritualism and totemism in human resource management" in *Human Relations,* vol.48, no.4, pp. 367-385; JAI Press for excerpts from K. Kamoche's "Toward a model of HRM in Africa", in Shaw et al (1993), *Research in Personnel and Human Resource Management,* pp. 259-278; Routledge for Tables 4 and 5 and excerpts from K. Kamoche's (1992) "Human resource management: an assessment of the Kenyan case", in *International Journal of Human Resource Management,* vol.3, no. 3, pp. 497-521.

Ken N. Kamoche
July 1999
Hong Kong

1 Introduction

In the last fifteen or so years, there has been a lot of interest in the subject of human resource management (HRM). This interest has been most intense in America and Europe where arguably, the seeds of contemporary HRM were first sown. Increasingly, attention has shifted to other parts of the world such as Asia. Africa has largely been ignored in these efforts. Granted, there have been a number of books focusing on developing countries which include reference to some African countries or cases (eg Jaeger and Kanungo, 1990; Kiggundu, 1989). However, there still remains a large gap in the international management field, as far as Africa is concerned. Blunt and Jones' (1992) book marked an important turning point, but one which, to the best of my knowledge, has not been taken any further by other researchers. There have, of course been some important contributions in various journals but a lot remains to be done. It is in this regard that this book is being offered.

This chapter is organized into three parts: the first part provides a background to the research by introducing the three key themes HRM, the paradigm debate and the Kenyan context. The second part covers the actual research process, ie the methodology and the difficulties associated with conducting research in a developing country context. The final part gives a general overview of the rest of the chapters.

Part One

The Author's Interest in the Subject

This book is the result of a decade-long effort to come to grips with the nature of management in Africa and to seek to understand how best to tackle the challenges of managing people on the continent. This effort has focused largely on Kenya, the country I am most familiar with, having been born and raised there. However, the insights yielded here have an important resonance with much of the rest of Africa, and these will be highlighted here. My first real attempt to explore these issues was during my graduate studies at Oxford University, starting with my MPhil. thesis

(Kamoche, 1990). My concern at that stage was firstly, to explore a terrain that had received little attention in the literature, and which had also tended to be treated as a low-priority organizational function: the management of employees. Organizations in Kenya have over the years defined their agenda strictly within the narrow confines of short-term productivity and profitability. The market/cost imperative has resulted in a preoccupation to minimize costs, adopt the "appropriate" technology, and increase market share. These efforts have not always paid sufficient attention to the needs of employees, nor have managers shown a great deal of interest in the implications of these strategic decisions on the management of people.

It was this state of affairs that prompted me to assess the nature of the Kenyan firms' employment practices in order to determine how they could be improved or altered to suit the needs of those most affected by them while at the same time meeting strategic objectives. The second objective of that earlier study was to find out what lessons a Japanese approach might offer to Kenyan firms. This involved travelling to Japan to interview executives of 13 of Japan's largest and most successful enterprises (selected from car-assembly, electronic, trading, construction, engineering and other major sectors) to try to understand the nature of *nihonteki keiei* (Japanese management). Fourteen Kenyan firms were also visited. The research found that while there was certainly a lot that Kenyan managers could learn from their Japanese counterparts, the transferability of Japanese practices was mediated by various cultural, technological and economic factors.

Eventually, I decided to focus more attention on the management practices of the Kenyan companies, and to look critically at the "Western" model because many firms that are beginning to adopt contemporary HRM are controlled by foreign, "Western" interests. The dearth of published work on the management of employees in Kenya also stimulated this research and it was hoped that the doctoral thesis (Kamoche, 1992) from which this book is derived would help to fill this gap. Thus, the doctoral research expanded the conceptual scope of the earlier study and involved a more incisive analysis of the nature of employment practices and the possible significance of these to theorists and practitioners.

What is HRM?

As noted above, there is evidence to suggest that the personnel function has been treated as relatively less important both in the literature and in practice, yet Kenyan organizations, like many others elsewhere, often proclaim that employees are their most important asset. The orthodox thinking seems to be that even in those companies with a well-developed personnel function and "progressive" HR initiatives, the commitment to develop such practices as recruitment, development and retention of staff is very much driven by the pressure for organizational performance. Such pressures have intensified in the 1990s, an era of major political change which saw the end of one-party rule, unprecedented economic malaise resulting from institutionalised corruption and political ineptitude, and a gradual deterioration in living standards. At the level of business, Kenyan industries which previously operated in a fairly protected environment have been hit hard by the economic liberalization which has resulted in more exposure to the turbulent world economy including the recession and massive direct imports of cheap foreign products. Against this background, the pursuit of personnel practices on a relatively informal and even *ad hoc* basis is clearly inappropriate in a country with high unemployment and an insufficiently skilled labour force.

Problems in the management of employees are further complicated by diverse socio-cultural and politico-economic considerations which are characteristic of a developing country. Foreign capital has continued to dominate the private sector, and not surprisingly, many of the changes in management style and approach have emanated from abroad. However, some of the practices that foreign firms have introduced have been at variance with existing socio-cultural circumstances, and are to this extent, inappropriate. It has therefore been found necessary here to characterize the context within which organizations are operating. This is essential because management is a socio-cultural phenomenon and not merely a set of universal practices which can be transferred with relative ease across cultures and different organizations. Kenyan managers and policy makers have keenly embraced foreign ideas and treated them as a necessary ingredient in economic success just because they are perceived to have "worked" in the West. It is argued here that the choice of management approach must give regard to clearly-defined situational circumstances.

The second major objective is the quest for clarity in the nature of the employment practices in question. Since the late 1980s, there has been a trend to replace the term "personnel" with "human resource management". Much of the impetus behind this trend is traceable to the parent companies abroad. A fundamental issue in the search for clarity is one of definition: what *is* HRM? A review of the contemporary literature on HRM reveals that it continues to be characterized by ambiguity and controversy both in theory and practice. Views vary as to the distinctiveness of HRM vis-a-vis traditional personnel management so-called. In some quarters, the arrival of HRM has been heralded as a great development in enlightened management. The more cautious see it as no more than an elaboration of the more familiar personnel approach, while to the more critical, it signifies a more subtle form of labour regulation and control. I have sought conceptual clarity by an examination of the main concerns of HRM as they emerged in the 1980s. In this regard I have adopted the key features of Guest's (1987) theoretical construct. In this discussion I have attempted to go beyond the normative-prescriptive level at which the model was initially fashioned, and the conceptual-analytical level as in Legge (1995). I have proceeded to apply the model at the empirical level to query the nature of HR practices in five organizations.

Multi-Paradigm Analysis

It is further recognized here that our views about the social world are predicated on certain fundamental assumptions we hold about the social world and how it should be apprehended. In this regard, I have adopted Burrell and Morgan's (1979) paradigms of sociological analysis to address HRM by commencing from an awareness of these fundamental assumptions. The framework is appropriate for our purposes here because it presents a very comprehensive survey of the basis of knowledge in the social sciences. It attempts to reach beneath the surface of social phenomena and discover how various forms of knowledge have come to be constituted in the realm of social enquiry. The framework enables us to examine the subject from four points of view. By varying the underlying assumptions, the *paradigmatic lenses* bring a different "picture" of HRM into focus. Moving from one paradigmatic frame to another thus enables the social theorist to define his subject of enquiry within the context of that paradigm, applying the language, concepts and tools of analysis appropriate for the paradigm in question.

It is posited here that much of the existing work on HRM, following in the tradition of other organizational research, has taken place within the functionalist paradigm. In sociological theory, functionalism is guided by the notion of purposive rationality in its quest for rational explanations for social phenomena. Its definitive concern is to find "practical solutions" for "practical problems". Thus it holds a distinct appeal for managers.

Similarly, organizational researchers have also found themselves drawn to functionalist analyses, thus helping to sustain functionalism as a dominant orthodoxy. There is a danger, however, that this dominance could lead to a one-sided and *ipso facto*, impoverished view of organizational phenomena.

The multi-paradigmatic approach adopted here therefore challenges this dominant orthodoxy and more importantly, seeks to explore the rich terrain that organizational theorists have tended to ignore, and thus enrich our understanding of the nature of HRM. Rather then merely offering contrasting images of HRM, we aim to demonstrate that the dominant orthodoxy, however useful, is merely one way of conceptualizing the phenomenon. This "monocular" approach is to a large extent responsible for the muddled conception of contemporary HRM; also, it is not well equipped to handle the very complex issues associated with managing people. The other three paradigms are offered, not merely as alternatives to the orthodoxy, but as additional "ways of seeing". The multi-paradigmatic approach therefore enables us to cross disciplinary borders and effectively draw from relevant literature from other disciplines.

In a nutshell, the purpose of this discussion is as follows: to seek conceptual clarity into the nature of HRM by adopting a multi-paradigmatic analysis to characterize the taken-for-granted normative aspects of HRM and what purposes it serves (functionalism), to understand its "hidden meanings" (interpretivism) and to discover whose interests it serves (radical critique). The use of Kenyan data to illustrate the above allows us to pursue the HRM debate from a fresh international angle.

Some Comments on the Kenyan Economy

Agriculture has traditionally been the mainstay of the Kenyan economy, accounting for over 30% of GDP. However, due to the slow growth or decline of agricultural export commodity prices and high prices of manufactured goods and crude petroleum, the terms of trade have declined over time, as illustrated in Table 1.1. A number of factors have combined to place adverse pressure on the economy. These include: extreme weather conditions fluctuating from prolonged drought to devastating floods leading to reduced agricultural output; political uncertainty; falling donor funding in the wake of widespread corruption and human rights abuses; deteriorating terms of trade; high inflation; the depreciation of the Kenyan shilling against major currencies; high unemployment (45%); a high external debt which stood at about $6.5bn in 1998 and a population growth rate of 2.5%. In the 1980s, tourism overtook coffee and tea to become the main source of foreign exchange. Currently, horticulture is the leading foreign exchange earner. In the mid-1990s, the tourist industry faced stiff competition from emerging Eastern European economies, and also from the opening up of post-apartheid South Africa. Security concerns and the deterioration of facilities and infrastructure have hampered recovery.

The country has seen renewed agricultural output in the late 1990s; for example in 1996 Kenya became the leading exporter of tea, surpassing Sri Lanka and India. Industry has traditionally been based on import substitution, but over the years, the manufacturing base has been strengthened to some extent. This has however, come under pressure from import liberalization where cheaper imports are competing for a relatively small local market. The population is currently estimated at about 30m. The only viable option left appears to be to manufacture for export. In this regard, there has been an export-campaign, including the setting up of manufacturing-under-bond systems and export processing zones, foreign exchange and trade liberalization, and some efforts toward privatization.

Part Two

Methodology

This section describes how the relevant research material (theoretical and empirical) has been collected, analysed and presented. The problems encountered in the exercise are also discussed.

The initial process involved an extensive review of the literature in the three key themes: HRM, sociological paradigms and management in Kenya. The first two were both exciting and presented no particular problem. Literature on management in Kenya was much harder to come by. Extensive searches in British and Kenyan libraries yielded very little relevant and/or useful literature on management in Africa in general. This was a blessing in disguise because it offered the opportunity to make a substantial contribution. Discussions with colleagues in various institutions in Britain, Africa, the United States and Australia helped me to refine my ideas and the research design. The ideas themselves went through a number of modifications - each day, every seminar/discussion brought new

Table 1.1 Kenya: Some economic indicators

Terms of trade[1]	1982	1983	1984	1985	1986	1987	1988	1989	1990	1991	1992	1993	1994	1995	1996	1997
All items	100	94	110	92	103	85	88	79	71	82	79	90	101	96	93	102
Non-oil items	100	88	108	87	93	75	79	70	62	71	71	81	91	96	95	108
GDP % growth rate[2]	3.0	3.1	3.7	4.9	5.5	4.9	5.2	4.9	4.5	2.1	0.5	0.2	3.0	4.8	4.6	2.3
Growth in Manufacturing	2.7	4.5	4.3	4.6	5.9	5.7	6.0	5.9	5.3	3.8	1.2	1.8	1.9	3.9	3.7	1.9
Inflation	20.5	11.5	10.2	13.0	3.9	5.2	8.3	9.8	11.8	19.6	27.3	46.0	28.8	16.0	9.0	11.2

Source: Economic Survey, various issues

insights which continued to open up new avenues for further research.

As noted above the initial research data comprise 14 Kenyan companies selected to cover a wide range of industries, from construction and engineering to consumer products, publishing, the hotel industry, chemical products, agro-industry and vehicle assembling. Out of these fourteen, 5 were eventually selected for more detailed study. In addition to the diversity in employment approaches these firms offered, the question of access was also vital in the selection. For instance, a consumer products company which had provisionally agreed to participate later refused to cooperate. This company had been identified in the previous survey to have a very "enlightened" HRM approach and would have constituted an interesting case for further research. An important reason for selecting the agro-industrial firm was because of the importance of agriculture in the Kenyan economy. An oil company considered to be at the leading edge of HRM decided, in the course of the research to scale down the amount of access that had earlier been granted, resulting in only a few meetings with the HR Manager. This yielded sketchy data and this case study was abandoned. Out of the five eventually selected, three appeared to have adopted a contemporary HRM approach to various degree; the other two formed an interesting contrast.

The first part of the research was carried out in 1989. At this stage the study was conducted mainly through interviewing senior officials in Personnel with the purpose of understanding their policy with respect to Personnel/HRM. These managers thereafter arranged for me to meet other managers in Personnel and other departments who provided more detailed information and other relevant data. Much of the empirical data for this study was collected in 1990/91. This took the form of initial interviews with senior Personnel/HR executives (Managers and/or Directors). The interviews were based on a semi-structured questionnaire, which was refined and elaborated after the 1989 project. Blunt (1983) notes that in the African context respondents feel uncomfortable with an overly formal approach especially because the old resent being questioned by younger people. According to this argument, the semi-structured or totally unstructured conversation allows the manager to "pass on" his experience/wisdom. This approach provided a basic structure while retaining the texture of a more flexible conversation thus allowing interviewees the latitude to furnish data that would not otherwise have been anticipated. It is also very important to build trust over a period of time.

The initial interview with the senior executive concentrated on issues like strategy or policy formulation, the role of the Personnel function in the overall organizational structure, management's views about HRM and the extent to which contemporary HRM was being implemented, if at all. This initial interview lasted an hour to an hour and a half. In the course of the time spent at each company, however, it was possible to speak to these informants again whenever necessary. Most of the rest of the research was conducted in the Personnel/HR department where relevant documents were examined with the help of employees. This enabled certain factual data to be checked against the views expressed in the main interviews.

Interviews were also held with managers in other departments, eg Training, Production and Marketing. In this way, it was possible to corroborate data. A "snowball sampling" approach was found expedient, whereby the key informants referred me to colleagues. Depending on accessibility, I allowed about 7-10 days at each firm. It often proved necessary, however, to make subsequent visits. I kept in touch with the managers for about a year to seek additional data and clarification. This brought the study closer to a longitudinal analysis rather than a static group comparison as at a point in time (eg Bulmer, 1977). Research was also carried out at the Ministry of Labour, including interviews with senior labour economists.

It was decided to structure the analysis on the basis of two key strands which were considered central to HRM: selection/recruitment and training/development. The Kenyan case problematizes selection in so far as various difficulties surrounding selection/recruitment were identified in the first study. These evolve around the high unemployment arising from slow industrial growth, and the concomitant high pressure on the few available opportunities. Inadequate commitment to training is a common feature in industry as a whole, which raises problems about the degree of competence-creation and the adequacy of existing skills for the challenge of national development.

Background Information about the Firms

Table 1.2 provides a summary of the case studies. The firms are discussed in more detail below.[3] The names have been disguised for confidentiality.

Table 1.2 A brief profile of the firms

Company	Size (No. of employees)	Employment practice
Autoco	395	Strong evidence of modern HRM, both in practice and language use.
Pharmaco	300	Evidence of a deliberate shift towards HRM, with a focus on training. The term HRD is preferred.
Mimea	23000	HRM mainly for management cadres, pursued in conjunction with TQM.
Chematox	186	"Traditional" personnel ethos.
Automart	649	"Traditional" personnel ethos.

As for unionisable staff, union membership was found to be very high. This is illustrated in Table 1.3.

Table 1.3 Union density

Company	Unionisable	actual %
Autoco	227	53.7%
Pharmaco	180	90.0%
Mimea	Approx 20000	*
Chematox	106	64.0%
Automart	363	90.0%

* No specific records of paid-up members are maintained, but management believes that the check-off system covers almost all workers.

The check-off system explains the high average density which is way above the national figure of 35%. Managers reported that workers, in their ignorance, tend to assume that union membership is a statutory requirement, especially when they are issued with check-off forms at recruitment. As a result, the awe and fear of officialdom associated with the act of "filling forms" gives a false impression.

Autoco

This auto-assembly firm was formed in 1975. It is a joint venture between an American auto-firm which owns 49% of the shares, and the State which owns 51%. It assembles passenger and heavy-duty vehicles from CKDs ("completely knocked down" kits) provided by a Japanese subsidiary of the

US parent company. It has an annual capacity of 3500 units on an eight hour shift, five days a week system. Thirteen different models are assembled on a single line, production shifting on a predetermined basis according to demand. It is hoped to shift eventually from CKD assembly to a Localisation Scheme. At the time of the research, local content stood at just under 50%, and comprises items like batteries, glass, shocks, springs, tires, exhaust systems and radiators.

The Japanese subsidiary provides original product/part specification, technical information and assistance within a Technical Assistance Agreement, and product/part testing. In addition to vehicle assembly, the firm also has a large Tooling Section which manufactures such assembling equipment as fixtures and jigs, for own use, local sale and export. Autoco is the second largest auto-assembler in Kenya and its products are exported across eastern, central and southern Africa. While the technical and production expertise has mainly come from Japan, financial and managerial control is exercised from Detroit. Since the mid-eighties, management has been pursuing HRM with the aim of "streamlining the employment and training practices" in the company as a whole. The main impetus for change has come from the parent company, through the American Managing Director, although management has also had to respond to local stimuli to develop and retain their workforce and ensure high customer service. HRM initiatives draw from the Quality of Working Life (QWL) ethos which the company fostered in the late 1970s. The Personnel Manager heads the Personnel department and also serves as the secretary on the Human Resource Committee, the HR policy-making body which comprises the Managing Director, the Sales and Marketing Director, the Finance Director and the Factory Director.

Pharmaco

Pharmaco is a pharmaceutical firm, a wholly-owned subsidiary of an American company. The firm was set up in Kenya in 1952. Initially, all the products were imported and the firm acted simply as a distributorship for its US parent company. A modern factory was completed in 1972 and today the firm produces a wide range of over-the-counter pharmaceutical products; these include products to relieve pain and fever, facilitate diagnosis, control infection and curb symptoms. Pharmaco also imports, manufactures and markets a wide range of prescription medicines. The firm's products are also marketed across eastern, central and southern Africa.

HRM in this firm was introduced in the late 1980s. This began with the realization at headquarters in the mid-eighties, that the existing management practices particularly in the "Pacific Rim" needed to be streamlined if the company was to remain competitive in subsequent decades. It was thereafter decided that changes would be made in the worldwide operations, hence the adoption of "World Class Management". This programme sets out how changes in the management of people are to be implemented. These initiatives have drawn heavily from the existing quality awareness programme. Previous efforts at formulating a "quality movement" (including quality circles based on a QWL ethos) failed due to lack of top management support and lack of adequate preparation and training on the part of the implementers.

The Employee Involvement initiative had also not gone beyond the formation of informal teams and attempts to foster a team spirit. But due to the definition of "excellence" first in terms of production and then marketing, these ideas never really took root. It was therefore decided that the strategic framework must begin with "people". This has seen the setting up of an HRM corporate function headed by a director and manager. According to the official policy, the introduction of HRM was necessitated by the realization that the problems inherent in the management of employees arose not from "personnel administration" but from the "development and retention" of employees. Hence an emphasis on HRD (Human Resource Development).

Mimea

This third company is a market leader in agro-industry. Mimea is 88% owned by a UK company; the remaining shares are in public hands. Mimea (K) was incorporated in 1925 with the purpose of marketing Indian tea in Kenya. Fifty years later, the firm had grown into a large agro-industrial enterprise, and a major producer and exporter of a wide range of products which are at the top of the national foreign exchange earners' list. Apart from tea, exports include coffee, carnations, sisal and agricultural chemicals. Mimea has 24 tea estates with a total of over 6000 hectares. The first major step towards diversification was the purchase of a coffee estate in 1931. At the time of the research, three estates with a total of over 500 hectares were under coffee - these were served by two factories. Some of the world's best Arabica coffee is grown on the firm's estates. Up to 120 hectares are under flower crops and 2000 hectares under sisal.

In addition to its own estates, the firm is also served by a network of out-growers who receive a wide range of extension services to maintain high quality. Research and Development covers crop nutritional and husbandry techniques and manufacturing processes. There have been some major breakthroughs resulting in high yields and better quality, eg in producing varieties of coffee which are resistant to coffee berry disease. Vulnerability to climatic conditions, disease and competition has necessitated the high-level research. For example, up to 8% of the annual tea yield may be destroyed by hail. Similarly, sisal has continued to face stiff competition from synthetic fibres.

According to the Personnel Director, Mimea has not formally embraced the HRM approach at the overall company level; HRM initiatives apply mainly to management - in particular, the management development programme - and to a lesser extent to office clerical and supervisory staff. In contrast, a form of welfarism has been found suitable for the rest of the farm labour force. Since 1975, a major programme to improve housing and living conditions for its employees has been in force. Thousands of houses for labourers and supervisors have been constructed by the engineering department. The company has also constructed schools on many estates which are subsequently handed over to the government educational authorities upon completion. Multi-purpose social centres have been set up, with the aim of providing a social centre for every group of 1000 people. Medical centres have been established on all major estates; these provide a back-up to the dispensaries serving the individual estates. The company also runs two hospitals.

Chematox

Chematox was established in 1940 to manufacture a broad range of chemical and industrial products. 66% of the shares are held by a UK company, 15% by a State-controlled institution and the remaining 19% are in public hands. The firm's products fall into three categories: industrial gases, health care and welding products. Over time, the firm has expanded into the steel-related industrial sector with subsequent increases in demand for their liquid gases and welding products. Industrial and health care gases require the highest quality and safety standards. This has resulted in high investments in cylinder testing and maintenance facilities, as well as ways to prevent product losses through 'vacuum distribution technology'. The firm ranks cost effectiveness and customer service as its key priorities.

There have been other developments in new technology, such as new applications involving product transfer systems, fibres technology and mechanical assembly. The firm has also enhanced marketing efforts in areas like fruit ripening applications, food transportation in a controlled atmosphere, livestock branding and product quality improvement in rubber-related industries. Operations also include poultry farming applications and the emerging opportunities in the steel and scrap sectors.

As for the management of employees, although managers felt that the adoption of HRM would improve the practice and redirect effort towards motivating and developing employees, a "traditional approach" to personnel management is still maintained. Market imperatives have placed immense pressure on the firm to invest in training in order to enhance competitiveness and customer service. However, much of the emphasis is on managerial development and higher level technical expertise. The organizational structure also gives some indication of the priority accorded the employee issues: the head of Personnel is known as the Personnel and Training Officer, and he reports to the Company Secretary.

Automart

Automart was established in 1949 with a franchise to distribute and service vehicles for a German firm. In 1963, it took on a franchise for a Japanese firm. It is a private company owned by European investors who between them hold 54% of the share ownership. The rest was reported to be in "private local ownership". For many years, the firm remained in the business of vehicle distribution and service, purchasing vehicle parts and other accessories from an assortment of suppliers. It has also taken some steps towards vertical diversification, the first of which was the acquisition in 1977 of a manufacturer of brake linings, pads and related products. This was followed in 1985 by the acquisition of a manufacturer of oil and air filters. These moves were necessitated by competitive market pressures which have continued to impose stringent cost imperatives. In the 1980s it became increasingly difficult to secure import licences because of governmental restrictions on the importation of whole vehicles. Managers construe this as governmental interference, which ultimately results in uncompetitive prices. Locally assembled vehicles are more expensive than imported ones mainly because of high production costs of the local suppliers of raw materials.

Although this firm also retains the "traditional" Personnel approach, the Group Personnel Manager, who reports to the General Manager, made some efforts to bring about "meaningful changes" in the management of employees, including trying to induce a shift towards certain aspects of HRM. One outcome was a new appraisal and payment system for shopfloor workers. Other efforts included trying to draw up a long term approach to the planning and development of staff, but these did not receive much top management support.

Some Caveats and Constraints

This study focuses on views obtained mainly from managers, and may to this extent seem to adopt a "managerialist" bias. Due to various constraints, including time, the views of ordinary employees and union representatives were not systematically sought except in so far as there was interaction with employees when studying and reviewing documents. It was, however, possible to expand the scope of the coverage through discussions with staff in other departments. An elaborate study of industrial relations is also beyond the scope of this book. However, the key features of industrial relations and the role of trade unions are characterized. An attempt is therefore made to establish the potential role of industrial relations in HRM initiatives.

It is also noted here that given the embryonic nature of the concept of contemporary HRM especially at the time of the research, it was sometimes difficult to determine exactly what managers meant by HRM. This was made even more confusing when the adoption of HRM appeared to represent no more than a change of terminology. In this regard, Noon's (1989) views about examining the actual practices irrespective of managerial intention are helpful. This allows one to move away from the more common approach of simply comparing claims and actual practice, and instead to examine specific practices in their own right. While giving regard to the contemporary definition of HRM, eg as in Guest (1987), the practices in the case studies were examined "as they were" in the first instance, in order to focus on the practices themselves, rather than on what the literature describes as HRM. This prevented the filtering off of valuable information which may not have fitted the working description.

In positing the concept of "grounded theory", Glaser and Strauss (1967) argue that researchers should gather, study and analyse qualitative data without the inhibitions of adhering to a grand theoretical schema. Other research methodologists (eg Bryman, 1988) have recognized the suitability of this approach when dealing with qualitative data. This project has benefited from these perspectives. Morgan and Smircich (1980) argue that the appropriateness of qualitative research derives from the nature of the social phenomena being explored. Morgan and Smircich (1980, p499) emphasize the need for:

> a focus of attention on the ground assumptions of social theory and research in order to transcend the abstract debate about methodology on its own account and the abstracted forms of empiricism, both qualitative and quantitative, that dominate the contemporary scene.

This enables the social scientist to discover what approach is suitable for what aspect of the phenomena having identified the "ground assumptions". For our purposes, this entails identifying what issues are problematized within the respective paradigms.

Various problems were encountered in the research, mainly in respect of the actual fieldwork. The first one was that of access. For the 1989 study, questionnaires were sent out to HR managers in 18 companies as a prelude to the subsequent fieldwork. Thirteen Japanese firms had agreed to participate. Only two of the Kenyan firms responded and this line of enquiry was abandoned. I therefore decided to make contact with the managing directors. Responses were few and slow to come. The whole process required endless letter-writing and telephone conversations both to persuade the managers to avail their time and to assure them that the exercise was for purely academic purposes. Gaining access at the latter stage of the research was less daunting because rapport had already been established with the firms; the difficulty in this case was in the proposed duration of the study. In one firm, a General Manager abruptly withdrew the permission initially granted on the grounds that it would take up too much company time. After some weeks of persuasion the key informants agreed to cooperate against the wishes of the General Manager.

Doing research in a developing country presents problems that test the researcher's patience and resourcefulness to the absolute limit. One of the main problems is managers' suspicions about researchers' purposes. This is because academic research has not yet gained wide acceptance and support in organizations in general. Some managers declared that they did not, as a matter of policy, entertain activities with universities. The reasons for this are intriguing as virtually all of these managers had university education, either locally or abroad. Perhaps the answer can be found in the general feeling that academic researchers offer little to the organizations, and merely take up valuable company time, pry into confidential corporate policies and appear to question managers' judgement and make them look foolish. In this regard, academic researchers are viewed with the same suspicion as other unwelcome guests such as tax inspectors, auditors, quality inspectors, health inspectors and so forth.

Managers are therefore highly protected by secretaries who always claim they are "in a meeting", and a lot of issues seem to fall under a protective shroud of "classified" or "confidential". A study of theses both in Oxford and at Nairobi University reveals that this is a deeply-entrenched problem in conducting research in developing countries. There is, for example, the fear that sensitive or confidential information may be made available to competitors, or to other unauthorized parties. This is perhaps more evident in the case of foreign researchers, or citizens based in foreign institutions as it is more difficult for managers to verify their credentials. Finally, there is a common problem of physical access: many companies are located in remote industrial areas or export promotion zones to take advantage of low-cost locations or tax benefits. The infrastructure in such places can be very unfavourable. Given the foregoing, the researcher therefore has to come armed with an awesome arsenal of persistence, persuasion, patience, honesty, humility, opportunism and pure luck.

Part Three

The Structure of the Book

This section presents a brief outline of the structure of the chapters. The next three chapters (chapters two to four) deal respectively with the three substantive themes identified above. While individually discussing specific frameworks for handling their respective subjects, these chapters also jointly constitute the overall framework within which the rest of the book is located. Chapters five to eight comprise the analyses within the paradigms posited in chapter four. It is in these four chapters that a *paradigmatic journey* is undertaken. Chapter nine, the Conclusion, brings all the various strands together. Brief outlines of each of the chapters follow below.

Chapter two considers the concept of human resource management. I examine various key issues, ranging from the origins of HRM to the emergence of 'strategic' HRM. It is argued in this chapter that in order to come to grips with the myriad debates and controversies, it is necessary to formulate a model of HRM, hence the positing of an *interpretation* of Guest's model. This leads on to a discussion of the African management context in chapter three, beginning with a look at Kenya. It is argued in this chapter that in order to determine exactly what are the employment needs and challenges in organizations, it is necessary to characterize the context within which the management of people takes place. This is expected to facilitate the formulation of an approach which is both effective and suitable.

The concept of multi-paradigmatic enquiry is formally posited in chapter four. This chapter begins with an expose of the concept of "paradigm" as derived from Kuhn (1962), and then proceeds to elaborate how the concept is employed here. Burrell and Morgan's (1979) paradigms are thereafter posited, followed by a critique of the paradigm concept and an examination of the application of paradigms to the African context. Chapters five and six constitute an analysis of HRM within the functionalist paradigm. Chapter five examines selection, recruitment and socialization while chapter six is concerned with training and development. Both chapters examine the HR practices of the firms in question on a thematic basis, aligning the discussion to the dimensions of the HRM model. Both chapters undertake the dual aim of analysing the extant practices within the context of the HRM model and illustrating the ways in which these practices are informed by a structural-functionalist ethos.

Chapter seven seizes the two paradigms of "the sociology of radical change" to advance a *radical critique* of HRM. Drawing from critical theory, and in particular the work of Gramsci, the discussion first centres on whether and to what extent HRM is the "new" workplace hegemony. It then proceeds to an analysis of HRM within the radical structuralist paradigm, paying more attention to the contradictions inherent in the political-economy. Chapter eight constitutes a discussion of HRM within the interpretive paradigm. The chapter argues that social phenomena must be understood from the point of view of social actors. The discussion draws from social anthropology to explore ritualism and symbolism in

HRM. It then draws from language philosophy to examine the role of rhetoric and totemism in scripting the reality of HRM.

The final chapter brings together the key themes and takes a final look at the issues that the discussion addresses. It recapitulates the arguments, identifies the implications of the findings for management theory and practice and suggests the scope for further research.

Notes

[1] Ratio of export price index to import price index at 1982 prices.

[2] At constant 1982 prices.

[3] This information is drawn from interviews and company documents. Permission to use these materials was granted on condition of anonymity.

2 Human Resource Management

This chapter takes an analytical look at the subject of human resource management (HRM) as depicted in the literature. In view of the ambiguity and controversy that have come to characterize HRM, one of the objectives of this chapter will be to seek conceptual clarity in the phenomenon in order to understand exactly what is meant by *human resource management*. The chapter comprises three parts. The first part is an overview of the emergence and nature of HRM. The second part examines the significance of a contemporary model of HRM, while the final part briefly outlines how the model is interpreted for the purposes of our discussion.

Understanding Human Resource Management

We begin by seeking to establish a temporal context for HRM. This exercise has to be seen in a historical context for two reasons: first, it enables us to fathom the "roots" of this organizational phenomenon and hence lead us to a more informed understanding of what it entails and what motive forces have brought it into being; secondly, this permits us to appreciate the nature of the dynamic political and exchange forces that are inherently built into social phenomena.

This overview also helps us to understand what HRM aims to achieve and what meanings people attribute to it. For Keenoy (1990, p370) it is "the conceptual euphemism to describe all the apparently transformative changes in the management of employment relations in the 1980s". Blunt (1990a) suggests that in the late 1970s and even into the early 1980s the discipline concerned with the human side of enterprise was largely regarded as moribund; it lacked status and influence and was preoccupied with house-keeping operational issues, not managerial or strategic ones (see also Legge, 1978; Manning, 1983; Thurley, 1981; Watson, 1977). Guest (1990) attributes the concern with status to the origins of personnel management "as an extension of scientific management or a form of welfare management". Legge (1995, p10) attributes it to "the contrast between the high aspirations of the normative model and of failure to deliver as reflected in the behaviourist model".

According to this argument, personnel management became a "trash can" into which unwanted tasks and low-potential managers could be dumped. If we accept this argument, then the concept of HRM, and in particular its quest for boardroom attention offers personnel practitioners the opportunity to emerge from the managerial doldrums. However, personnel management does not constitute a uniform set of practices. Tyson and Fell (1986) identify three models: "clerk of works", "contracts manager" and "architect". The "architect" model has a strong resonance with contemporary HRM.

If it can be demonstrated that HRM is the latest stage in the development of personnel practices, or the latest manifestation of a concern with the management (and control) of people at work, then it may help to explore the forces that have over time shaped the direction and intensity of this preoccupation. These may be traced back to "scientific management" and Frederick Taylor's attempts to rationalize tasks with machine-like precision in his "time and motion" studies. These were efforts to reshape the tools of control available to management, and even today, it is widely felt that much management thinking is still guided by a rationalistic philosophy. The human relations school sought to eliminate the dehumanizing elements of work at the shopfloor and meet the needs of workers. The Hawthorne experiments in turn highlighted the importance of the "group" and interpersonal relations (hence "social" man) which Taylor's "individualist-rational-economic" man ignored. It is noteworthy, however, that at the core of these studies was the concern with "productivity". Further concern with the individual's needs found expression in industrial psychology - the theories of motivation and job satisfaction.

An important development was that of the *psychological contract* between the employee and the organization, which constituted one of the earliest attempts to formalize the notion of a congruence of interests by establishing "mutual understanding" (eg Schein 1988). Another dimension of this "matching" concept was in the socio-technical school of thought which aimed to restructure work in such a way as to match the social system to the technical system (Trist and Bamforth, 1951). Other relevant management conceptions have been Organizational Design (OD), Human Resource Accounting (HRA), and the Quality of Working life (QWL). The latter two have been the most recent precursors to HRM. With respect to QWL, this is borne out in two of our case studies, Pharmaco and Autoco. Popularized for example by Flamholtz (1985) HRA was the ultimate quest for legitimacy through quantification. QWL came into prominence in the 1970s, and two of its proponents, Davies and Cherns (1975) argued that this "humanization of work" was the key to devising appropriate social policies and workable responses to the problems arising in the transition from the industrial to the post-industrial era. QWL was seen as urging a programme of organizational and social change; Burrell and Morgan (1979, p.182) observe that:

> Social change within the wider environment is such that people are beginning to demand more satisfying work, and that organizations need to make operational and managerial subsystems congruent with these demands. This is a familiar theme, which has long been the concern of neo-human relations theorists...; the quality of working life movement represents a logical development of these traditions.

In their advocacy of a new approach to industrial relations, Kochan et al (1986) seem to equate QWL with HRM. However, Hendry and Pettigrew (1990) claim that HRM differs from such other constructs as OD, QWL and even personnel management in the way it was initially formulated: it was inspired by the crisis in American management in the face of Japanese competition. This involved the drive to restore competitiveness, reformulate organizational cultures and develop a more strategic management approach. The so-called "excellence movement" (eg Peters and Waterman, 1982) also created an atmosphere of confidence and hope, and subsequently, "human resource management was reborn, repackaged, and elevated to the boardroom" (Blunt, 1990).

The foregoing gives some idea of the changing face of the management of people. It is noteworthy that one of the outcomes of the "HRM movement" is the pressure to explain HR activities in terms of their financial implications. Broadly, this refers to the "organizational imperative" (Kamoche, 1994), which refers to the inherent industrial practice of subjecting activities to the profitability and productivity test, such that activities are considered desirable only to the extent that they make a tangible and quantifiable contribution. This creates a problem for human resource activities whose contribution is not readily evident. As a result, there remains some doubt about the real reasons behind the rise in interest in HRM. It is submitted here that this interest is a combination of a number of factors: the need to respond to an increasingly demanding labour force, the need to invest in training and career development in the face of competing commitments, the tightening of managerial control as a response to competitive pressures, the quest for enhanced status for HR practitioners, consultants and academics, and the need to derive a tangible and potentially strategic contribution from the workforce.

Strategic Human Resource Management (SHRM)

The last twenty years have witnessed a growth of interest in strategic planning in the face of mounting competition in industry. The importance of a "strategic" dimension has been recognized in all the main organizational functions, from marketing, information technology to manufacturing. It can also be argued that the claim for HRM to be meaningful only to the extent that it has a "strategic" stance accords well with the theme of the enduring quest for status amongst members of a disciplinary community. The earlier proponents of SHRM suggested that like any other management function, HRM must fit a suitable strategy (eg Tichy *et al,* 1982; Hendry and Pettigrew, 1986; Miles and Snow, 1984; Schuler, 1989). Tichy *et al* go so far as to suggest that HRM must be seen as the *third* key element in organizational activity, after Chandler's (1962) model of strategy and structure. According to this argument, the critical managerial task is to align the formal structure and the HR systems so that they are incorporated within the formulation of the strategic objectives of the organization. Tichy *et al* identify three key dimensions in the concept:

-   devising an organization-wide selection and promotion system that supports the organization's business strategy
-   creating internal flows of people that match the business strategy, and
-   matching key executives to the business strategy

The above line of thinking culminated in the "matching model" of SHRM in which Fombrun et al (1984) for example tried to match human resource strategies to business strategies. This approach has spawned a large number of studies which together constitute a "situational-contingency" framework in which HR strategies flow from and are shaped by the respective business strategies. An obvious weakness in this framework is that is does not allow that HR strategies are capable of driving the business strategies, thus in effect denying the proactivity potentially inherent in individuals' initiatives. These approaches have also been criticised for being too prescriptive, lacking real empirical support, and making simplistic assumptions about the tenability of a strategy-HR "fit" (see also Boxall, 1992; Mabey and Salaman, 1995; Purcell and Ahlstrand, 1994; Tyson, 1995).

Much controversy still remains about whether and how HRM contributes to firm performance. Some observers have reported a positive relationship between financial performance and the degree of integration between corporate strategy and HR functions (eg Fox and McLeay, 1992). Others have found inconclusive evidence of a direct link between HRM and performance (eg Bamberger et al, 1990; Whipp, 1992).

Recognizing the strategic dimension is important in that it signals to management the advantages that might accrue from treating people as a resource that will yield benefits if invested in appropriately. Additionally, it ensures that HR issues enjoy top management support especially in the introduction of new measures and strategies that impact on people. Such situations include mergers and acquisitions, introduction of new technology, internationalization and culture change programmes. The reality of SHRM has been a mixed bag: while some managers recognize the strategic value of employees' contribution and have shown a commitment to invest in people, others think of HR as a cost to be kept down. The difficult economic realities of the 1980s and 1990s have seen unprecedented cost reduction measures achieved through "retrenchment", "downsizing" and "business process re-engineering". While cost reduction is often inevitable, the enthusiasm with which it has been pursued in some cases raises serious doubts about whether firms have sufficient capacity to meet the challenges of the 21st century in terms of the knowledge-creation.

Toward a New Perspective on SHRM

The SHRM debate has progressed from considering how personnel management differs from HRM to exploring how HR can lead to sustainable competitive advantage. This has seen the emergence of the resource-based view of the firm which was initially developed in the strategic management literature. Much of this can be traced back to the writings of Penrose (eg 1959) who highlighted the strategic value of firm "uniqueness" which is derivable from the heterogeneity of a firm's productive services. As such, firms can configure or reconfigure their assets and unutilized resources in a way which distinguishes them from other firms' asset configurations. What makes the process even more potentially rewarding is that it is not clear to competitors exactly where the source of success lies. Penrose sought to explain how firms expanded through the utilization of resources both within and outside the firm. These insights have today provided scope to explore how firms can achieve sustainable competitive advantage through the utilization of "human resources". Within the discussion of strategic management, the resource-based view of the firm is now familiar territory.

From an earlier paper by Wernerfelt (1984) the basic theme has been to explore how this view of strategy enables us to treat the firm as a bundle of resources, tangible and intangible, and the role they play in product/market competition (eg Barney, 1991; Dierickx and Cool, 1989; Grant, 1991). More recently, attention has turned to HRM in order to show how the resource-based view can enhance our understanding of the strategic value of human resources. Kamoche (1994) sees the resource-based view as an alternative to the industry-based view of strategy which has engendered the dominant notion of the "organizational imperative". Many HR activities, processes and functions are not directly measurable, which renders the industrial organizational view of strategy largely inoperable in HRM.

According to Kamoche (1994: 41), the emergent resource-based view helps us to "take account of the nature of human resources by focusing on the subjectivity, ambiguity and creativity that characterize HRM". Wright et al (1994) and Kamoche (1996) examine the features of this model, and the conditions in which human resources can be a source of competitive advantage: if they are valuable and scarce relative to other resources, and are not easily substitutable or imitable. This elaborates the concept of "uniqueness". Mueller (1996) suggests that strategic assets are generated by "social architecture" – on-going skill formation activities, informal learning and tacit learning.

The utilization of resources raises questions about how the benefits arising therefrom are distributed. This is the issue of "appropriability" which, while recognized in the strategic management literature, has not been fully explored in the SHRM literature. In this regard, Kamoche (1996) identifies the weaknesses in the situational-contingent model which ignores the incongruity of interests in social relations. The application of the resource-based (or resource-capability) theory must therefore take into account the diversity of interests amongst organizational stakeholders, and the important role the industrial relations literature has played in addressing and mediating such interests.

This discussion has been taken further by Kamoche and Mueller (1998) who propose an appropriation-learning (A-L) perspective in which the emphasis is not merely on generating strategic assets. Rather it should involve individuals in the knowledge-creation process, with opportunities for individuals to learn and acquire knowledge for their own personal and career development.

Appropriation is about how firms retain the added value from the utilization of resources; as for HRM, the firm's capacity to retain such added value is constrained by the fact that the firm does not have an absolute proprietorial claim over the knowledge employees possess. In an increasingly high-tech world, the issue of knowledge-creation will attract more and more attention eg in redefining the meaning of work, and affording individuals more scope to define how they utilize the knowledge attributable to themselves. The challenge for individuals is not merely to strengthen surveillance and other control mechanisms, but to seek a clearer understanding of the complexities surrounding "ownership" of knowledge, including the question of property rights.

In search of a model of HRM

Despite the plethora of models that have been put forward by various writers there has not been much evidence of a "theory of HRM". Models of HRM tend to be either prescriptive or descriptive. Difficulties have, however, been expressed regarding the manner in which these two approaches have been adopted. Hendry and Pettigrew (1986) suggest that HRM has from the beginning been highly normative - it provided a diagnosis and proposed solutions. They single out Beer et al (1985) and Walton and Lawrence (1985) as normative in the way they laid down a manifesto and theoretical framework for the teaching of HRM at Harvard.

Guest's Model of HRM

Guest's (1987) conception of HRM is adopted here because of the way it tries to capture the nature and ethos of HRM as commonly understood. In a manner that parallels the descriptive-prescriptive approach to model-building, Guest (1989) argues that HRM can be derived empirically or conceptually: empirically through an assessment of the practices of firms which either claim to practice HRM or have at some point been identified as exemplars of HRM. A conceptual analysis on the other hand is based on a set of assumptions about what constitutes appropriate management of human resources. In devising his model, Guest aims to develop a set of testable propositions leading to prescriptive policies. He then goes on to present a model in the form of "four policy goals", which he sees as the main dimensions of human resource management. The key elements (goals) of this model are integration, commitment, flexibility and quality. We summarize the key features of each below.

Integration   Integration consists of four components:

- the need to link HR to corporate strategy, which also calls for top management support
- the need for coherence within HR policies and with other policies
- involvement of line managers
- the integration of all employees into the business and the importance of goal congruence

Much of the essence of this dimension has been discussed above and will not be repeated here. It is noted here that whereas the role of HRM in strategy formulation cannot be overemphasized, its impact will be mediated by the importance that an organization attaches to strategic management itself. Similarly, the involvement of line managers may be curtailed by structural constraints.

Employee commitment   Developing a feeling of commitment to the organization is predicated on the assumption that committed employees will be more satisfied, more productive and more adaptable. This goal seems to be plausible in the way Beer et al (1985) identify it with self-worth, psychological involvement and identity for the individual. It is, however, associated with several problems. First, commitment to what? Though most writers refer to commitment to the organization, multiple and possibly competing commitments should be considered: career, union, family, workgroup and other such commitments; these in turn span different levels of analysis, from individual to group and department. Much of the literature associates commitment with "organizational goals and values". The definition of the goals and values is also treated as unproblematic, as is the assumption that organizations have clearly defined goals which are shared by all members (Coopey and Hartley, 1991). This essentially unitarist conception of the organization disregards the existence of multiple interest groups and inherent political processes.

A second issue concerns the form of commitment. This relates to the actual conceptualisation and form of commitment. Various definitions of commitment have been offered: (for a literature survey, see for instance Angle and Perry, 1986; Coopey and Hartley, 1991; Mowday et al, 1982). Coopey and Hartley suggest that there are two dominant definitions in the literature: definitions involving *behavioural acts and consistencies*, and those which focus on *affective attachments and identifications*. The latter connote a sense of devotion, loyalty or allegiance. This is typified by Porter et al (1974) who relate it to the relative strength of the individual's identification with, and involvement in, a particular organization. Buchanan (1974) and Mowday et al (1982) also stress the notion of "attachment to" and "identification with" the organization. Porter et al (1974) identify three elements in attitudinal commitment: a strong desire to remain a member of the organization; a strong belief in and acceptance of, the values and goals of the organization; and a readiness to exert considerable effort on behalf of the organization.

The behavioural variant, on the other hand, is about the individual's perception of the value of remaining in an organization, which is expressed in an unwillingness to leave the organization (Coopey and Hartley, 1991). Salancik (1977) sees it as the binding of individuals to certain acts through public statements of intent, personal acceptance of responsibility, irrevocability of decisions and clarity of behavioural goals. It should be pointed out, however, that choosing to remain with an organization (continuance commitment) may be the result of factors other than job satisfaction and high performance, eg lack of choice, or high unemployment (see also Meyer and Allen, 1988).

Rather than polarize the two conceptual approaches, Coopey and Hartley argue that both have value and could be integrated into a single approach which recognizes that commitment can develop either through affect or through behaviour. It must be recognized, however, that organizations must also demonstrate a commitment to employees, through managerial actions. These might include fairness over pay and promotion methods (eg Hendry, 1995), or no lay-off guarantees. In their Appropriation-Learning perspective, Kamoche and Mueller (1998) point out that the stability assumed in the quest for "organizational commitment" is becoming untenable in an increasingly unstable and uncertain employment climate. In an era of job insecurity and the constant threat of being "retrenched", our traditional view of commitment will have to change.

Flexibility/Adaptability   Flexibility is seen as providing the capacity to manage planned organizational change and enabling the organization to be adaptive and responsive in the face of unanticipated pressures at all levels in the organization. Guest advocates organic structures whereby the organization avoids rigid, hierarchical, bureaucratic structures, prevents powerful, entrenched interest groups from developing, and where there are no inhibitive demarcations among groups of workers or between individual roles. This echoes Burns and Stalker's (1962) organic as opposed to mechanistic structures.

Three forms of flexibility are identifiable: functional, numerical and financial flexibility (eg Atkinson, 1984; Atkinson and Meager, 1986). Functional flexibility is achieved through the possession of "flexible" skills among the workforce and the willingness to move freely between tasks. This should be facilitated by the provision of training and development. Numerical flexibility refers to changes in headcounts and the maintenance of a workforce which is reduced and increased with relative ease according to changing needs. Financial flexibility aims to institute rewarding systems that vary with performance. The economic and competitive realities of the 1980s saw the emergence of the so-called "flexible firm" at the heart of which concept lies the distinction between the "core" and the "peripheral" workers. The "core" consists of those who are treated as a "valued" resource and who conduct the organization's key activities. The emphasis here is on functional flexibility – the "core" are constantly equipped with new skills.

According to Atkinson (1984) the peripheral group is divided into two; the "first peripheral group" are also full-time employees, but they enjoy a lower level of job security and less access to career opportunities, than do the "core". They include the clerical, supervisory, component assembly and testing staff, with *plug-in* rather than *firm-specific* jobs. When they acquire vital skills in line with functional flexibility, a second peripheral group is likely to emerge – mainly consisting of part-time workers. The retrenchment phenomenon has gradually redefined the flexible model as organizations strive to contain labour costs at all levels, in effect blurring the core-periphery distinction. It s also noteworthy that the flexibility model is not without some contradictions, eg in the conceptualization of the "core" and "peripheral" groups, and how people are treated in pursuit of the model (eg Blyton and Morris, 1992).

Quality This final feature has three inter-related dimensions:

- The quality of staff: hence the need to recruit, develop and retain staff with high levels of ability, skill and adaptability.

- The quality of performance and the need to set and maintain high standards. This requires standards and goals of performance to be identified and agreed. In order to ensure high commitment, trust and motivation, management policy and practice must also maintain high quality standards and be perceived as such by employees. This also calls for appropriate systems of communication including some sort of grievance system.
- The public image of the organization must also measure up to a high standard, in particular its human resource policies. A reputation for high quality policies/practices, in the way the organization treats its employees and other stakeholders is an important mechanisms for attracting the "right" people.

Guest's model has been criticized for taking little account of contextual circumstances; it is hoped to resolve this weakness in the model by giving some attention to the situational circumstances in Kenya. In a critique of HRM, Keenoy (1990a, p373) asserts that:

> One of the singular successes of the HRM rhetoric has been to establish the impression that there are "excellent" and "successful" companies which, irrespective of the socio-economic contexts in which they operate, have achieved that position by practising something akin to the kind of activities Guest elaborates and that such practices are a key ingredient of becoming "excellent".

He goes on to suggest that Guest's model should be treated as an ideal-type of generic HRM to conduct a comparative analysis of qualitatively different forms of employment policy and public practice to identify the multifarious constraints which stand in the way of achieving the ideal. The model is used here to query the nature of diverse employment practices, but not to establish how it might be achieved. The model is thus more useful as a tool to *organize* the research findings in a way that permits relevant patterns and trends to be identified in each and every specific case. In this regard, the concern of the next chapter is to explore the nature of the socio-cultural and politico-economic context within which organizations operate in Kenya, and how these factors might mediate the practice of HRM.

A Summary of key HRM Features

This section spells out the features of our HRM model as derived from Guest's model. The features hopefully provide a "litmus test" denoting those aspects of managerial activity which for our purposes constitute the yardstick against which the extant practices might be measured. The extent to which organizations comply with these particular aspects will subsequently indicate the extent to which they are practising HRM as herein defined and as commonly understood. Additionally, this should provide some indication as to what and how much would need to be done in order to adopt HRM practices if indeed these are considered desirable and feasible. Also, by juxtaposing the extant practices within the Kenyan organizational context against Guest's conceptual model, we will be able to test the tenability and validity of the latter.

The model is not merely a checklist of procedures that organizations should follow. It aims to spell out, in the first place, what we would expect to find in an organization that is practising HRM, irrespective of a claimed intent to do so. It is not suggested here that these are the things organizations *should* necessarily be doing. Using Guest's model to assess how a newspaper enterprise has adopted HRM practices in response to competitive market forces, Noon (1989) focuses on what is being practised *irrespective of declared managerial intent*. He asserts that this avoids the well-aired problem of attempting to assess whether what is done is what was intended, yet allows the examination of the practice against the theory. In a similar vein, Storey (1992) observes that crucial developments are often neither designed nor presented as specifically HRM initiatives and that the thrust may derive from total quality management or from a perceived need to enhance the organization's image in the area of customer care.

Integration

-   a broad corporate strategy which spells out the organizational long-term goals and the procurement, development and use of resources necessary to achieve them
-   integration of the human resources dimension into the corporate strategic planning process (eg through a HR manager/department)
-   well-integrated policies and practices, hence internal coherence of the HR dimension (eg the link between selection, appraisal, training and rewarding)

- coherence of HR with other areas of policy
- top management support (eg board representation)
- more active involvement of line management in the implementation of HR policy
- integration of employees into the organization eg through socialization (the inculcation of "organizational values"), and the inculcation of company-specific skills in development
- initial training at induction which also serves as a prelude to a more systematic training programme
- an integrative company-wide appraisal programme
- a trend towards individual arrangements through a merit system (complemented by a special status-seniority element that reflects particular rigidities in a straightforward merit system and perceived organizational commitment)

Commitment

- values that embody the ethos of the organizational goals; (these may be articulated in a Mission Statement which actively guides policy formulation)
- the implications of these organizational values on relevant "stakeholders" (eg employees, customers, suppliers, the state and the public at large) and the ability to attract suitable employees
- identification of perceived individual values, in particular attitudes to the organization's goals and values
- attempt to achieve compatibility through "reciprocal commitment"
- assessment of adherence to "organizational goals and values" (especially at appraisal)
- inculcation of attitudes deemed to be compatible with perceived organizational values

Flexibility

- pursuing rigorous recruitment procedures for core employees, on the one hand, and less formal, and even *ad hoc* procedures for the peripheral workforce
- use of temporary workers to create a buffer peripheral workforce as a hedge against market uncertainty

- hiring casual and temporary workers mainly for unskilled and semi-skilled jobs
- establishing a flexible-hours system for part-time workers, which is strictly determined by organizational manpower needs
- maintaining numerical flexibility for the peripheral workforce and functional flexibility for the stable core staff
- job rotation and multi-skilling to facilitate rapid re-deployment where and when necessary
- designing jobs for adaptability in a flexible firm

It is suggested here that the core-peripheral distinction might be configured as in Figure 2.1.

Figure 2.1 A four-tier hierarchical structure

Level	Constituents
Tier 1	management trainees (and other managerial jobs)
Tier 2	supervisors office clerical staff accountants technicians marketing staff
Tier 3	salesmen skilled artisans mechanics craftsmen machine operators full-time farm workers
Tier 4	part-time workers contractual workers casual labourers

Tier 1 comprises the managerial "core". The "peripheral" is more problematic; it consists of Tiers 3 and 4 and, depending on the activity and context, Tier 2 can either be described as core or peripheral. This will be elaborated in chapters five and six; however, our concern will be to identify how employees fall into the various categories in particular cases rather than to rigidly follow the distinction.

Quality

Although doubt has been raised above about the centrality of "Quality" to HRM, it is however, important to consider how it might affect the viability of the chosen approaches.

-   are there clearly laid-down procedures for recruitment and development (or are these *ad hoc* exercises resorted to only when the need to recruit or develop arises)?
-   do the recruitment and development procedures address explicit policy objectives (eg integration, commitment and flexibility)?
-   can product quality be enhanced in relation to the improvement of HR initiatives, such as in linking HRM to TQM (the Total Quality Movement)?
-   if it is required to reduce turnover (or absenteeism, level of grievances), are steps effectively taken to ensure, in the first place, that the relevant HRM policies will achieve this, and secondly, that this actually has been achieved?

Conclusions

This chapter has sought to outline what HRM means and what it entails. This has been a quest for conceptual clarity in an organizational phenomenon that has come to be seen as ambiguous and controversial and which has led to the tautological use of the term "HRM" to describe any "new" ideas in the management of people at work. By presenting an introductory overview of the "human side of enterprise", it has been argued that there are several key themes which are identifiable in the emergence of HRM from the 1980s. The chapter also examined the need for a model in order to make sense of what it is we are really dealing with. In this respect, Guest's theoretical construct was presented; the discussion then proceeded to interpret this model in a way which seems appropriate for assessing the practice of human resource management in Kenya.

3 Management in Africa

This chapter considers the nature of management in Africa. We begin by examining the theory and practice of management in Kenya in order to establish the context within which the research was conducted, and then propose a model for managing people in Africa. The discussion draws from the available literature and from discussions held with managers in the case studies. This chapter therefore presents essential background material in order to characterize the issues that impact on management practice in a developing country context.

The Kenyan Management Context

There are two important strands in this discussion: first, the tendency for the country to import western management practices; the second strand is the need for suitable practices. Western management techniques have been introduced by expatriate managers, African managers who have been trained in the west or who have had a Western-style education, but as it has often been pointed out (eg Onyemelukwe, 1973), these practices have not always been appropriate in the African context. Jaeger and Kanungo(1990) observe that management practices from the west have become "sacred cows" for industrial development; developing countries are advised and feel themselves that they must adopt Western thought and practices to achieve "rapid economic prosperity". Doubt remains about the effectiveness of these practices. These writers therefore advance the case for an indigenous management which takes account of the relevant environment, which they characterize in terms of three major aspects: economic and technological, political and legal, and socio-cultural.

The introduction of management practices like HRM/HRD is largely a consequence of foreign investments. The case material itself reveals that many of the changes being introduced in the management of people emanate from headquarters abroad. A historical perspective helps to illustrate the tradition of espousing foreign practices, and consequently leads us to question their appropriateness. Do they take into account the real needs of the organization and those of the members who comprise it, or are they simply brought in because the parent company abroad says so, or because of some faith in the ability of the potent "magic" from the west to cure organizational ills? In the past, expatriate managers ignored local cultures and were sometimes known to allow racist and intolerant attitudes to determine their management styles (eg Onyemelukwe, 1973). Techniques like Management By Objectives (MBO), psychometric tests, QWL and so forth, are often introduced with little due regard to the contextual circumstances. This chapter emphasizes the need to formulate practices that are not only cognizant of the context but which also draw from relevant local resources. It is hypothesized here that the practice of importing western norms and values has prevented the formation of a management style that draws on the indigenous circumstances and cultural ethos.

A Historical Perspective

This section addresses the first theme identified above. Management practices in Kenya have evolved in tandem with the growth of capitalism and industrialization. It is important to identify the origins and evolution of these trends in order to understand the management challenges and how they have come into being. The introduction of western capitalism brought with it a broad assortment of practices that embodied the industrial ideology. The resultant exercise of control by multinational corporations has greatly influenced the present-day management theory and practice.

Swainson (1980) traces Kenya's links with western capitalism to the late 19th century. She observes that from the outset of British rule, a European settler class was established in Kenya and with the development of a market economy, other forms of production became subject to the needs of capital. Much of this initial capital was channelled into agriculture principally to finance the growing of cash crops on large settler farms and this helped to establish agriculture as the mainstay of the economy. The colonial system of segregation both encouraged and fostered a dual policy of peasant (African) and large scale (European) agricultural production whereby the peasant mode of production not only operated principally as a marginal, subsistence and hence non-marketed form of production, but was also coerced into providing cheap labour for the European settler farms.

Capital that was channelled into industry found a logical starting point in agricultural primary processing thus offering an outlet for the vast amounts of food products coming from the plantations. While the settler and foreign firms remained within the area of plantations and import/export trade, the

Asian merchant capital dominated the sphere of retail trade (Swainson, 1980). The evidence shows that the colonial government stifled the development of indigenous African industry. This was achieved by a combination of credit limits and legislation which included rules to limit litigation to collect debts, attachment of property for the payment of debts, and restriction on collecting money by African associations (see Kim, 1986).[1] Following this argument, these policies thus began the process of stifling local entrepreneurialism. It is difficult to tell, however, whether local entrepreneurs would have created an "indigenous" management approach.[2]

Post-war Entrenchment of Foreign Capital

Both the limited size of the internal market and the shortage of money capital from either the government or private sources prevented the development of an industrial base before 1939 (Swainson, 1980). Existing investment was in the hands of settler entrepreneurs.[3] During the period 1945-1963 international capital became more prevalent in Kenya, thus consolidating the position of foreign investors (Swainson, 1987). Kenya attained independence in 1963. Langdon (1981) identifies the period 1967-73 as one of accelerated multinational entry. This was made possible by a wide range of incentives and a favourable investment climate: assurances of monopoly powers in some cases, generous tax conditions, and the fostering of alliances with the polity. The investment climate after the oil-shock recession of the 1970s made the country less attractive but investments picked up again in the early 1980s. By the mid-1980s, foreign investments accounted for about 70% of value added in manufacturing (Bhushan, 1988).

It is posited here that the influx of foreign (predominantly western) capital further consolidated the management practices that the settler class had already engendered. Right from the outset, the capitalist mode of production appeared to thrive on managerial authoritarianism, leading to the institutionalization of adversarial employee relations. The colonial policy of fostering foreign investment at the expense of local entrepreneurialism clearly echoed the agricultural policy which supported "settlers" in cash-crop production and restricted local people to subsistence. Some local entrepreneurs reacted to these restrictions by combining political activity with business. In this regard, Marris and Somerset (1971, p68) suggest that: "business itself was sometimes as much an expression of nationalism as an economic venture in its own right...(Projects) were attractive as symbols of African progress, rather than profitable." An example is the Luo Thrift Society started by Oginga Odinga and others.

Swainson points out that although the colonial government made some effort to redress the imbalance it was particular firms (eg East African Breweries, Unga Flour, BAT, etc) that initially helped to stimulate African trade by extending wholesale facilities to African traders. It was only after independence that local people were able to play a more active role in the economic activities. This processes was further boosted by the policy of "Africanization" in the 1960s and 1970s, and the creation of joint-ventures through institutions like the Industrial and Commercial Development Corporation (ICDC).

The Personnel/HR role and function

In analysing the characteristics of the personnel function in Third World countries, Poole (1982) notes that since personnel management has evolved largely as an administrative or managerial specialism, its contours and substance may be expected to reflect, in some measure, the orientations and perceptions of the managerial personnel rather than being merely a product of political, economic or organizational change itself. It is suggested here that the perceptions and orientations are informed by diverse cultural and value considerations.

In an earlier assessment of personnel practices in Kenya, Henley (1977) notes that the initial role of personnel practitioners was very much a public relations one, especially amongst the Africans who were being co-opted by multinational companies following the policy of Africanization. In addition to drafting into supervisory positions those African clerical workers who showed an aptitude for administration, those appointed to personnel positions were those who could liaise with the intelligentsia in mutually symbiotic alliances, especially in expediting various operations through bureaucracies, securing work permits for expatriates and so forth (Henley, 1977; Langdon, 1981). Akinnusi (1991) has also noted that the personnel function in Africa was the first to be indigenised for reasons of expediency; African chiefs were relied upon as recruiters of labour, and subsequently, as pacifiers of the same in the face of vociferous demands and complaints. Table 3.2 illustrates the key considerations in the evolution of personnel/ HR in Kenya.

Figure 3.1 Key features in the evolution of personnel/HR

* *Pre-independence* (before 1963) - volatile labour market and political context

dual role
- African : forced labour, "wage slavery"
- European: special treatment/privileges

Asians mainly involved in trade and commerce

* Post-independence "Africanization"

* *Criteria for appointments into Personnel*

- aptitude for administration
- literacy (especially proficiency in English)
- record-keeping (clerical) skills
- obedience - respect for authority structure
- political connections/public relations - ability to secure work permits; liaising with a politically sensitive Labour Ministry

Personnel thus evolves as a routine, administrative and political activity.

* Centrality of the Welfare role:
- pressure from kin and clansmen for favours in jobs and promotion
- taking account of migrant workers (rural-urban drift)
- creating solutions for infrastructural problems

* Organizational priorities - Personnel seen as "low-status", reflecting the dominance of finance and technology - high pressure for productivity and profitability
* "dealing with" unions

* Effect of QWL (late 1970s) - pressure to humanize work practices, hence:
- HRM: "emergent" from late 1980s
- HRD: training seen as the key priority

In Search of an "Appropriate" Approach[4]

This section specifically addresses the need for an approach which is suitable for the purposes of organizations in Kenya. Various studies of management in Africa have stressed the relevance of context and suitability. Blunt and Jones (1992) have highlighted the importance of suitability in adopting Western management practices. Blunt (1990b) adopts a contingency approach in considering organizational effectiveness in developing countries, and emphasizes that a contingency approach must be built around a core of organizational and value imperatives. In assessing the relevance of western organization theories in Kenyan agricultural administration and their implications for other organizations, Leonard (1977) emphasizes the need to specify the contingencies under which theoretical propositions are expected to operate rather than the development of highly abstract "laws" of behaviour. Onah (1981) notes that management cannot be practised in a vacuum, and is affected by the socio-economic variables of the country in which it is practised.

The foregoing implies a contingent orientation to effective management practice. In this regard, Miller's (1987) contingent configuration of *imperatives* or "powerful influences" yields some interesting insights in our conception of *context*. These are: *environment, structure, leadership* and *strategy*. In their discussion of developing country contexts, Kanungo and Jaeger (1990) propose a configuration of the external and internal factors influencing organizational effectiveness, including *economic/technological, political/legal* and *social/cultural*. From the foregoing it seems inevitable that the adoption of foreign practices should be contingent upon the contextual circumstances. The following are considered crucial factors in the formulation of the "context" for HRM in Kenya. This broad framework incorporates both the internal and external considerations in order to emphasize the interrelationships between them.

* socio-cultural factors
* competitive environment
* industrial relations
* the State

These are discussed below.

The Socio-Cultural Factors

This discussion is about the issues that define the beliefs, norms, practices and interrelationships particularly between management and subordinates. We first consider the "us-and-them" attitudinal cleavages in Kenyan society. The most important manifestation of this is in the management-subordinate divide. Miller (1984) sees this phenomenon within the broader context of increased stratification by social class, greater differences between rural and urban dwellers, discrimination against women and some minorities such as pastoralists, and major differences in access to such amenities as health and education. According to Miller (1984), this split includes, on the one hand, those who constitute the higher economic echelons, and who benefit from a patron-client system; on the other hand we have the lower rungs of the economic system, or those who are not in the system at all. This stratification has worsened as the gap between the rich and poor has widened in the 1990s. With a per capita GDP of $310 it is estimated that more than half the Kenyan population of 30 million are living below the poverty line.

Stratification is also evident in managerial attitudes; certain commentators have observed the tendency of managers to be intolerant and even arrogant. Waweru (1979) describes a wide range of complaints by workers which include the "arrogant and disrespectful" attitudes of managers. It has been claimed that African communities exhibit a high power distance, (eg Jaeger and Kanungo, 1990; Seddon, 1985). As such, "wisdom" and "the right to rule" are ascribed to the elderly or to those in positions of authority. This results in a relatively high degree of acquiescence in authority such that the power hierarchy is legitimized by cultural norms. In the organizational setting, the "boss" is an all-powerful being. This situation can be traced back to the abrasive and often brutal styles adopted by colonial managers.

A related aspect is that of managerial authoritarianism, which has tended to be attributed to the colonial era (eg Waweru 1975). Although traditional African communities might exhibit a high power distance, this did not necessarily mean authoritarianism; rather, as we argue below, the power hierarchy was sustained by a system of paternalism. Managers in the case studies agreed that an abrasive style was prevalent in the country and that it persisted because it was considered *effective*. Leonard (1977) found that the Kenyan agricultural elite's conception of a good supervisor was a "remote, demanding and authoritarian figure"; he also argues that authoritarianism can in part be attributed to insecurity. In a similar vein, Onyemelukwe (1973), attributes it to managers' fear of eroding their authority by familiarity towards subordinates. This parallels the "us-and-them" cleavages identified above. This leads us to wonder whether indeed authoritarianism can offer any real and sustainable advantages. For Damachi (1978) the emergent authoritarianism in African business is highly centralized, hence any form of delegation of authority is usually to relatives and trusted close friends.

The kinship ethos in the African extended-family system can be said to have bred a form of "authoritarian paternalism". Workers thus expect to be "looked after" and are therefore in turn willing to accept that their superiors should exercise an inordinate amount of control (see also Seddon, 1985). A similar situation has been observed in Asian countries like Thailand: the "take care" culture (Kamoche, 2000). While the system generates a beneficial welfare culture, it also, unfortunately impedes individual initiative and creativity. Corporate welfare includes a wide range of fringe benefits such as subsidised canteens, low-interest loans, discounts for staff purchases and so forth. An HRM approach with a welfare-paternalist element may, on the basis of this argument, go down well with employee expectations.

"Ethnicity" is an important consideration for African societies which are characterized by cultural heterogeneity and extended family ties. Some observers have been content to dismiss the consequences of ethnic dysfunctionalism without trying to understand fully how and why it has come about. In his description of the environment for business in Africa, Onyemelukwe (1973, p25) observes that there are basic values which govern the life of these communities:

> In the first place, there is a heavy accent on family-blood relatives, the group of kinsfolk held together by common origin and common obligations. The family is conceived of as a large number of people, many dead, some living and countless numbers yet to be born. Every individual is taught to accept his place in this group and to behave in a way to bring honour to it. Emphasis is placed on helping others in sickness and health, success or failure. A family member fulfils his obligation not by acquiring for himself but by giving to other members.

Ethnicity at the workplace might manifest itself in various forms: straight favouritism in recruitment and promotion, or in the search for ethnic homogeneity perhaps, as Blunt (1980) contends, as an adaptive response to alienation at the workplace. Particularist practices (especially favouritism on ethnic and kinship lines) are in effect the opportunity for the individual to discharge his obligations to kith and kin. This creates the negative spectre of "tribalism". "Tribalism" does not refer to the multiplicity of ethnic groups, or indeed to the natural affinity that members of one tribe feel to one another; instead it refers to the relationships between people from other tribes (Leys, 1975). Leys argues that the foundations of this phenomenon were laid by the colonialists through their divide-and-rule policies and by the introduction of capitalist modes and relations of production, which subsequently gave rise to new forms of insecurity, and obliged people to compete with each other at the national level.

In his analysis of migrant labour, Blunt (1980; 1982) has attempted to develop a "kinship solidarity" thesis whereby ethnic homogeneity can supposedly be encouraged to counter alienation at work and to provide a sense of belonging amongst people whose language and culture unite them in the face of city-life tribulations. Ethnic homogeneity supposedly provides the companionship of kinsmen and fellow tribesmen and offers psychological support to migrant workers. Blunt implies that kinship solidarity might offer a useful base for the institution of autonomous workgroups, which might in turn help to resolve the participation problem. While this position has *prima facie* appeal in fostering organizational practices upon extant socio-cultural realities, it is doubtful whether the perpetuation of ethnic-based practices is tenable in a country where tribalism is widely acknowledged as one of the most serious social-political problems, and where "tribal clashes" nearly precipitated a civil war in the early 1990s.

It is suggested here that semi-autonomous workgroups can be aligned to the communal-groupism ethos as this goes beyond ethnic considerations. The group-collectivist ethos is prevalent in Kenyan society, and in organizations as well as in the wider community, this often manifests itself in the spirit of "harambee" - pooling of resources to help relatives and friends and share financial burdens. Clearly, personnel/HR practitioners must be aware of ethnic considerations and the pressures placed on those in wage employment. Blunt and Popoola (1985) suggest that managers should be insulated from, or indifferent to kinship pressures. The existence of this dilemma creates a particular problem in the search for "integrative practices" in HRM.

The Competitive Environment

Under the "competitive environment" we include a broad range of issues that directly impact on organizational performance. We consider the way the business environment and business decisions affect the management of human resources. The generic term "competitive" as used here denotes a concern with the way organizations compete. It therefore includes the availability and use of technology, organizational structure, and the use of financial and other economic resources in strategic management. Although these factors will not be discussed here at length, it is important to emphasize the effect they have on the different organizations' treatment of the human resource.

It is, for example, generally held that the institution of modern HRM practices is a costly undertaking because it entails the commitment of financial resources especially through rewarding and development. This view was supported by managers in the case studies. This has implications on the extent to which HRM initiatives can be taken in the small and medium sized (mainly indigenous) firms with limited financial resources. Organizational structure and type of technology impact on HRM with regard to the structure of work and job design; this means that approaches and practices may vary between departments and even jobs, thus illustrating the difficulty of conceiving of HRM as a standard set of practices. A good example is the "core-peripheral" structure which was found to be a central feature in the case studies.

The need to pay keen attention to strategy is underpinned by the uncertainties that bedevil the business climate in developing countries. Describing this volatility, Blunt (1983) asserts that changes in the continent are probably greater in magnitude, more varied and numerous, and occur more quickly, than elsewhere in the world. The nature of these uncertainties has also been characterized by Munene (1991) who has observed that various socio-economic and political factors combine to create an environment which is manifestly hostile to business. Unfortunately, there has not been a strong tradition of long-term strategic management in industry in Kenya. Views from managers in the case studies supported Kiggundu's (1989) argument that the volatile environment in developing countries makes long-term strategic planning very difficult; failure to use strategic management to respond to such an environment only makes organizations more vulnerable.

This weakness goes back to the 1960s and 1970s when the government fostered a policy of import substitution ostensibly to discourage imports and establish a local manufacturing industry. But rather than give the much-needed impetus to a nascent industry, this policy created a protected and largely inefficient local industry (eg Langdon, 1987). According to this argument, protection gave rise to complacency, and it was not uncommon especially in the formative years of industrialization for organizations to lobby the government persistently for all manner of protection, from stiff import tariffs to export guarantee schemes. There is now an initiative to shift to export-oriented industries although the country's export strategy is still vague. It is expected that this will provide a growth impetus to manufacturing, which currently accounts for only about 15% of GDP, and employs 10% of the workforce; the principle economic activity, agriculture, accounts for 30% of GDP, and employs 78% of the workforce.

The relative weakness of long-term strategic planning is also explained by the fact that the subsidiaries of the MNCs have to a large extent relied on head office in matters of strategy and policy-formulation. This generally means that subsidiaries are subject to very tight reporting requirements and have very little time to engage in long-term strategic thinking. This has in turn created a culture of "passive compliance" (Kamoche, 1997) where subsidiary level managers merely follow guidelines from headquarters and concern themselves with strategy implementation while leaving strategy formulation to the headquarters. Reliance on parent company guidance indicates the removal of the responsibility of strategic planning from the local management. This sort of "guidance" was found at Autoco, Pharmaco and Mimea with respect to the institution of personnel/HR changes. On the whole, market uncertainties, inadequate information, and a reliance on informal planning and decision-making structures have tended to create some form of short-termism reminiscent of "logical incrementalism" (Quinn, 1980). This was exemplified by Automart's notion of *Management by Deciding* and Chematox's *juggling with policies* (considered in subsequent chapters). This has implications on the viability of "strategic HRM". It must be pointed out though, that the use of such approaches may simply reflect the inappropriateness of more rationalist ones in situations characterized by high uncertainty and complexity.

The weaknesses in strategic management can also be attributed to the enduring drive to survive the challenges of the "external environment". Organization theory in Africa is dominated by the "external environment" paradigm. There is an underlying assumption that organizational success is predicated upon managers' ability to understand and control external environmental factors. The "environment" itself has been characterized in a number of ways. For example, Munene (1991) distinguishes between the "task" environment and the "general" or "institutional" environment. Munene analyses and measures the nature of the external environment to determine how it influences decision making and goal attainment. He finds that both external (eg transactional failure, unpredictability and uncertainty) and internal (eg red tape and family cliques) characteristics combine to create organizational inertia and to prevent viable organizational forms.

The "internal" dimension has received less attention relative to the "external" dimension in organizational analysis in Africa. In some cases, the opportunity to analyse the internal organizational context comes up against the dominant logic of the external environment. For example, some writers lament the focus on the "internal organizational processes" which they claim has led to a neglect of an understanding of the complex external environment (eg Blunt & Jones, 1992; Kiggundu, 1989). This internal focus appears to refer to efforts to improve performance through the use of foreign techniques. It seems to have little to do with the firm's configuration of resources, capabilities and organizational routines (Nelson & Winter, 1982). The ultimate image is that of an external environment which is manifestly hostile to management.

This encourages a reactive approach to planning which is anchored primarily in the industrial organization perspective and which only addresses the nature of the external hostilities and how these can be overcome. As such, the internal circumstances of the firm are seen as unproblematic. The question of strategic choice and the strategic options available from internally generated resources and capabilities is largely ignored. This approach is in part responsible for the neglect of the knowhow and expertise held internally in the field of HRM. This has meant that the potential strategic value of human resources and the unique cultural attributes have not been fully acknowledged or realized since the greatest imperative has been organizational survival.

Industrial Relations

This section provides a background to industrial relations in the country, and seeks to explain how the extant IR climate has come into being; this in turn will shed some light on how the management-labour interface with regard to appreciating the "context", can best be mediated. A more detailed characterization of industrial relations in Kenya is found in the extensive literature (eg Sandbrook, 1975; Singh, 1969, 1980; Chege, 1988).

Worker organization and protest began in the early colonial period when a consciousness of the need to rise against the oppressive colonial regime began to sweep across the country. The first forms of such organization were actually political associations rather than trade unions. The agenda of the most prominent association in the early 1920s, the East African Association included, *inter alia*: removal of the "colony" status which Britain imposed on Kenya in 1920, free elections to the Legislative Council, reduction of taxes, abolition of the hated "Kipande" identity card, the campaign against forced, unpaid labour, and increases in wages (Singh, 1969). It follows from this argument that industrial conflict and worker protest were thus defined *ab initio*, by the combination of political oppression and industrial exploitation. Only the staff of the government and railways (European, Asian and African) could form staff associations. Artisans and labourers were not allowed to organize, in case they demanded to form conventional trade unions. According to Singh (1969), trade unions first arose on a large scale among Asian workers, initially in the railways and in the construction industry. This was exemplified in the Railway Artisan Union formed in 1922. This union closed down in 1923, and some of the leaders were deported to India.

Conventional trade unions began to appear amongst African workers in the 1940s. Their agenda effectively married the political and the industrial, whereby key leaders like Bildad Kaggia, Chege Kibachia and Fred Kubai and many others organized strikes to attain political as well as industrial objectives. The first major union, the African Workers' Federation (AWF), was formed in 1947. That same year the AWF organized a major strike in Mombasa, whose main grievances (as in many other strikes thereafter) were, *inter alia*, the government's indifference to racial discrimination in the wage system, the rampant disrespect shown to African workers, and the "indirect slavery" bred by a low wage economy (Waweru, 1984). This strike heralded the militancy that was to continue well into the 1950s in the wake of the Mau Mau independence struggle. Unions suffered persecution by the State throughout the colonial era and in spite of their militancy, remained a weak force in the face of industrial and political challenges.

The role of the union movement became rather ambiguous after independence. Indeed, some union leaders either abandoned the movement altogether or used it as a stepping stone into a political career (see Sandbrook, 1975). Furthermore, according to Sandbrook the new government showed itself to be just as concerned to control organized labour as the colonial regime had been. Unions were now being urged to exercise self-restraint in the interest of "industrial stability for economic development". Concern with industrial stability also signaled the government's sympathetic attitude towards employers and suspicions about union militancy. In 1965, the Central Organization of Trade Unions (COTU) was formed in order to establish a viable industrial relations climate. The other objective was to unify the union movement which was at the time torn between two warring unions, the Kenya Federation of Labour (KFL) and the Kenya African Workers Congress (KAWC). The Industrial Relations Charter (IRC) was enacted in 1962 and was subsequently followed a number of "Tripartite Agreements" signed by the KFL, the Kenya Federation of Employers (KFE), and the Kenyan government. The IRC sought, among other things, to establish a framework in which the three parties would be involved in promoting trade unionism and settling disputes.

The Tripartite Agreements in particular aimed to settle disputes peacefully and to avoid disruptive activities. By requiring mutual concessions from employers and unions (eg prohibiting wage demands for a period of 12 months in return for a 10% labour intake), they enhanced the corporatist nature of industrial relations in the country. Over time, the government-employer alliance has resulted in a tightening of the restrictions on union activities. This includes the banning of strikes by governmental decree and exhortations to striking workers to return to work or lose their jobs. The Trade Disputes Act also introduced sweeping changes in dispute resolution and effectively restrained unions from adopting too militant a stand (Chege, 1988). Ogolla-Bondi (1980) classifies the restrictions into five categories:

(1) Restrictions on the scope of the right to organize; registration
(2) categorically precludes associations that are remotely "political".
(3) Limitation of the extent to which legitimate interests can be pursued.
(4) Prohibition or restriction of industrial action, especially as in designated "essential services".
(5) Regulating the constitutional form and internal administration of trade unions; this is laboriously spelt out in the Trade Unions Act.
(6) Co-optation of union leaders: support in parliamentary elections and appointments to governmental corporations.

The Trade Disputes Act lists a wide range of "essential services" which are barred from unionising, including water, electricity, postal, hospital, air transport and air traffic control, posts and telecommunications, teaching and so forth. These restrictions have, however, been breached from time to time. There are various other controls on union operations, covering things like supervision of union elections, submission of financial and election reports, and so forth. Furthermore, the principal officers of COTU are appointed and serve at the pleasure of the President of the Republic. These factors raise doubts about the independence of the trade union movement in the country. They describe what Siddique (1989) refers to as an "inclusionist-corporatist" framework of industrial relations.

The tendency for African governments to substantially narrow the range of trade unions' activities is well-documented in the literature. The government's position has been strengthened further by the imperative to achieve economic development with minimal disruption from union activities including strike action. This has, from time to time, been achieved through draconian laws and force. Kaniki (1981) observes that independent governments have tended to continue the legacy of showing an eagerness to use police brutality and similar forms of state repression to control workers on strike. With regard to Kenya in particular, Chege (1988, p182) points out that fear of retribution ranks high as a reason behind the relative tranquillity in the country's industrial relations.

> This applies especially to union leaders fear arrest for calling "unofficial strikes". To the rank and file however, the biggest fear is that of being sacked for striking... The large and ever-growing reserve of unskilled and semi-skilled job seekers waiting to fill any openings has actually strengthened the employers' hand at the lower end of the job market by making it easy to replace militant skilled labourers.

The role of unions in the contemporary HR activities remains a moot point. So far there has been little effort to involve unions in the changes, and managers do not anticipate any significant shift in union involvement. The issue is compounded further by the concern about the adversarial nature of the employer-labour relations (eg Waweru, 1984). Nationwide teachers' and bankers' strikes in 1998 reveal the existing climate retains a high degree of mutual mistrust, and have also demonstrated the political nature of industrial action by direct involvement of the government by imposing "solutions" be decree. Managers have traditionally held union leaders in low esteem, and are often heard to complain about their "low education" and "lack of understanding" of the basics of business. Union leaders on the other hand accuse managers of insensitivity, and being concerned with the ruthless exploitation of workers. These tensions seem to indicate that the introduction of HRM practices which embody a unitarist ethos will encounter serious difficulties.

Additionally, the general inadequacy of participative mechanisms and low degree of constructive communication (especially between management and unions) does not bode well for a viable HR climate.[5] At first glance, this scenario would seem to suggest incompatibility between industrial relations and HRM but it must be remembered that besides the stipulations of the IR Charter, it is in the government's interest to sustain a "well-regulated" trade union movement in order to ensure "industrial peace".[6] Secondly, considering the degree of politicisation of the union movement (both in terms of governmental interference and the trade union leaders' political agenda), a total sidelining of trade unions is impracticable.[7] In view of the above, management must give due attention to the potential role of unions in HRM initiatives. This may involve the delineation of specific collaborative initiatives - identifying areas of joint participation, such as re-grading and job re-design in functional flexibility, and training. This might entail the use of joint committees to handle specific HRM issues, with the support of the union. The success of such initiatives depends on the prevailing IR climate and managerial attitudes

The Role of the State

The purpose of this section is not to prescribe a role for the government in the institution of HRM practices but to assess the implications of such a potential role. Officials in the Ministry of Labour indicated that they were closely watching the developments and expressed concern that *HRM may be an attempt to break unions*. Their apprehension is due in part to the suspicions surrounding the adoption of unitarist HRM mainly in the US and the possibility of such practices being imported by MNCs. Suspicions were further raised when a vehicle assembly plant in Mombasa tried to implement an extreme form of numerical flexibility which consisted of hiring a big proportion of its workforce on six-month renewable contracts. This was found to be illegal and stopped after government intervention. Ministry officials were concerned about the possibility of similar practices being introduced under the guise of HRM.

Proposing a specific role for the State in HR initiatives continues to exercise the minds of various observers. In the earlier days of HR theorizing, Beer et al (1985) advocated legislation "to make the stakeholder concept a reality" but nevertheless expressed doubt about the feasibility of active public policy in the USA, given the existing property relations. Walton (1987) wonders how HRM can improve productivity and facilitate change without the governmental support of the kind found in Japan under MITI (the Ministry of International Trade and Industry). Similarly, Kochan et al (1986) refer to the "new trends" in industrial relations in the USA as experiments which require the active support of public policy for sustained diffusion and institutionalization. The question of legislation is echoed in Guest's (1987) claim that for HRM to flourish in the UK, the impetus would have to come from the political context. This idea is repeated in Keep's (eg 1989) call for public policymakers to offer incentives for training and development. In this regard, Kamoche and Mueller (1998) suggest that there is further scope to search for "macro-level" solutions to the development of people rather than relying on the hope that organizations will take training and development seriously. It is now recognized that the State has a potentially pivotal role to play especially in providing a framework within which investments can be directed into training and developing people. This is exemplified in Singapore where the State has played a direct role in driving industrialization and economic progress through education and training, and also in Germany's system of industrial apprenticeships.

In the Kenyan case Waweru (1984; 1979) offers a cogent advocacy of the radical restructuring of property relations as the only way to develop viable work practices; this is a call for the workers to own the means of production. Given the existing politico-economic structure, however, this solution does not seem feasible. A capitalist mode of production has been firmly entrenched in the industrial process. Furthermore, the State's commitment to industrial investment is backed by a wide range of favourable incentives to foreign investors, including repatriation of profits, guarantee of property rights, tax allowances for locating in the rural areas and in industrial estates (Export Processing Zones) and so forth. The role of the State may be viewed in the broader context of an "industrial relations system".

In this regard, Siddique (1989) posits a model of industrial relations for the Third World in which the State is accorded a dominant role. He argues that the restricted industrialization process in the colonized countries which essentially sought to cater for the interests of the home country was inappropriate and failed to absorb the rapidly growing population leading to labour surpluses. This reduced the economic bargaining power of the working classes, who were subsequently forced to supplement their income from the "pre-capitalist" agricultural sector. This created a problem of commitment to the industrial way of life. Some evidence of this may be found in the post-independence "back to the land" presidential exhortation which was designed to reverse the rural-urban migration.

Siddique's Marxian analysis holds that the dualistic economic structure has led to an uneven effect of capitalist development on the population, including an inadequate proletarianization of the workers, which Marx argued was central to the emergence of a capitalist mode of production. The "weak" class formation has supposedly made both the *insufficiently proletarianized industrial working class* and the *undeveloped bourgeoisie* less powerful than in the industrialized West. This allows the State to play a dominant role, as evidenced by the corporatist framework that emerged after independence. As noted above, the trade union movement was co-opted into this framework. It is this pre-eminence of the State in the Third World economy which prompts Siddique to conceive a model of industrial relations in which the State necessarily plays a dominant role. The merit in this model is that it depicts the inter-relationships of the three key stakeholders (the proletariat and bourgeoisie so-called, and the State); it also emphasizes that the role of the State has to be seen not as a contemporary phenomenon but rather from a historical perspective.

The post-independent Keynesian role has been in decline in recent years as exemplified in the privatisation of state enterprises, and the decline in the provision of basic facilities like health and education under the IMF and World Bank sponsored view that these should increasingly be left to "market forces". Unfortunately, this recommendation rings hollow in a country where "market forces" are constrained by state bureaucracy and widespread corruption and where half the population live below the poverty line. It is noteworthy that managers in the case studies saw little need for a role for the government beyond ensuring compliance with legislation. However, the Training Manager at Autoco felt that the government might persuade firms to institute welfare and benefit programmes that assist the workforce directly. We argue here in way of conclusion that the role of the State in HRM should include creating opportunities and incentives for management and unions to engage in more constructive debate on the impact of business decisions on HRM; legislative protection against the potential excesses of management; a more visionary policy on education and skill-formation at the national level, as well as a more coherent industrial strategy.

Toward a Model of HRM for Africa[8]

This section builds on the foregoing to explore the case for a model of management that is suitable for the needs of Africa in general. Management theory in general has been heavily influenced by economics and American organizational psychology with an unrelenting quest for "facts" and generalizable, universalist theories. Redding (1994) has identified an epistemological problem in this genre - "the bankruptcy of empirical positivism" (p345). There is a long intellectual history stretching from early "scientific management" to the seminal work on rationality in formally constituted organizations (eg Selznick, 1948; Simon, 1957) to latter-day strategy analysis which often takes on a clinical punctiliousness in Business School case studies. However, in spite of the dominance of functionalist/positivist analyses, Western scholarship has gradually come to acknowledge the existence of alternative viewpoints, including Simon's "bounded rationality", the influences of subjective, social and informal aspects, ethnographic and interpretivist studies, and the role of language and power. Other noteworthy perspectives include Marxist theory and the radical humanist critique - see for example Habermas' (1972) "communicative distortion", and Marcuse's (1964) critique of technology and logic.

To understand the African thought-system and its impact on industrial practice, it is necessary to appreciate how the African worker makes sense of the world through symbolism and to some extent, mystical thinking. He draws from proverbial social thought and organizes his life in a system of reciprocal social relationships where the family is the core unit (see for example, Ahiauzu, 1986; Horton, 1967; Mobana, 1960; Nzelibe, 1986; Otite, 1978). Nzelibe (1986:11) argues that: "whereas Western management thought advocates Eurocentricism, individualism, and modernity, African management thought emphasizes ethnocentricism, traditionalism, communalism, and cooperative teamwork". It follows therefore that if meaningful debate is to be maintained between these two perspectives, there should be more analysis of the African thought system. In this regard we examine the implications of adopting "western" models vis-a-vis the unique characteristics in Africa.

The (Ab)use of Foreign Concepts and Practices

It would be naive to reject foreign concepts outright. The unrelenting pace of industrialization and globalization through multinational corporations and management education would not permit it. It is essential, however, to set out some difficulties in the use of such approaches and to identify clearly those that are suitable. We argue here that the unquestioning use of "western" models of management in Africa merely stifles the incentive to examine critically the real needs of organizations on the continent. The question of relevance has been a recurring theme in the literature (Damachi, 1978; Jaeger & Kanungo, 1990; Kamoche, 1993; Onyemelukwe, 1973). In this regard, the relevance of western concepts has been seen vis a vis the African culture. It should be pointed out that in spite of the relative uniformity in the essence of "African thought-system", "African culture" is in reality a melange of about 2000 "sub-cultures"/linguistic groups that fall into Bantu, Hamitic, Nilotic, Arabic, Asian, European and other such categories. Some countries like Cameroon have over 200 ethnic groups while Kenya has about 40.

Democracies and military dictatorships exist side by side. Marxist and "free market force" ideologies shape the industrial arena. This diversity casts some doubt on the feasibility and usefulness of universal constructs. "Western" concepts are potentially useful if they can offer insights about the range of options available for crafting organizations and enhancing their effectiveness. The particular circumstances, needs and constraints that typify the African business context should define the appropriate agenda for action by specifying desirable organizational structures and systems, showing how resources are to be secured and distributed, and making strategic choices, including identifying what elements of foreign concepts are appropriate.

The role of culture and cross-cultural management have been extensively discussed in the literature (see for example Adler, 1986; Hofstede, 1980; Laurent, 1986; Tayeb, 1988). The complex nature of culture, in particular where this involves comparative analyses finds expression in the convergence/divergence debate and the need to pay attention to both emic (culture-specific) and etic (culture-common) aspects of organizational phenomena. Child (1981) recognized the powerful effects of culture in the processes of organizing and human behaviour, such as authority, style, participation and so forth, as opposed to structure, strategy and technology. This requires researchers to be sensitive to the emic aspects in cross-cultural and comparative research and to eschew methodologies and conceptual premises which are a-contextual and universalist. The adoption of foreign practices depends not only on cultural but also on political, institutional and structural factors. Tayeb (1995) argues that a combination of national culture, labour relations, social stratification, educational system, pressure groups and so forth contribute to the "repertoire" available to the country. The diversity of these characteristics on the African continent poses immense challenges to any effort to adopt foreign practices.

A noteworthy critique is offered by Abudu (1986) who argues that the effects of colonialism and ill-conceived industrialization in Nigeria (and much of Africa for that matter) produced a culture which is neither local nor foreign, but "a hybrid monstrosity". This implies that efforts to conceptualize an African "context", "culture" or "society" should be undertaken with caution. It is important to pay attention to the challenges at the level of the firm - while retaining the broader, macro-picture - before we can begin to offer standard recipes. It is with this in mind that the concept of internal resource heterogeneity is offered here.

Cultivating the Internal Resource Base: the Way Forward?

Penrose (1959) argued that the uniqueness of firms arises from the heterogeneity available or potentially available from their internally held resources. This perspective enables us to shift the emphasis in organizational analysis away from the dominant external environment paradigm, to the level of the firm. As noted above, the external environment paradigm misconstrues the heterogeneous nature of African society and ultimately casts firms in a reactive mode to a putative hostile environment. In positing the paradigm of internal resource heterogeneity (IRH) we acknowledges the dimensions of the African thought system identified above. Ahiauzu (1986) has demonstrated how the African industrial worker brings his indigenous thought-system to the workplace and uses it in "interpreting, constructing, and ascribing meanings to things, structures, and processes at the industrial workplace" (p47).

Industrialization in much of Africa is only about forty years old, and the individual's way of life, including his work behaviour is still largely determined by "traditionalism". This has to do with "accepted customs, beliefs, and practices that determine accepted behaviour, morality, and the desired characteristics of the individual in African society" (Nzelibe, 1986, p11). Nzelibe argues further that for the African, all modalities and realities are interrelated and phenomenally interactive. Therefore, there can be no separation between the worker's "private"/family life and his industrial work life. His work behaviour should be understood in terms of the meanings he attaches to the immediate world around him. Thus the pace of modern industrial life, the complexity of industrial technology, impersonality of relations, the non-recognition of traditional forms of status based on age and social hierarchy and so forth, are examples of factors that the African worker perceives as alienating manifestations of "Western" management.

A shift towards the worker's frame of reference is a useful starting point in adopting the IRH. A more comprehensive approach involves a consideration of the entire range of resources and capabilities within the ambit of management. This requires a particular configuration of resources and a capacity to deploy them (eg Barney, 1991; Grant, 1991). The interface between strategic management and HRM should thus be understood in terms of what the firm can do (capabilities) with the skills, abilities and talents (resources) of its employees and managers (Cappelli & Singh, 1992; Kamoche, 1996; Mueller, 1996). The notion of "capabilities" highlights the behavioural rather than the structural aspect of strategy (Stalk, Evans & Shulman, 1992). It parallels Child's (1981) comments on cultural effects cited above. This is important for the perspective being developed here because structure connotes a static element, while behaviour connotes proactivity and what people actually do.

The resource-capabilities perspective builds on some of the earlier work on how HR can support strategy, eg through reward policies, career management, managerial expertise, selection and training (eg Evans, 1986; Fombrun et al, 1984; Hendry & Pettigrew, 1986). This literature is relevant here in the implementation of HR strategy. Figure 3.2 illustrates a processual model for the strategic management of HR in Africa. This begins with strategy formulation where both external and internal environments are carefully considered. This model differs from extant approaches mainly on two counts: the attention given to the internal environment, and the incorporation of the African thought-system through the "HR ethos".

This model indicates that the strengths of the organization evolve around the concepts of core competences (see Prahalad & Hamel, 1990), corporate values and culture. This is consistent with IRH. The second phase in strategy formulation is to identify a viable strategic approach. This model proposes a shift away from the extant strategic approaches (passive follower, political manipulation and cost reduction) to an "evolutionary" resource-capability approach. It is important to acknowledge the political dimension of strategy (eg Mintzberg, 1985) in so far as it describes the social context within which resources are allocated; however, manipulation and patronage involve a much more invidious element.

According to Mueller (1996), valuable strategic assets are not generated by senior management's codified policies alone. For him, sustainable competitive advantage is brought about by "'social architecture' that results from on-going skill formation activities, incidental or informal learning, forms of spontaneous co-operation ... and tacit knowledge" (p777). We interpret this approach as combining the resource-capability view located within IRH and continuous learning; the complementary roles of formally constituted planning mechanisms and and serendipity. The strategic thrust thus moves away from cost reduction to innovation, quality management and selective investment in the long term. HR policies subsequently flow from business strategies as predicted by the "matching model" of HRM (eg Fombrun et al, 1984).

Figure 3.2 A processual, strategic model of HRM for Africa

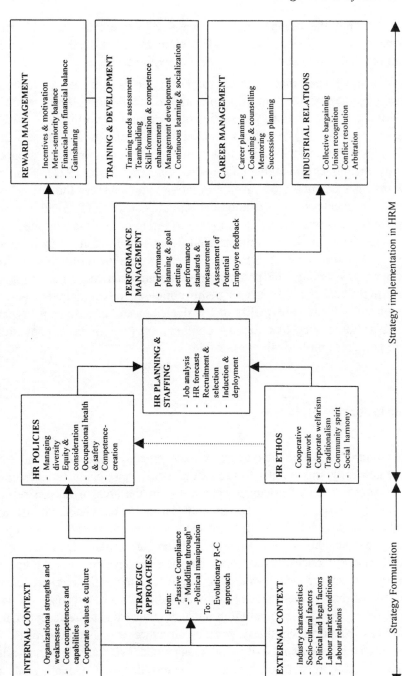

INTERNAL CONTEXT
- Organizational strengths and weaknesses
- Core competences and capabilities
- Corporate values & culture

HR POLICIES
- Managing diversity
- Equity & consideration
- Occupational health & safety
- Competence-creation

HR PLANNING & STAFFING
- Job analysis
- HR forecasts
- Recruitment & selection
- Induction & deployment

PERFORMANCE MANAGEMENT
- Performance planning & goal setting
- performance standards & measurement
- Assessment of Potential
- Employee feedback

REWARD MANAGEMENT
- Incentives & motivation
- Merit-seniority balance
- Financial-non financial balance
- Gainsharing

TRAINING & DEVELOPMENT
- Training needs assessment
- Teambuilding
- Skill-formation & competence enhancement
- Management development
- Continuous learning & socialization

CAREER MANAGEMENT
- Career planning
- Coaching & counselling
- Mentoring
- Succession planning

INDUSTRIAL RELATIONS
- Collective bargaining
- Union recognition
- Conflict resolution
- Arbitration

STRATEGIC APPROACHES

From:
- Passive Compliance
- " Muddling through"
- Political manipulation

To:
- Evolutionary R-C approach

HR ETHOS
- Cooperative teamwork
- Corporate welfarism
- Traditionalism
- Community spirit
- Social harmony

EXTERNAL CONTEXT
- Industry characteristics
- Socio-cultural factors
- Political and legal factors
- Labour market conditions
- Labour relations

Strategy implementation in HRM

Strategy Formulation

Underpinning the policies is what we refer to here as the "HR ethos" germane to the African context. The elements of this ethos are derived from the discussion above on the African thought system.

We argue here that in order for HR policies to make a meaningful impact on the management of people, and to secure the commitment of the workforce, they have to be sufficiently grounded within the worker's thought and value system. For example, teambuilding as a form of training will be accepted to the extent that teamwork is consistent with groupism, familysm and communalism (see also Onyemelukwe, 1973). Similarly, reward systems should be based on motivational schemes that are relevant to the worker's sociopsychological circumstances and which combine merit pay and some degree of seniority to reflect socially-sanctioned forms of status. This has been demonstrated in empirical studies (eg Kamoche, 1992b, Onyemelukwe, 1973). Firms have to weigh the motivational effects of merit pay against the potential resentment from the older employees who might feel their loyalty is being doubted. It is anticipated that this model will improve the quality of HR decisions and initiatives in Africa in so far as the choice of policy or combination of policies is contextually valid and epistemologically defensible.

Conclusions

In an attempt to define the *context* of management in Kenya first, and Africa more generally, this chapter has sought to assess those characteristics crucial to an appreciation of organizational needs in the area of human resource management. The chapter began by considering the entrenchment of foreign capital and the deleterious effects of the practices introduced in the colonial era. This helped to explain the origins of apparently inappropriate management practices. It was noted that the repressive conditions created by the colonial regime, which worked in league with the settler entrepreneurs set the tone of management practice. Bureaucratic forms of organization which had little regard for the socio-cultural context thus came to be accepted, up to today, as the norm. Similarly, various structural and statutory restrictions prevented the development of indigenous practices so that subsequent efforts to rectify these imbalances, such as "Africanization" while creating business and employment opportunities for local people, had little meaningful impact on management practice and management style.

In examining the broader context within which the practice of management is carried out, we discussed four key features: socio-cultural, the competitive environment, industrial relations and the State. These factors differ in significance and implications, but they must be given sufficient attention if we are to develop and pursue practices that reflect and are sensitive to the organizational challenges in the country. A consideration of these contextual factors will take managers closer to the formulation of practices that meet the condition of *appropriateness*. It is with this in mind that we have offered the concept of internal resource heterogeneity.

Notes

[1] Kim (1986) observes that the restrictions included a limit of Sh 200 on borrowing from non-Africans; the colonial government could give an exemption under special circumstances, but this was liable to be withdrawn at the slightest sign of involvement in "political agitation".

[2] In his analysis of the growth of a managerialist class in Kenya, Kim (1986) reveals that the post-independent Africanization process was used as a tool of accumulation by already propertied African businessmen and politicians, who often acted in league with or as front men for foreign investors. Africanization cannot therefore be considered an adequate opportunity for the development of an indigenous managerial approach. African investors of the 1970s were already well schooled in the extant methods which had been introduced in the colonial era.

[3] The colonial government's investment policy in Sessional Paper No. 77 of 1956/57 set out the importance of importance of private enterprise and a pivotal role for the State. This was reinforced by the independent government in Sessional Paper No 10 (1965), which promulgated the manifesto for "African Socialism", which in reality translates into a laissez-faire market economy.

[4] Parts of this section were published in Kamoche, K. (1993), reprinted with permission. Permission was also granted by Elsevier Science for sections reprinted from Kamoche, K (1997).

[5] In the case studies, suggestion systems were treated as important communication arrangements at Autoco and Automart; in the other cases, managers claimed that they were abused or used for "trivial welfare complaints".

[6] Trade unions offer the government an opportunity to exercise control over the workforce particularly through the appointment of union leaders and the concomitant cultivation of vested interests in the union movement. The other important form of protection is that of statutory union recognition.

[7] Trade unions in Africa tend to have some form of affiliation with the political system, usually through co-optation. Henley (1989) argues that many African leaders, after Lenin, treat trade unions as the "transmission belt" of the party. In Kenya, the transmission belt has from time to time included numerous civil institutions, including women's movements, youth associations, etc.

[8] This section is reprinted from International Business Review, Vol 6, with permission from Elsevier Science.

4 Multi-Paradigm Analysis

This chapter presents the sociological paradigms of analysis within which the study of human resource management is to be located. The paradigms used here are treated as "analytical lenses" with which to survey the landscape of HRM in Kenya in order to enrich our understanding of this phenomenon. Different issues are problematized by the different paradigms; the robustness of a multi-paradigmatic analysis therefore arises in the possibilities to assess the gaps left in the analyses in alternative paradigms and to address the implications that a shift in perspective brings to light. The multi-paradigmatic approach has been adopted in various studies, eg: the analysis of personnel images of the future of work, (Gowler and Legge, 1986a); the study of organizational phenomena in a fire service (Hassard, 1985; 1987), and the analysis of management accounting research (Hopper and Powell, 1985). The first part of this chapter outlines the nature of a paradigm and specifies how this concept is employed here. This draws initially from Kuhn's notion of a paradigm. Burrell and Morgan's framework will then be posited. I then offer a critique of the concept of a "paradigm" and proceed to examine the suitability of the B/M framework to the African situation.

The Nature of a Paradigm

Thomas Kuhn

Thomas Kuhn is largely credited with the introduction of the term "paradigm" into common parlance. Kuhn's *The Structure of Scientific Revolutions* (SSR 1962; 1970a) sought to explain how progress is made in the natural sciences, and to understand what forces determine the nature and direction of progress. By examining the history of science, he asserts that scientific research tends to be guided by sets of practices and beliefs that constitute a conceptual and instrumental framework and which are accepted by a particular scientific community. He defines this as "normal science" (SSR p10), which means research based on past achievements that "some particular scientific community acknowledges for a time as supplying the foundation for its further practice." Kuhn (SSR 10) argues that the classic achievements of science shared two essential characteristics:

> Their achievement was sufficiently unprecedented to attract an enduring group of adherents away from competing modes of scientific activity. Simultaneously, it was sufficiently open-ended to leave all sorts of problems for the redefined group of practitioners to resolve.

He terms achievements that share these characteristics "paradigms". The term paradigm has subsequently come to be interpreted in many different ways. Indeed, according to Masterman (1970), Kuhn uses the term in at least 21 different senses. She concedes, however, that these senses do not necessarily contradict each other, and may in some cases elucidate others. Masterman attempts to clarify the nature of a paradigm through the following re-categorization:

1. **Metaphysical paradigm or metaparadigm**: something far wider than, and ideologically prior to theory: it is a whole *weltanschauung*.

2. **Sociological paradigm**: this category corresponds to Kuhn's "disciplinary matrix" which broadly refers to what members of a community share that accounts for the relative fullness of their professional communication and the relative unanimity of their professional judgement.

3. **Artefact or construct paradigm**: this refers to the use of a paradigm "in a more concrete way", and includes the concrete accomplishments of a scientific community.

For Masterman, the artefact paradigm is the most important conception of a paradigm, because it is directly related to puzzle-solving. Masterman's aim is to re-focus Kuhn's notion of a "paradigm" in a practical, utilitarian sense. Within the context of "normal science", according to this argument, a paradigm is an artefact which can be used as a puzzle-solving device, not a metaphysical world-view. This view is indeed consistent with Kuhn's assertion that the scientist is a solver of puzzles, not a tester of paradigms. But it must be noted that Kuhn's case for puzzle-solving is seen against the futile exercise of "testing" a paradigm within "normal science"; testing occurs only after persistent failure to solve a puzzle has given rise to a crisis and when this sense of crisis has evoked an alternative candidate for a paradigm (SSR 145).

It would seem, however, that belief in "normal science" can actually lead to dogmatism and ultimately hinder progress. Popper (1970) contends that a "normal" scientist should be pitied; he argues that the uncritical, acquiescent approach to routine problem-solving is a great danger to science. Instead he advocates "revolution in permanence". We argue, in this regard, that Masterman's legitimation of the value of artefact paradigm through recourse to "normal science" appears unsuitable for our purposes. Similarly, the use of "construct" or "artefact" paradigm is rather restrictive. Masterman concedes that this conception of a paradigm is less than a theory, since it can be something as little theoretic as a single piece of apparatus. Our discussion is therefore more concerned to interpret "paradigm" at the sociological level. It is not claimed here that these conceptions of "paradigm" are unconnected.

We suggest that the metaparadigm constitutes the philosophical world-view, the *weltanschauung* within which the basis of knowledge is located. This subsequently informs the creation of views amongst a community of scholars as they go about their business of applying artefact or construct paradigms to solve puzzles. The notion of sociological paradigm encapsulates two dimensions: the beliefs, values and practices of practitioners of a discipline in a particular community which parallels Kuhn's "disciplinary matrix", and the "world-views" in socio-philosophical writings as in Burrell and Morgan.

Burrell and Morgan

This section introduces Burrell and Morgan's (B/M) framework. Their main proposition is that social theory can be conceived in terms of four key paradigms based upon different sets of metatheoretical assumptions about the nature of social science and the nature of society. They argue that assumptions about the nature of science can be thought of in terms of the subjective-objective dimension, and assumptions about the nature of society in terms of a regulation-radical change dimension. These two dimensions in turn define the four paradigms: "functionalism", "interpretive", "radical humanism" and "radical structuralism". These are illustrated in Figure 4.1.

Figure 4.1 Paradigms of sociological analysis

Sociology of radical change

	radical humanism	radical structuralism	
subjectivism			objectivism
	interpretive	functionalism	

Sociology of regulation

Source: B/M (1979) Reprinted with permission from Ashgate.

The four paradigms define one's mode of theorizing and reflect one's position with regard to what Burrell and Morgan see as the four basic sets of assumptions about the nature of the social world and the way in which it may be investigated. These are depicted in Figure 4.2.

Figure 4.2 The subjective-objective dimension

The subjectivist approach
to social science

The objectivist approach
to social science

Nominalism   <------ **ontology** ------> Realism

Anti-positivism <----- **epistemology** -----> Positivism

Voluntarism   <----- **human nature** -----> Determinism

Ideographic   <----- **methodology** -----> Nomothetic

Source: B/M (1979) Reprinted with permission from Ashgate.

According to B/M, assumptions of an *ontological* nature are about the very essence of the phenomenon under investigation: "reality" is either external to the social scientist (ie it is of an "objective" nature) hence "realist", or it is the product of human consciousness, hence "nominalist". *Epistemological* assumptions are about the grounds of knowledge. Positivism holds that knowledge is hard, real and can be transmitted in tangible form; anti-positivism sees it as softer, more subjective, spiritual, and experiential. Assumptions about *human nature* are mostly about relationships between human beings and their environment. They are either deterministic: man responds mechanistically to the external world, or voluntarist: man plays a central role in shaping his circumstances. According to B/M the above assumptions have methodological assumptions about how the social world might be investigated. Treating the world as objective reality invites nomothetic methodologies which focus on relationships between the various elements, and a search for general laws. However, the subjective experiences of individuals lend themselves to ideographic methodologies.

The B/M framework offers two alternative views of society. The sociology of regulation seeks to explain why society holds together and emphasizes order and stability. The sociology of radical change on the other hand is about diverse interests, conflicts, control and distribution of power. The sociological tradition from which this is drawn is well articulated in the "order-conflict" or "consensus-conflict" debate (eg Dahrendorf, 1959; Lockwood, 1956).

Multi-paradigmatic analysis enables us to examine social phenomena from different perspectives and thus gain a rich understanding of the nature of the subject of enquiry. The use of a multi-paradigmatic analysis will be demonstrated by placing different "paradigmatic lenses" upon the terrain of HRM. This will help us to determine what "images" come to light, how these different perspectives reveal gaps and weaknesses in the orthodox conception of HRM, and how we can begin to understand the bases of the meanings that different people attach to HRM. In this regard, the paradigms will be employed here to depict the conceptual nature of the phenomenon given the underlying assumptions of the paradigm under review.

A Critical Look at the Nature of a "Paradigm"

The B/M framework is a useful analytical schema for unlocking the meanings embedded within the different approaches to social theorizing. It enables us both to query the grounds of knowledge and to enrich our understanding of social phenomena. It will be argued here that while this framework has considerable implications for the appreciation of the nature of organizations and different forms of organizational reality, its utility in this sense is mediated by two key issues:

1. The conceptual scope and substantive content of the framework, and
2. The particular social (and other) context within which multi-paradigm analysis is being conducted.

The first point can be broken down further into three parts:

* the appropriateness of the two-by-two matrix
* paradigm completeness and consistency,
* paradigm closure, incommensurability and relativism

These issues are treated in turn below.

Scope and Content

The appropriateness of the two-dimensional matrix The first aspect of the conceptual scope is the categorization of social phenomena along two dimensions which B/M conceive of in terms of "assumptions about the philosophy of science and the nature of society". B/M sought to devise a schema that would permit them to delineate perspectives that are founded upon mutually exclusive views of the social world. The four strands of the subjective-objective dimension are considered in this analysis to be vital components of the nature of social science and as constituting a useful template for querying the ways in which the social world may be investigated. One point that requires some attention, however, is Pinder and Bourgeoise's (1982) questioning of the application of ontology. They argue that it is not a question of ontology to query the existence of organizations, or any other thing. For them this is the task of science. Ontology, for them, is the study of being *qua* being, ie the study of existence irrespective of any particular existing things. They therefore propose the term "existential presuppositions", which refers to the set of assumptions about what exists.

   Willmott (1990) claims that the fundamental flaw in the B/M framework arises from the assumption that theories and perspectives are actually determined, in structuralist fashion, by the pre-existence of four "mutually exclusive" paradigms. He further criticizes the sense of dividing the vast intellectual terrain into "four paradigmatic enclaves" and argues that a more defensible approach would be to recognize both the diversity of assumptions guiding analysis and the ways in which they may be combined. He contends that in differentiating between the political leanings of analysis towards "regulation" and "radical change", B/M specify a dualism in which there is no room for any ambiguity about the "political impulse and impacts" of various modes of organizational analysis. Willmott offers alternatives to the restrictiveness of the object-subject trap through attempts to overcome the dualism of subjectivity and objectivity in theory (eg Berger and Luckman, 1967, and Giddens, eg 1976), and in practice (eg Freire, 1972). We consider these below.

For Berger and Luckman social reality is the product of a process involving a continuous series of subjective and objective *moments*. They seek to explicate how and why subjective meanings (externalization) become objective facticities (objectivation) which then "act back" as they socialize present and future generations (internalization). For Giddens, however, there is only one moment - *the moment of reproduction.* Giddens's theory of structuration shows how the subjective and objective social realities are integrated in a duality of structure. Giddens (1976; p121/2) posits the *duality of structure* in terms of how social structures are both constituted *by* human agency, and yet at the same time are the very *medium* of this constitution. For example he shows how as a "structure" language both describes the general rules of syntax and how language is constituted through words, and at the same time creates distinct speech-acts. The duality of structure therefore becomes evident in the observations of people's actions, ie social outcomes which are at the same time operating as the medium through which the outcomes become possible.

It is evident from the foregoing that this dynamism in the social process defines a fascinating recursiveness which has not been captured in the B/M matrix. Freire's (1972) concern is with the practical manifestations of dualism in the "experience of oppression and the fear of freedom." In his theory of oppression and emancipation, subjectivity and objectivity can exist side by side and are therefore not in dichotomy. The significance of this criticism is that the two-by-two matrix should not close off debate on issues and approaches that are not underpinned by the two axes it identifies.

Paradigm completeness and consistency The ability of each of the above paradigms to capture effectively the salient world-views and intellectual traditions that are perceived to constitute the conceptual scope of the paradigm is a matter for debate. On the nature and uses of a paradigm, Burrell and Morgan (1979, p23) assert that:

> It is a term which is intended to emphasize the commonality of perspective which binds the work of a group of theorists together in such a way that they can be usefully regarded as approaching social theory within the bounds of the same problematic.

Unity within the paradigm is seen in terms of the basic and often "taken for granted" assumptions. These are said to create very specific boundaries between groups of theorists, such that each paradigm is complete and enjoys internal consistence. This view accords with the association made above between "sociological paradigms" and Kuhn's "disciplinary matrix": what practitioners within a particular discipline have come to accept as shared values and ways of handling phenomena. This study will not query the appropriateness of the socio-philosophical schools of thought within the B/M framework; to this extent, the model will be taken as given but the next section will argue the case for an extension of its substantive scope.

An important point that arises from the foregoing is that of consistency in the mapping of the schools of thought. Two commonly cited cases of supposed inconsistency are: the location of the action frame of reference within the functionalist paradigm, and Marx's so-called "epistemological break" (eg Hassard, 1987; Hassard and Pym, 1990; Reed, 1985). Various writers have argued that the action frame of reference as articulated by Silverman (1970) clearly belongs to the interpretive paradigm (eg Willmott, 1990; Reed, 1985). However, B/M assert that although Silverman adheres to a highly voluntarist view of human nature, his conception of the social world is informed by an ontology, an epistemology and a methodology characteristic of the subjectivist region of the functionalist paradigm, (especially in Silverman and Jones, 1976). Such cases of supposed "ontological oscillation" and migration yield potentially fruitful insights for inter-paradigm debate. This is evident in the more familiar case of Marx.

It is widely held that Marx's work shows a clear-cut "epistemological break" from his earlier concerns with Hegelian idealism to "scientism". This view has been attributed mainly to the writings of Althusser who sought to highlight the empirical-structuralist nature of Marx's work and its concern with radical as opposed to the earlier ideological concerns. Others believe there is a definite and consistency in Marx's work. It is suggested here that the epistemological break so-called has to be seen not simply in terms of a concern with problematics in social change *per se*, but in terms of the assumptions underlying the *mode* of social change. This is in turn predicated on different loci of interest: consciousness vis-a-vis contradiction.

The epistemological break cannot in itself be treated as the definitive feature in the distinction between the two paradigms of radical change. With this in mind, the critique of HRM developed in chapter seven will draw in general from the *totality of capitalist structures*, and the distinction made between the two paradigms will be predicated on the way Marx initially develops his problematic around *consciousness* and then focuses more attention on *contradiction*. This discussion will in essence describe a paradigm journey rather than a synthesis of paradigms. Undertaking "paradigm journeys" on the basis of putative "epistemological breaks" will hopefully lend some legitimacy to the possibility of diversity in intellectual traditions.

Paradigm closure, incommensurability and relativism   This section now examines in more detail the possibility of meaningful debate between paradigms. B/M (p23) assert that:

> Each of the paradigms shares a common set of features with its neighbours on the horizontal and vertical axes in terms of one of the two dimensions but is differentiated on the other dimension. For this reason they should be viewed as contiguous but separate – contiguous because of the shared characteristics, but separate because the differentiation is ... of sufficient importance to warrant treatment of the paradigms as four distinct entities.

There appears to be a certain amount of ambiguity in B/M's conception of inter-paradigm debate. They are not clear as to how we might reconcile "contiguity" and "differentiation". Furthermore, they argue (p36,) that "some *inter*-paradigm debate is ... possible", but hold out little hope for this by stating that "relations between paradigms are perhaps better described in terms of 'disinterested hostility' rather than 'debate'".

B/M claim that the paradigms are mutually exclusive. This view is reinforced by their argument that in their pure forms, the paradigms are contradictory, since they are based on at least one set of opposing meta-theoretical assumptions. B/M see Kuhn's notion of "revolutionary science" as accounting for the low incidence of inter-paradigm journeys. Kuhn contends that scientists seldom seek alternatives, and they will retain a particular paradigm so long as the tools it supplies continue to prove capable of solving the problems it defines (SSR, p76). It is only when they begin to lose faith in a paradigm that scientists consider alternatives. Accordingly, the transition to a new paradigm is often necessitated by a crisis, or a sense of malfunction which is a prerequisite for revolutionary science.

B/M are concerned that the failure of the interpretive and radical paradigms to develop fully is because theorists operating within them have adopted a reactive stance with regard to the functionalist orthodoxy. It is this that leads them (B/M, p397) to advocate a form of "isolationism" whereby:

> Each of the paradigms can only establish itself at the level of organizational analysis if it is true to itself. Contrary to the widely held belief that synthesis and mediation between paradigms is what is required, we argue that the real need is for paradigm closure. In order to avoid emasculation and incorporation within the functionalist problematic, the paradigms need to provide a basis for their self-preservation by developing on their own account.

The hermeticism inherent in the above stance raises questions of incommensurability and relativism. This again might be traced back to Kuhn's (SSR, p103) contention that: "The normal-scientific tradition that emerges from a scientific revolution is not only incompatible but often actually incommensurable with that which has gone before." Kuhn, (1970b) has subsequently revised his views on incommensurability by offering the scope for communication. This, according to him, would still not solve the problem of comparison, which remains in spite of mechanisms of translation.

The notion of incommensurability assumes a new complexion in Jackson and Carter's (1991) separation of the paradigms of Kuhn and those of B/M: they argue that the former are *diachronic* while the latter are *synchronic*. Following this argument, incommensurability in Kuhn's paradigms is resolved on the temporal dimension in a convergence of previously divergent theoretical perspectives; B/M's paradigms, on the other hand, "exist simultaneously and in perpetuity - the incommensurability which characterizes relations between the paradigms is irremediable" (p116). They further state that resolving incommensurability in B/M through the Kuhnian normal-revolutionary sequence would only lead to the establishment of a new dominant orthodoxy and epistemological authoritarianism, the very fallacy that B/M warn against.

Jackson and Carter's defence of incommensurability on this count appears plausible. However, their inclusion of incommensurability of goals is debatable: they assert that the "inhabitants" of the different paradigms do not share the same objectives. This position may hold if we follow Kuhn's diachronic paradigms. However, whereas the "inhabitants" of particular paradigms may indeed define their problematics strictly within the confines of their paradigm, it is also conceivable that theorists in different paradigms address the same aspect of social (or other) phenomena while defining it in the language and intellectual tradition, and employing the "tools" of their respective paradigms. This is also the case in multi-paradigmatic analysis. The important point in Jackson and Carter's argument is that of the rejection of a synthesis of meta-theoretical perspectives, a point that B/M also stress.

Hassard (1987, p.10) sees the problems of incommensurability in terms of *how progress is signalled or standards met.* He asserts that:

> We are left in a relativist vacuum whereby theory communities are pictured in hermetic isolation, capable of only talking past their professional enemies: they are (seemingly) attributed equal status in explaining social and organizational phenomena.

This sounds like a call for the establishment of an over-arching framework with which we can weigh paradigms against each other, or their perceived "value". Not only does this view invite some new conception of a dominant paradigmatic orthodoxy, it does actually seem like a mis-interpretation of the multi-paradigmatic scheme. An overarching framework might possibly help to resolve the question of comparability, but it also essentially represents a certain paradigmatic position and thus further compounds the issue of "evaluating" paradigms since "value" is paradigm-specific. This is the view taken by Feyerabend. The notion of genus-species might offer an interesting insight as to how different paradigms might be seen to constitute "parts" of a broader whole, which nevertheless stand as entities in their own right.

In our analysis, *paradigm incommensurability is not conceived of as a problem.* Jackson and Carter's notion of the diachronic nature of Kuhnian paradigms shows how an inadequate or inferior paradigm is superceded by a more "useful" one. In B/M's synchronic case, such a comparison is untenable. The fact that the paradigms are underpinned by opposing meta-theoretical assumptions implies that their incommensurability is given. Trying to reconcile such incommensurability is an exercise in futility. We must be constantly aware, however, that the paradigm itself has been defined in terms of the patterning of underlying meta-theoretical assumptions, which reflects individual choice and is *changeable.* Therefore, the "borders" between paradigms are by no means sacrosanct.

Two ways out of hermiticism may be offered (see also Maruyama, 1974). First, through inter-paradigm debate which would enable theorists to understand the "language" of other paradigms and to appreciate how other theorists negotiate their problematics. This may result in paradigm elaboration, the re-definition of borders and paradigm shifts. The second option is through multi-paradigmatic analysis, whereby the social theorist revolves the analysis around the different paradigmatic locations. This permits us to move away from what Maruyama (1974) describes as the tendency of professional practitioners, social scientists and many others to consider society uniculturally, and to adopt a monocular view of phenomena. The danger that Maruyama sees is that people can become trapped in their own paradigms, ie "monopolarized". This could lead to a rejection of other ways of "seeing" and interpreting reality. Maruyama recommends the "cross-paradigmatic process" as a way of improving communication between those in different paradigms: this involves "demonopolarization" and "transpection", ie thinking in the other person's paradigm, and likewise allowing others to think in one's paradigm.

We conclude this section by noting that an assessment of the relative merit of different world-views must be related to the particular context within which the phenomenon is being investigated. This is because the perceived value of forms of knowledge is defined by the expectations and needs of each particular community as well as their value-systems.

The Significance of "Context" in Multi-Paradigm Analysis

Our concern with "context" in this section is to engages B/M's focus on the intellectual tradition in Western civilisation. This implies a critique of historical ethnocentrism in the framework. Their analysis is based almost entirely on the Western (mainly Western European and American) intellectual tradition, except for some of the material in the radical structuralist paradigm which has been developed in the (former) Soviet Union with philosophical roots in Marx's work. Apart from brief mention of a few "alternative" worldviews like Castaneda's alternative reality and Zen philosophy, we are given little indication about how other non-Western worldviews might have enriched this framework. Without suggesting that B/M should have attempted a review of the entire socio-philosophical thought from around the world, they might perhaps have considered the implications of their analysis for organizational theory outside the Western tradition. It is a little surprising that despite the world-wide rise in interest in Japanese management practices that started in the 1970s, they make no mention of the possible effect of such views as Zen philosophy on Japanese management thinking.

The important question that arises from the foregoing is: if this framework *is* ethnocentric in conception and substantive scope and content, what value does it have for the analysis of phenomena outside the (and indeed within a heterogeneous!) Western socio-philosophical context? Does it have value in the analysis of phenomena where the fundamental assumptions and world-views pertinent to these phenomena are informed by totally different conceptions of knowledge? As noted in chapter three, an uncritical acceptance of the model(s) of HRM or indeed any other form of social phenomena in the Kenyan context is both questionable and potentially disastrous. It is now proposed to apply the same critique to the B/M framework. A re-assessment of this framework to such an extent as to incorporate socio-philosophical perspectives from Africa, for instance, is beyond the scope of this study. That is not to say that such an exercise would be futile for our purposes; on the contrary, the elaborate review of the sociological and philosophical perspectives in Africa (and elsewhere) would greatly enhance our appreciation of the application of sociological paradigms and the contextual significance of different forms of knowledge. This would also enable us to assess the social relations in the production of knowledge, the neglect of which, as Clegg (1982) points out, is a weakness of the B/M framework.

What this critique reveals is firstly, the need to be aware of the limitations of this framework, and secondly, the implications of trying to "see" an African (or quasi-African) phenomenon through "Western" eyes. In this regard, Shweder (1991) raises the interesting question about whether, in general, we can justify others' conception of the world within the framework of our own rationality. This calls into question the predominance of the Western rational perspective and the risk involved in imposing a Western logic on phenomena in other parts of the world. A sharper critique of this perspective is found in Means' (1988) rejection of what he calls the "European" tradition to impose its logic on the Indian Americans and other peoples in general. Some African writers have advocated an "Afrocentric" perspective in place of the "Eurocentric" one. Keto (1989) for example criticizes the latter for imposing hegemonic dominance on the study of African history. He proposes an "Afrocentric" perspective not merely to replace the former or to deny the validity of other perspectives but to provide a focus for scholarship that explains the world "through the prism of African eyes and experience".

The comments made in the earlier sections of this critique assume more relevance here: the duality of the subjective-objective and the regulation-radical change perspectives in Western sociological thought may be sustained, but it may well be that other tools of analysis, or indeed other configurations of sociological analysis, are relevant in the African context. Horton's (1967) earlier attempts to depict and contrast patterns of African and Western "world-views" focused on continuities and contrasts between "traditionality" and "modernity" and the Popperian use of "closed" and "open" systems. These categorizations initially appeared to pave the way for a useful intellectual exercise. Unfortunately, they did not yield much and have actually been dismissed as naïve and unsound. In a subsequent paper, Horton (1982) admits that his earlier views were highly contentious; in particular his use of Popperian terms distinguished between static "traditional" thinking and dynamic "modern" thinking. A re-appraisal of the criticisms now leads him to the view that the typical "traditionalist" world-view is far more open to change and external influence, and the typical "modern" world-view is less open to change than he had earlier allowed (eg p210).

Horton had also claimed that traditional settings exhibit a special anxiety about threats to the established body of knowledge. Others have pointed out, however, that this sort of anxiety is not peculiar to traditional settings, but is equally present at the heart of "modernity" (eg Feyerabend, 1975), as exemplified in the suspicion directed at new ideas, especially those that challenge conventional wisdom. Horton had also drawn a controversial contrast between the absence and presence of an awareness, on the part of individual thinkers, of alternative theoretical frameworks. Hs more recent work seeks to replace this contrast by one which emphasizes "lack of inter-theoretic competition in the traditional setting" as against "prominence of such competition in the modern setting". Evidently, there is a need for greater clarification in these and related issues which pertain to the nature and conception of different world-views.

This points to the need for further research in the African context, on the nature and scope of socio-philosophical "world-views" and how these might inform the study of organizational reality. The discussion on the African thought system in the previous chapter goes some way to addressing this shortcoming. The absence of a suitable, literary intellectual tradition makes this task particularly challenging. It is anticipated that researchers will be able to formulate research approaches that bring together comparative sociological and philosophical schools of thought derived from the African experience. This will be the ultimate test of the suitability of "Eurocentric" perspectives in the African, or any other context. Formulating or identifying appropriate paradigms of analysis must take into account both the nature of the traditional African society and the ways in which it has changed in the wake of "modernization".

While it is important to begin with an appreciation of the African thought system which some observers associate with symbolism and mystical thinking as discussed in the previous chapter, it is important to broaden the intellectual net to capture, inter alia, the organization of African societies at the political and administrative levels; the factors governing the generation of knowledge for example in terms of developing appropriate technology to manage productive activities, and in particular the society's beliefs about their ability to achieve such ends; the nature of social relations at the interpersonal and institutional levels and their implication for achieving change in society, and so forth. Clearly, this is a huge task which requires a multi-disciplinary approach but one which will no doubt go a long way towards addressing the recurring concerns about what is or what is not suitable for the African organizational context.

Conclusion

This chapter introduced the concept of multi-paradigmatic analysis. In order to clarify some of the confusion about the nature and meaning of a "paradigm", we examined Kuhn's conception of a paradigm, and specified the use of this term for our purposes. In this regard, Masterman's re-categorization of Kuhn's use of "paradigm" was posited as a useful starting point, and the "sociological" version was identified as the most salient one. This chapter also presented a critique of the paradigm debate and identified some of the key contentious issues both in Burrell and Morgan's framework and in the paradigm debate as a whole. The discussion suggested ways in which some of the problems immanent in the debate, eg those arising from hermeticism and relativism, might be resolved. The critique also pointed out the need to exercise caution in treating the B/M framework as an universalist approach to the analysis of social phenomena; questions have been raised about its structure and substantive content. To this have been added certain misgivings about the framework's universalist appeal given that it has drawn principally from the Western intellectual tradition. It was proposed that there is wide scope for further research in the socio-philosophy pertaining to other parts of the world where an application of the framework may be attempted. In this regard, we identified the case of Africa and proceeded to propose some strands that researchers might consider in articulating a relevant epistemological approach for analysing African organizational phenomena.

With regard to the use of a multi-paradigmatic analysis of HRM, our purpose is not necessarily to encourage debate between HRM theorists operating in different paradigms, but to discover how different meta-theoretical perspectives affect the way we apprehend the phenomenon of HRM. The challenge here is to strike a balance between generating "forms of knowledge" that enhance our appreciation of the phenomenon under investigation and which lay no particular claim to some orthodox truth on the one hand, and the need to demonstrate some form of *progress* in the generation of "forms of knowledge" on the other hand. It is not proposed here to provide a "true" picture of the nature of HRM from each of the paradigms as this presupposes that some such "true" picture exists. Nor is it intended to use the paradigms as ways of formulating different views of the subject which are thereafter synthesized into a "whole". It is proposed rather, to consider the paradigms as "different ways of seeing", without ranking them in terms of their "perceived usefulness". The "value" of the images and accounts that each paradigm generates is seen in terms of enriching our appreciation of the nature of the subject matter, revealing the gaps in understanding what the subject comprises, and determining how different views of what constitutes HRM might inform the conception and execution of approaches to the management of people at work.

As Barley (1980) observes, B/M's conceptual map is less concerned with guiding us from here to there in the everyday world of organizations than it is with helping us see that world from various vantage points. Giddens's (1976, p144) notion of "mediation through negation" might help to elucidate the foregoing: whereas it is not proposed here to offer the non-functionalist paradigms simply as alternatives to the orthodoxy or simply on the basis of the putative inadequacy of the functionalist one, there is a need to be aware of the shortcomings or limitations of each paradigm. This makes us aware of how paradigms might mediate each other, thus perhaps anticipating the beginnings of some form of inter-paradigm debate as well as the implicit recognition of the relative merits of the different paradigms.

5 An Analysis of Recruitment within the Functionalist Paradigm

This chapter focuses on the generic practices of recruitment and selection in the case studies, which include identifying the staffing need, interviewing, deployment and socialization. We begin with a brief introduction to the functionalist paradigm and its relevance to HRM, and then proceed to provide a thematic analysis of the dimensions of HRM in the firms in question.

Functionalism and HRM

B/M trace the origins of functionalist sociology to the work of Auguste Comte, who was essentially concerned with the knowledge of human and social unity towards the creation of a new social order. This knowledge was to be predicated on the "positive" method prevalent in the natural sciences; biology in particular provided many analogies. B/M (1989, p42) observe that:

> Comte thus laid the foundations for the mode of social theorising characteristic of the functionalist paradigm. Based upon the "positive" model of the natural sciences, utilising mechanical and organic analogies, distinguishing between statics (structure) and dynamics (process), and advocating methodological holism, Comte initiated important ground rules for a sociological enterprise geared to an explanation of the social order and regulation.

Under Darwinian influence, Herbert Spencer made a further contribution to the positivist tradition by developing in more detail the implications of the biological analogy for sociology, and in particular the analysis of *structure* and *function* (B/M, ibid). These and other writers have contributed to the theory of society as self-regulating by showing how parts or aspects of the society serve to sustain the whole. The themes of structure and function have been developed further by anthropologists like Malinowski and Radcliffe-Brown. Radcliffe-Brown (1952) argued that the social life of the society is defined as the functioning of the social structure. For him, the social structure consists of a set of relations amongst unit entities and is sustained irrespective of changes in such entities, ie, even if some people leave the society, through death or otherwise, the fundamental structure of the society remains. For functionalist theorists this is a very strong defense of stability and the continuity of society, and by analogy for our purposes here, organizations.

The theories B/M cite (eg social system theory, social action theory and objectivism) share the objective of explaining why society holds together, and in this, they are underpinned by the notion of purposive rationality. The organizational schools of thought associated with these theories are therefore united by their concern with order and stability. These are: social system theory and objectivism, the action frame of reference, bureaucratic dysfunctionalism and pluralist theory. The "orthodox approach" tends to adopt theories and models of organizational functioning, to focus on "areas of empirical investigation, that are oriented towards managerial conceptions of organisations, managerial priorities and problems, and managerial concerns for practical outcomes" (Salaman and Thompson, 1973).

The functionalist theorist seeks to provide practical solutions to practical problems, and thus generate knowledge which can be *used* in real situations. The functionalist perspective is therefore committed to a philosophy of social engineering as a basis of social change (B/M, p26). However, while the rational perspective is good at explaining (ie prescribing) how organizations *should* work, it fails to explain why they do *not* work as they should (Bolman and Deal, 1984). This discussion therefore aims to establish how managers approach the HR question in a practical way; how they achieve stability and order through HR policies and practices which are underpinned by a purposive rationality, and how therefore, the "human resource" serves a structural-functionalist purpose.

A Brief Outline of the Standard Practice of Recruitment

The standard practice involves a set of procedures that seem to be uniformly adhered to in the companies visited, although some variations were noted. More often than not, an absence of on-going manpower planning means that staffing needs are only addressed when a position falls vacant or when the need to create a new position arises. A line manager fills out a requisition form detailing the job specifications, and this is ratified by the head of the department and Personnel. Personnel then go about advertising, internally and/or externally. Internal recruitment is designed to encourage advancement from within. Managers reported a preference for internal recruitment which fosters the internal labour market. Otherwise, external sources include other companies, training institutes and other such colleges, or the Ministry of Labour, especially for unionisable jobs. The Personnel Manager then goes through the applications and prepares a short-list which is then forwarded to the recruiting department. High-potential candidates are then invited for interviews. The panel of interviewers consists of one or two officers from the recruiting department including a technical adviser where necessary, the head of Personnel/HR, and a General Manager. An offer is subsequently made to the most suitable candidate(s). New recruits are taken through an orientation programme which in the case of the managerial cadre often involves attachments to various departments before final deployment to an area of functional specialization.

The foregoing illustrates the general practice for non-unionisable employees and the managerial/supervisory cadres. The recruitment of unionisable workers is in principle similar but differs in some respects: the head of the department need not be directly involved, and the exercise may be handled by the Factory Manager. Furthermore, it does not involve orientational rotation. The hiring of casuals and temporaries is even more *ad hoc* and informal: they are ordinarily "picked up from the factory gates" or hired "by word of mouth".

A Thematic Analysis of Employee Selection

The discussion here is based on the components of Guest's model. The dimensions of this model constitute a frame through which the recruitment practices in the five companies are examined. The discussion begins with those companies which come closest to the normative model (Pharmaco and Autoco), and goes on to those which seem farthest from the model (Chematox and Automart); Mimea is somewhere in between. Figure 5.1 presents a summary of the key issues in recruitment on a case-by-case basis.

Figure 5.1 A summary of the case material on recruitment

INTEGRATION   COMMITMENT   FLEXIBILITY

PHARMACO

INTEGRATION	COMMITMENT	FLEXIBILITY
- Integration of HR within corporate strategy through HRM dept and HR Committee - management support through HR Director - steering role by US parent company - differential socialization	- organizational values influence selection - subjective perception of suitability - commitment through semi-formal workgroups and team working - projection of distinct image - quest for employees who will identify with firm's success	- varying degrees of rigour in recruitment of different cadres - temporary/casual labour for unskilled and semi-skilled jobs - small peripheral buffer

AUTOCO

INTEGRATION	COMMITMENT	FLEXIBILITY
- integration of HR through HR Committee - planning subject to budgetary constraints - differential socialization focused on company objectives, work and team - some US parent company influence	- nurturing teamwork and a team spirit - teamwork seen as route to organizational commitment - quality teams foster unitarism - remuneration seen to impinge on commitment	- varying degrees of rigour in recruitment - temporary/casual labour for unskilled and semi-skilled jobs - small peripheral buffer

MIMEA

INTEGRATION	COMMITMENT	FLEXIBILITY
- board representation by Personnel Director - focus on management succession planning and recruitment - lower tier planning based on sales projection - broad welfare agenda - differential socialization	- welfare paternalism: seen as route to organizational commitment - identification with firm supposed to build a sense of identity	- varying degrees of rigour in recruitment - temporary/casual labour for unskilled and semi-skilled jobs - large peripheral buffer - high impact of foreign demand and seasonality - ethnic balance to avoid tensions

Figure 5.1 (cont'd)

CHEMATOX

- Personnel's indirect top management access through Company Secretary - small role for Personnel/Training - "juggling with policy" within budgetary constraints - short-term personnel and manpower planning - sharp management-employee divide - differential socialization	- technical competence considered viable way to identify with the firm - status system supposedly hinders commitment to the firm	- varying degrees of rigour in recruitment - temporary and casual labour for semi-skilled and unskilled jobs - small peripheral buffer

AUTOMART

- Personnel's indirect access to top management through General Manager - centralized top management control - management inertia in HR change - ad hoc "Management by Deciding" for short-term manpower planning - differential socialization	- organizational values linked to customer service - commitment to customer satisfaction seen as route to organizational commitment - lack of commitment seen in terms of a "thieving sub-culture" - attitudinal cleavages seen to hinder commitment	- varying degrees of rigour in recruitment - temporary and casual labour for unskilled and semi-skilled labour - artificially large temporary workforce

The Goal of Integration

The goal of integration, as noted earlier, consists of the following: corporate and HR strategy, coherence of policy, management support and employee integration. The case material is examined under these sub-titles.

Human resource strategy As argued in chapter three, the strategic dimension as commonly understood has not in general been adequately developed. This position was, in the main, supported by the case material. This has subsequently tended to determine the agenda for personnel issues. The setting up of human resource committees at Pharmaco and Autoco is designed to address this weakness. Traditionally at Pharmaco, the personnel issue did not receive much attention in corporate planning, and it is this which prompted the introduction of "HRM/D", headed by a HR Director and

HR Manager. The purpose is, *inter alia*, to "develop and maintain a team of talented, motivated and skilled workforce" through the linking of the HR function to corporate strategy, and particularly through the influence of the HR Committee.

The HR Committee ensures that the HR dimension receives attention at Board level not only in terms of the specific ways in which the management of employees is to be conducted, but also in respect of the way corporate decisions affect employees. This includes measures to recruit "high-quality" employees, specific analyses of how best to utilize the existing expertise through appropriate deployment and redeployment, and the pursuit of a more systematic development programme. However, on the grounds of confidentiality, specific details were withheld. A Human Resource Committee also handles HR issues at Autoco. The purpose of the committee is to "review the policies and procedures for maintaining competent labour in the long-term". Its agenda also includes the more operational, lower-level decisions that encompass the selection policy, promotion and advancement policy, rewards and welfare.

The focus of HR strategy at Mimea is management development, and to attain this end, this company maintains fairly comprehensive two- to five-year plans for management needs and development. There is no specific HR committee; however, the Personnel Director represents personnel in the policy-making body, the Executive Directors' Meeting, and is able to highlight the implications of corporate decisions on personnel and to identify necessary changes and personnel needs. Management at Mimea is very clearly defined as the "core", as seen against the other staff. There is little planning for the other staffing needs; this is handled more or less on an *ad hoc* basis. Planning for unionisable staff and casual workers is based on sales projections.

Planning at Chematox is done by the Business Management Committee, which consists of the Managing Director, heads of departments and business managers. The Company Secretary represents Personnel. Chematox's five-year Corporate Plan is structured along six sectors: business; diversification; people; computer and insurance; safety and finance. The Operations Director reported that the company is "a bit thin" on corporate planning because of the "vagueness" of the business environment in the country. This supports the argument, in chapter 3, about the state of strategic management in the country. The corporate plan does, however, attempt to spell out clearly broad corporate policies and objectives relating to the six key sectors. These are supposed to guide short-term policy making which is made difficult by market fluctuations. The "people" sector was said to be given very little attention, such that personnel planning is limited to taking account of short-term manpower needs and the review of existing policies like recruitment and rewarding. An interesting observation is "parent company guidelines" were reflected not only in financial reporting deadlines but even in such operational areas as the use of aptitude tests for recruitment. The Personnel/ Training Officer explained that this helps them to conform to "international standards".

At Automart, planning is the concern of the Budget Committee, which comprises departmental heads; as in Mimea and Chematox, there is no specific personnel/HR committee. The General Manager (Management Services) represents Personnel on the Budget Committee. Automart presents a more extreme picture of *ad hocracy*, whereby the General Manager claimed that the company has no *corporate ethos*, and that corporate planning does not go beyond routine short- and medium-term sales and financial projections. This company was like a family business ran by a very powerful Chairman. The Personnel Manager had attempted with little success to bring the personnel issue closer to the Board by introducing a long-term perspective to recruitment and development. In this, the board was seen as "unenthusiastic". The other probable reason was the Personnel Manager's lack of direct access to the Budget Committee; he reports to the General Manager. This case parallels that of Chematox and illustrates the importance of access to top management. The Personnel Manager reported that there was a long tradition of *ad hoc* decision-making, whereby managers managed "by *deciding*", as opposed to "making decisions". He explained this to mean making on-the-spur-of-the-moment decisions with inadequate information and little institutional support. "Management by Deciding" is found expedient because of the organizational uncertainties and low level of environmental predictability.

Coherence of policy Coherence of policy emphasizes the organizational need for a systematic approach to managerial activity, ie an approach which draws from the functionalist assumptions of stable, integrated structures which serve some specific purposes and above all, maintain continuity in the system as a whole. An important issue problematized within this paradigm is that of sustaining continuity in the organizational *system*. Thus, HRM constitutes a set of social relations which are a part of the integrated whole. The degree to which HR policy coheres with other areas of policy indicates its contribution to the maintenance of the system.

The HRM/D policy at Pharmaco entails careful attention to both organizational and departmental growth vis-a-vis staffing and skill requirements concerning all staff, as well as the delineation of long-term goals. Coherence in policy was therefore seen in terms of linking "individual specifics" to "company specifics". An issue that raises some concern is that of running a personnel and an HR function *in tandem*. To avoid conflict, duties are clearly demarcated: the Personnel department is concerned with the "traditional" issues of administration, procedures and labour relations, while the HR function deals with strategic and developmental issues. This is illustrated in Figure 5.2.

Figure 5.2 Personnel and human resource functions at Pharmaco

PERSONNEL	HRM/D
Maintaining headcounts details	Coordinating the corporate HR strategy
Wage and salary administration	Appraisal and Remuneration policy
Benefits administration	Career advancement
Personnel record-keeping including	Training and Development
statistics on statutory deductions	Planning for HR needs which involves
Retirement	vetting all proposed recruitment
Labour relations	Job redesign

The Personnel Manager was instrumental in instituting these changes because of his concern about the relative neglect of the human resource and in view of employee dissatisfaction with management-labour relations. However, the subsequent structural changes seemed to reduce the status of his position. While the Personnel Manager was sympathetic to trade unionism, the HR Manager, on the other hand, exemplified the more common hostile attitude; he reported that he would prefer to deal with a Japanese-style Enterprise Union or better still, no union at all.[1]

At Autoco the HR dimension which caters for all the staff is incorporated into the Corporate Plan through the HR Committee as a way of ensuring the formulation of policy in line with organizational strategies. The formulation of the Corporate Plan involves all the departments and is coordinated by Finance, which signals the impact of financial considerations on planning. Manpower needs are subject to strict budgetary constraints. It is worth pointing out that management had also adopted a new consensual policy formulation procedure similar to the Japanese "Ringi" system, which aims to ensure the coherence of inter-departmental policy and greater involvement of managers in policy formulation.

The systematic management succession planning at Mimea does not cohere with the less formal and *ad hoc* recruitment of other cadres. Similarly, the recruitment practice for the "fourth tier" is more evident because of the size of the casual labour force. In the farms, depending on the severity of the unemployment problem, the Farm Manager may be compelled to line the hopefuls up and select every fifth person, for example. According to management at Chematox, the "vagueness" in the business environment in the country requires "clever juggling" with policies. This juggling takes place within budgetary constraints, and it is significant that the strategy-making body at this company is called the "Budget Committee".

A variant of "juggling" at Automart, *Management by Deciding* was a convenient substitute for a more systematic approach to policy formulation. Commenting on the lack of coherence in the disparate inter-departmental policies, the Personnel Manager conceded that there was a need for more communication between managers, and between managers and the Board. In these three companies, very clear distinctions were made between management and other cadres. Following the general view that HRM is something *for managers*, the existing approaches indicate that the focus on management has been an enduring one. Nevertheless, those companies like Pharmaco and Autoco with explicit HRM initiatives, are now giving more attention to other cadres.

Management support This section is concerned with the degree of support that personnel/HR initiatives were receiving from management, and especially top management. At Autoco and Pharmaco, moves towards HRM were initiated by top management through HR Committees with prompting from the American parent companies. The Personnel Manager at Pharmaco reported that there had been pressure from the employees to introduce practices that were "more responsive to their needs". In this company, while the HR initiatives are centralized in the HR department, line management are involved by aligning their personnel responsibilities to the corporate development strategies, eg in the planning of departmental staffing requirements, identification of necessary policy changes and the actual selection. There is also an attitudinal dimension whereby all managers are required to accept their role with regard to the management of employees within the corporate HRM/D concept and to seek a change of culture.

In all the other cases line management involvement in personnel/HR activities was not expected to undergo any major re-orientation. Top management support of HR initiatives at Mimea is through the Personnel Director. As noted earlier, Personnel has only indirect access to top management in Chematox and Automart which reflects the relatively lower status of the personnel function. Automart represents a case of top management inertia with regard to the Personnel Manager's attempts at change. In general, top and line management involvement is effected in recruitment through ratification of appointments.

Employee integration Employee integration is considered here with regard to socialization. The *prima facie* purpose of integration within this paradigm is to match employees to jobs, ie to establish a viable "fit" in such a way as to enhance predictability and eliminate potential conflict. We distinguish between preparatory training at induction and socialization as a process of integration. The former mainly involves learning new skills; the latter is concerned with the inculcation of organizational values and to the extent that it seeks to foster the organizational climate, it complements the role of recruitment through retention. Louis (1980) defines socialization as the process by which an individual comes to appreciate the values, abilities, expected behaviours and social knowledge essential for assuming an organizational role and for participating as an organizational member.

Schein (1978) sees entry into the organization, from the point of view of the individual, as a problem of breaking in and joining up, while from the point of view of the organization it is a process of induction, basic training and socialization of the individual to the major norms and values of the organization. This process should lead to a viable "psychological contract". The process of socialization is evidently an important integrative tool, one that involves a series of activities such as "reality shock", "surprise" (ie the difference between anticipations and actual experiences) and "sensemaking" (Louis, 1980), and "normalizing the setting" (van Maanen, 1977), which refers to the knowledge required for people to locate themselves within the organizational "space". However, to the extent that the functionalist paradigm denies the existence of the power dimension, and treats conflict as an aberration, socialization serves to smother conflict or allow it to manifest itself within predetermined limits. Individuals are therefore *integrated* into the organization in order to create a sense of togetherness. Ultimately, socialization and organizational culture serve to establish goal congruence and to confirm and legitimate the unitarist nature of HRM.

A form of differential socialization is evident in all the companies, whereby the managerial/supervisory cadres are taken through a systematic socialization programme at the point of hiring. The management trainee socialization is the most sophisticated. It often involved a series of meetings where the initiates are introduced to various senior managers who speak about the company values and the need for commitment and a sense of belonging. The socialization of unionisable staff is less rigorous and often simply involves a single meeting with senior management. Part-time and casual workers take on their duties with little ceremony. Subsequent (post-hiring) socialization involves a broad range of social and welfare activities, such as sports, year-end parties, and company newsletters. At Pharmaco, the annual Open Day is the most important event in the socialization scheme: it brings together family members for a wide range of activities. In this company, sporting teams take product names; this is designed to further enhance a sense of identification with the organization.

Socialization in the one-week management trainee orientation programme at Autoco proceeds as follows. The first part covers:

The company history
The organizational structure/chart
The Mission Statement
The operating philosophy, and
The organizational goals and objectives

The second part is described as follows in the Employment records:

The main concern at this stage is to get the new hires to appreciate the roles of the various departments in achieving company objectives. The departments are covered one-by-one and an effort is made to present the organization as a unified entity in which the individual has to find his place and endeavour to make his contribution to the attainment of organizational objectives in whatever department or role he is deployed to.

The final part serves to:

Inform the new employees mainly about what the company offers in way of: security services, the medical programme, the training programme, the company "benefits" programme, and industrial relations.

This orientation programme also stresses "commitment to one's work" and the need to communicate as a team. The notion of the "team" is the kingpin in integration at Autoco. Juxtaposing this elaborate integration scheme with the almost non-existent initial socialization of other cadres reveals yet another manifestation of a multi-tier system that in effect defines the organizational social hierarchy. Subsequent forms of socialization, however, aim to redress and even to mask the inequalities immanent in this stratification; as argued above, this is a logical position in the functionalist paradigm.

At Mimea, the *socialization* component of the initial integration of management trainees has the following objectives:

Figure 5.3 Objectives of socialization at Mimea

1. To acquaint participants with the company history, goals, policies and organizational structure.

2. To present/clarify the basic information the new employees want and need to know about the rules and regulations, benefits, procedures and conditions of employment.

3. To build the employees' sense of identity with the company and make them proud to work for the company.

Source: Employment records

Part three above highlights the concern to establish a congruence of interests and to elicit commitment to the organization. The company also maintains a broad post-recruitment integrative ethos which is most evident in sporting activities and the provision of a broad array of welfare and social facilities. These facilities include Social Centres which contain social halls, reading and games rooms, and a cafeteria; two hospitals which complement numerous dispensaries for the individual estates; housing for much of the estate workforce, and primary schools for their children. Mimea therefore best exemplifies a welfare paternalist approach to the management of employees, and thus introduces a new perspective to the question of HRM: that of the relative importance of welfare paternalism in an African context. The Personnel Manager and Director at Mimea felt that the complexity of the socio-economic challenges that African workers face demand a great welfare commitment from management. The position becomes more relevant when it is recalled that a "welfare state" in the conventional sense does not exist in Kenya: unemployment benefit is non-existent, extended family pressures place an enormous burden on the employed, and the precarious state of the economy has resulted in an inadequate provision of social amenities. This makes it almost imperative for the employer to take account of the above tenets of social well-being. The contemporary "western" model of HRM assumes that these issues have *already* been taken care of. The case of Mimea is an interesting form of dualism: "modern" HRM for the "core" management cadre and welfarism for the rest. It should be pointed out, however, that investments in "welfare" are entirely discretionary and are subject to financial considerations. They may also be a tool to achieve behavioural control where divergent interests clearly exist (see also Watson, 1986). Chematox was the only company without sporting activities, and managers admitted that this was a weakness in so far as sports do create a sense of "togetherness". There was little commitment either in management or amongst the staff, to organize sporting activities. Managers also admitted that there was a sharp divide between management and workers, which the organization was doing little to bridge. The only evident "team-fostering" activities were the Christmas lunch, in which managers serve the drinks (in a case of symbolic role reversal), and the canteen, where they have a standard menu for all, although they have segregated seating (separate seating arrangements for management and other staff).

Managers at Chematox take pride in the supposed socializing aspect of the newsletters which carry news on events, newcomers, changes in individual status, births and so forth. They believe this helps nurture a "family-like" atmosphere. The Operations Director reported that a "status system" was built into the organizational structure; he also conceded that the almost non-existent social interaction only worsened things. He felt that "too much teamwork introduces individual slack", and that excessive social interaction "loses its surprise element" through over-familiarity.[2] A production engineer who had left the company and re-joined as a senior manager attributed the lack of social cohesion to the inequalities in the rewarding system; his comments reflect this:

> Workers tend to lack a sense of belonging mainly due to their remuneration. My case, as a manager is alright; I cannot complain. But workers will tend to feel left out.

At Automart, although the typical tools for enforcing goal congruence are used - eg socialization at recruitment, sporting activities, year-end parties and a newsletter - managers lamented the lack of an integrative organizational ethos and culture, such that the "us-and-them" attitudinal cleavages immanent in employer-employee relationships made the objective of goal congruence rather remote. For example, management trainees undergo a very comprehensive induction and socialization programme, which lasts for up to twenty two months. The Staff Relations Officer reported that management attempts to solve the "class-conflict problem" by getting the workers to accept that they earn as much as their productivity.

This approach emphasizes the centrality of the contribution to organizational objectives as the rationale for *membership*, and its integrative character emerges as a form of control. A case that illustrates the difficulty of achieving integration was when management decided not to award the year-end bonus (which was, as is often the case, an example of profit-sharing at the discretion of management), causing the workers to boycott the Christmas party. The shop stewards themselves attended, ostensibly to catch the boycott-breakers, and the occasion was marked by unusual tension. Basing his view on his general mistrust of union leaders, the Personnel Manager claimed that the former were deliberately misleading the workers. It is ironical that an occasion of socialization where the congruence of interests was to be re-confirmed in effect offered the arena within which *incongruence* was in fact enacted.

Summary

As noted earlier, the extent to which HRM is incorporated into the overall corporate strategy depends in part on the importance that organizations attach to strategic management itself. The weaknesses in strategic management were attributed to, *inter alia*, the policy of import substitution, the traditional dependency on parent company direction and some amount of managerial inertia and complacency in the face of environmental uncertainties. In line with the resultant tendency toward *ad hocracy*, recruitment requirements are seen in terms of manpower planning for the foreseeable future (this applies to Chematox and Automart, as well as Mimea - with regard to non-management cadres). This reveals a weakness in ensuring that organizations have the "right" people in the "right" jobs, in years to come. The adoption of HRM at Pharmaco and Autoco is helping to establish a "fit" between the management of employees and other areas of corporate strategy. This indicates the beginnings of a move towards strategic HRM.

The dimension of Integration with regard to coherence of policy and management support has also revealed differences of nature and degree in the case studies. Organizations have tended not to acknowledge the interrelationships between HR/personnel policy and other areas of policy, such that long-term investment decisions for example, fail to take adequate account of personnel implications. This indicates that organizations have not in general given much attention to the potential of human resources to serve the structural-functionalist purpose of sustaining the system. This is one of the issues that led Pharmaco and Autoco to institute HRM/D: their acknowledgement of the potential role of employees in "organizational effectiveness". Line management involvement entails the participation of line managers in identifying departmental staffing needs, initiating the recruitment exercise and sitting on the interview panel. This seems to serve the purposes of these organizations, and managers expressed doubt about what other possibilities may be imputed for line management involvement at the recruitment stage.

If, however, there can be more involvement of line managers in corporate decision making, then planning for the human resource can also be devolved to line managers. The creation of a pervasive ethos of HRM especially at Pharmaco is evidence of the way in which managers can re-orient themselves to their HR responsibilities. There was general agreement that success in a re-orientation of HRM required top management support; only Pharmaco, Autoco and Mimea had made concrete efforts in this regard. The multi-tier socialization practice reflects organizational stratification. The assumption of stability and order that underpins the functionalist paradigm would suggest that organizations do not readily recognize and admit to the existence of inequalities. This was indeed observed to be the case: such inequalities were either denied or rationalized away. A review of the newsletters reveals that they are mainly written for the English-speaking well-educated office staff to whom copies are mainly provided. Year-end parties and sporting activities were seen as a good opportunity to iron out differences. On the whole, however, given the stratified approach to socialization, the full benefits of socialization as an integrative tool are not being fully realized.

The Goal of Commitment

The Goal of Commitment pertains to efforts to spell out specific organizational values and the "organizational direction", and the subsequent matching of organizational values to perceived individual values in such a way as to establish a viable "fit".

Pharmaco best exemplifies the Features of Commitment. The company has a Mission Statement and a statement of organizational values both of which seek to embody the ethos of the organization's goals. The significance of these statements is mainly stressed during appraisal where it is easier to relate individuals' personal values to those of the organization as revealed through their actual performance. At recruitment, however, in addition to technical and academic competence, there is a greater reliance on managers' subjective perception of "acceptability"; the organizational values are therefore designed to harmonize and direct this perception towards some degree of *objectivity*. Figure 5.4 illustrates the main tenets of these statements.

Figure 5.4 Key features of Pharmaco's mission and values

THE MISSION

1. A team committed to creating distinctive solutions

   for the needs of mankind.
2. Measuring success by the criteria of:
   * market leadership
   * superior financial returns
   * an environment of trust and personal growth
3. Accomplishing these objectives through the dedication of people and resources to continuous improvement

THE VALUES

1. Creation of a winning team
2. Being customer-driven
3. Dedication to continuous improvement
4. A sense of urgency
5. Acting responsibly

The HR Manager was emphatic about the need to inculcate a strong sense of commitment to the organization especially through "workgroups". They try to achieve this by exhorting employees:

-   to be dedicated to all that they do,
-   to identify with the success of the company,
-   to avoid a conflict of interests by
    basing their business conduct and decisions on
    the best interests of the company
-   to avoid all activities and behaviour which
    would be detrimental to the image of the company

The company has taken some initial steps to realize organizational commitment by spelling out the organizational values. However, at the level of recruitment, this has not quite been actualized though managers claim to be influenced by these values when identifying the "right" candidate. It is noteworthy that the notion of "teamwork" is given prominence at both the theoretical and practical levels: both Statements begin with the concept of a "team" and its significance in bringing about success. At the practical level, work is organized on the basis of semi-formal "workgroups".

Similarly at Autoco, steps have been taken to spell out the organizational values - including the formulation of a Mission Statement. But this has not been formally extended to the conscious quest for a "fit" in individual-organization attitudes/values. Managers recognized the problem of low commitment but were not entirely sure how this could best be resolved. Figure 5.5 illustrates the key aspects of the Mission Statement.

The Personnel Manager suggested that one aspect that may be impinging on organizational commitment is *pay*. Remuneration is considered an ubiquitous bone of contention, and management does not believe that this can ever really be resolved, since "people will never feel they are being adequately remunerated", as the Personnel Manager put it. There is a greater concern in this company with the notion of "teamwork" and "team spirit", which is perhaps more realistic and effective than "commitment" in engendering a sense of congruence and an identification with the corporate ethos. The organization emphasizes teamwork (hence a definition of the desired organizational structure) in achieving the strategy of growth and the goal of customer satisfaction.

Figure 5.5 Aspects of Autoco's Mission Statement

1. To be customer driven
2. To provide employees with competitive compensation and benefits;
3. To continually increase employees' skills and abilities through training
4. To create an environment where all may contribute to the fullest of their abilities
5. As a Corporate Citizen to strive to make a positive economic and social impact on the country
6. To provide a fair return to shareholders

Teamwork is typified in the shopfloor "quality teams" where workers are referred to as "quality makers". A production manager described the agenda of the quality teams as quality/production and welfare. The former refers to reviews of the previous day's quality and productivity standards while the latter refers to the tendency for workers to discuss personal and family-related issues. From the point of view of both management and workers, the teams served a vital purpose and also helped to legitimize the unitarist ethos that management was keen to foster. It was also believed, according to the production manager, that once the workers developed a sense of identity in their quality team, they would subsequently develop a sense of commitment to the "Autoco team". Something that offers the workers a sense of identity, allowed them a "welfare" forum and was task-related, would appear to be a more viable approach to merging the interests of management with those of the employees than the mere quest for *organizational commitment*.

The quest for Commitment at Mimea was found not to be an explicit organizational objective. It is implicitly sought at recruitment whereby the selection committee judges one's suitability for a position on the basis of expectations about their career advancement opportunities and potential to make a contribution to the organization, and also on the basis of the subjective interpretation of *recruitment guidelines*. Some aspects of these guidelines are presented in Figure 5.6, followed by an example of the way selectors arrive at their decision. Figure 5.6 relates to those who are expected to advance to the managerial grade, hence the managerial/supervisory "core". For lower grades, eg unionisable workers, there is a greater focus on technical suitability, and there is the expectation that corporate welfarism will engender the requisite commitment as seen in a previous section.

Figure 5.6 Guidelines for selection at Mimea

1. Possession of the intelligence, communication skill, and clarity of thought and creativity necessary to cope with the function's technical aspects.
2. Ability to mature sufficiently to reach full management grade within two to three years; ie, is the candidate "an independent thinker; does he have effective personal contact and self-knowledge?"
3. Is the candidate considered to have the right personality to reach middle management by mid-thirties; ie, is he a potential group leader, does he have an impact on others? and does he have motivation and assertiveness?
4. Is the candidate likely to reach senior management?

Source: Recruitment manual

The recruitment of a factory management trainee

Mr. X was a school teacher who wanted to change his career. The comments below are taken from interviewer notes. Those selectors who found him suitable offered such reasons as the following:

He was pleasant of personality, and was rational in thinking as a result of his experience as a teacher.
He appeared to have a sense of responsibility and supervisory skills which would make a contribution to management.
He was sociable and intelligent, and had good communication skills.

Views about his unsuitability included:

He was academic and therefore not practical. Since he had never worked in a company, he would be slow to learn the operations of a business enterprise.
He appeared to have little direction in life, and the reason for wanting to change career was not clear.

In this situation where technical competence is of little help in arriving at a decision, organizational members define their preferences on the basis of compatibility of interests and values, hence a "fit", while avoiding traits that are seen as unacceptable. Wood (1986) notes that managers tend to have criteria that range from the very specific which relate to successful performance of the job, to broader ones which relate ultimately to the organizational culture. This reflects the technical and social aspects of jobs, respectively. The notion of "acceptability" has been elaborated by Silverman and Jones (1976) who illustrate the subjective formation of organizational criteria used to identify those who are perceived as "suitable" and rejecting those who demonstrate "abrasive" behaviour.

Although management at Chematox recognize the need for an integrative ethos, Commitment is not a central organizational concern. Similarly, the normative propositions find little expression: the corporate ethos has not been translated into organizational values that the employees can identify with. The initial selection categorizes applicants into "possibles", "doubtfuls" and "rejects". The initial stage, as in the majority of cases, is simple and merely procedural: testing whether qualifications meet the job specifications. Aptitude tests are taken seriously: these cover arithmetic, proficiency in English and in the case of shopfloor workers, mechanical construction and comprehension of pictorial forms provided by the UK parent company. The desired individual characteristics have been defined only in terms of the usual criteria: academic qualification/technical competence and the subjective notion of "suitability". Suitability pertains to the desirability to conform to organizational requirements, including *fitting in as an active member*. At Automart, *organizational values* with regard to the kind of employer the company wishes to be are seen in terms of high quality customer service. Hence the only values that the company seeks to project are those concerned with its relationship to customers. The effect of this is that commitment has come to be defined in terms of customer service. Thus, at selection, management looks out for such qualities as ability to communicate effectively, personal appearance and presentation. Other criteria include: perceived leadership and supervisory qualities, sociability, technical competence and self- confidence.

These were initially designed for those in Sales and Marketing, but the ethos has been generalized across the organization. This is the sense in which "commitment to the organization" is perceived in Automart. The problem of a lack of commitment was often repeated: the General Manager for instance related it to a general lack of commitment to institutions in the country, which he attributed to selfishness and greed. He also attributed the theft of company assets (especially spare parts, and the tendency for some mechanics to take unauthorized leave to do private repair jobs with company tools and parts) to "greed in Kenyan society as a whole and a deeply-entrenched *thieving sub-culture*". Other managers shared the view that workplace pilfering may be attributed to the generally low wages which in turn breed low living standards and widespread poverty. Both the Personnel Manager and the General Manager doubted the possibility of eliciting commitment to the organization given the workers' fundamental identification with the union, and the supposed lack of commitment to institutions. It appears, therefore, that "Customer service" is treated as a convenient device to indirectly elicit "commitment" to the organization.

Summary

It is evident from the foregoing that whereas management, in the main, recognizes that there is fundamentally a problem of *Commitment* to the organizations, it is only at Autoco, Pharmaco and Automart that the propositions of our model come closest to being realized. Various reasons for low organizational commitment were offered, including the supposedly entrenched us-and-them attitudes. The existence of unions was almost invariably seen as inimical to organizational commitment, and many managers wished for non-unionism.

It would seem theoretically feasible to articulate employment-related organizational values (eg in a Mission Statement) and desired individual values and attitudes, and then "match" these two in order to select the *right* employee for the *right* job, in line with unitarist-functionalist thinking. Although this would not quite resolve the "commitment problem" which is much more complex than this, it would possibly eliminate some of the sources of contention with regard to suitability. This is what Pharmaco aims to achieve.

In view of the controversies surrounding *Commitment* that have been expressed above and in chapter two, it is suggested here that *Commitment to the organization per se*, while desirable within the functionalist paradigm, is likely to be a difficult goal to achieve. Furthermore, its viability might be seen by management to be mediated by its ability for example to enhance productivity and eliminate undesirable behaviour like pilfering. The former would be difficult to demonstrate. Similarly, sheer commitment to the organization would not resolve the issue of an undesirable "counter-culture". The problem is a much more complex one involving social morality, poverty and wage inequalities.

Both Autoco and Pharmaco were concerned to establish the concept of teamwork, the significance of which has been pointed out above.

Organizations might, from this point of view, circumvent the ambiguities and contradictions immanent in "commitment" by fostering teamwork and a team spirit. In an analysis of the use of the concept of teamwork at Autoco, Kamoche (1995) argues that this is a more viable alternative to commitment because it has direct implications for workers' day-to-day wellbeing. A healthy team spirit would serve the dual purpose of addressing individual socio-psychological needs and form the basis for the pursuit of organizational objectives at the group level without unduly antagonizing the union. Developing the critique of commitment, Kamoche and Mueller (1998) question the underlying assumption of predictability and stability in attitudes and behaviour (which are at the heart of commitment) in this era of organizational uncertainty. In their concept of appropriation-learning, the emphasis should be on "commitment to learning" whereby the knowledge thus generated is beneficial to both the individual and the organization.

Numerical Flexibility

Interest in flexibility arises from the need to establish how the concept might be interpreted by organizations seeking adaptability to unanticipated pressures. The analysis here will focus on the organizational recruitment practices that are aimed at controlling headcounts according to changing needs. Following the argument that the "core-peripheral" distinction is a central feature in the concept of Flexibility, it was hypothesized in chapter two that organizations would pursue rigorous recruitment procedures for "core" employees and informal or even *ad hoc* procedures for the "peripheral" workforce. This was largely found to be the case: organizations maintain fairly elaborate procedures for the recruitment of Tier 1 staff who are integrated into the organization in the hope of creating a reliable, committed permanent workforce. The practice found in all the cases involved a rigorous search which is sometimes conducted initially by specialist recruitment agents; interviews are held with various cadres of management, and as noted earlier, the initial socialization is also a fairly elaborate exercise. The rigour in recruitment declines as one goes further down the multi-tier structure.

Casual worker hiring was found to be very informal: they are literally picked up at the factory gates depending on short-term labour needs. As compared to the other tiers who enjoy security of tenure, this fourth tier is for our purposes here, the *main* peripheral group which serves as a buffer against market uncertainties. The crowds of job-seekers waiting at factory gates is indicative of high unemployment. It also reflects the leeway managers have to manipulate the numerical flexibility of their workforce. Waweru (1984) argues that the high level of unemployment which has subsequently strengthened the employers' hand at the lower rungs of the labour market, has been responsible for the recklessness with which management treats the employment of workers in general, and which has also weakened the union movement because of the fear of job loss in the event of "illegal" strike action. The worsening of the economy in the 1990s has made the situation of workers more precarious. The hoards of unemployed who roam the streets find themselves drawn into hawking and crime. The very keen concern with cost minimization is seen even among the clerical and factory core in the use of overtime to avoid fresh hiring. Other forms of numerical flexibility involve student vacational jobs which are the nursery bed for future recruitment and fixed-term hiring.

The respective figures for casual and temporary workers were:

Pharmaco	2%
Autoco	2.5%
Mimea	8.7%
Chematox	2.6%
Automart	16.9%

Managers in all the five firms reported that they practiced the form of flexibility described above. This also included another central feature of Flexibility described in chapter two: hiring casual and temporary workers for unskilled and semi-skilled jobs, and treating these staff as a buffer against market uncertainty. Mimea and Automart are the two cases that warrant some concern. At Mimea, numerical flexibility is largely determined by foreign demand for the company's exports; furthermore, it is tied to the seasonality of agricultural produce.

The other noteworthy aspect of casual labour is the concern with ethnic composition: managers try to attain an "ethnic balance" to avoid tribal tensions in the rural farming areas. This illustrates the effect of ethnic considerations in the organizational context. In hiring farm casual workers at Mimea candidates are asked to line up, and selected on a random basis. Similarly, where a particular ethnic group is dominant in one area, the farm manager might allocate a given percentage of vacancies to this group, while the others share out the rest in some random fashion. In this way, the organization is able to circumvent the charge of ethnic particularism at selection, and project the image of objectivity and equity to the job seekers.

The high figure for Automart is accounted for by the long delays in ratifying appointments by the Chairman. Since people in this situation are liable to be dismissed at short notice (they are treated as being on probation), they can quite rightly be seen as a peripheral buffer. It is not inconceivable that this was indeed the intended effect. Some of these workers had been in this "limbo-like" state for more than a year. This official laxity perhaps reflects a casualness in the treatment of employment issues. This is in keeping with the *ad hoc* approach to planning in Automart. It is a short-term response to market uncertainties, designed to ensure organizational stability and system continuity.

The cost rationale is evident in avoiding the recruitment of casuals and temporaries on a permanent basis.[3] In addition to this being a rational solution to the specific problem of market uncertainty which in Kenya constitutes a serious threat to business, this approach also accords with the functionalist conception of an external reality to which organizations *respond*. Flexibility is therefore designed to meet the challenges that are posed by these externalities in order to enhance predictability and *order*. Casual labour force was hired for unskilled and temporary tasks such as packing and unpacking, loading and off-loading, grounds maintenance and cleaning. Other forms of temporary work include part-time secretarial work, industrial student and apprenticeship attachment and various forms of absence cover. Some non-core activities were undertaken through sub-contracting, eg printing of documents, office cleaning, catering and transportation. Mimea also sub-contracts for clearing and ploughing new land.

It is concluded here that the practice of numerical flexibility as defined by our normative propositions is a common feature in organizations in Kenya. This practice is seen to be economically viable because the maintenance of a peripheral workforce enables organizations to avoid fresh hiring, especially for unskilled and semi-skilled jobs, thus helping to keep labour costs down. By encouraging a stratified employment system, it raises the question of integration, and further compounds the contradictions inherent in the concept of "Integration" as a whole. This stratified approach is justified on structural-functionalist grounds, and is reflected in the seriousness with which the recruitment of each particular level is treated.

Quality in Recruitment

Given the difficulty in moving beyond the prescriptive in this dimension, some thoughts are offered here as to how Quality might be understood. The suggestions made in the normative model relate to rigour of procedures, pursuing specific HRM activities, product quality and effective review and control of HRM activities. These would help to enhance quality in the three key areas: quality of staff, quality of performance and the public image of the organization. The rigour in the recruitment exercise might offer some idea of quality in terms of qualifications, skills and experience where applicable, in establishing suitability for the job. Rigour was found to decline down the multi-tier hierarchy, and this has some implications for the "quality" of staff vis-a-vis the job requirements. It would be necessary too, to define "suitability" in terms of a "fit" between the individual and the organization.

The notion of the "quality of staff" would still be problematic. It would be difficult for instance, to demonstrate causality between labour turnover and "poor quality" of staff, except to speculate that where labour turnover results from theft and indiscipline, then it may be assumed that the organization had hired "undesirable" staff. Job retention may also reflect "institutionalization", whereby labour becomes immobilized through occupational role integration (Gowler and Legge, 1972), rather than "high" or "good" quality of staff, or "commitment". The propositions that management policy and practice be perceived to be of high quality by subordinates and for the enhancement of an organization's "image" and "reputation" through the way it treats its employees are essentially prescriptive. It is proposed here that these quality objectives are achievable through the pursuit of specific dimensions (integration, commitment, flexibility, teamwork, and so forth), by paying particular attention to the individual employee characteristics that would facilitate the achievement of HRM initiatives.

The linking of product quality to the quality of staff and the practice of management may be achieved through TQM (the Total Quality Movement). Wilkinson et al (1991) indeed identify TQM as consistent with a move towards a strategic form of HRM whereby the "soft" side of TQM is concerned with creating *customer awareness* within the firm. "Quality awareness" at Autoco is focused on shopfloor quality circles where employees work in teams; the circles meet every morning before work commences to discuss the previous day's productivity and quality issues and to set the day's targets. Teamwork sees a high level of competition, and prizes are awarded monthly; a company-wide reward of free lunch is offered to all employees in the event of a defect-free unit. Cash prizes are also awarded for cost-saving suggestions. The quality movement is based on a strong "customer satisfaction" ethos where the Managing Director has striven to define "customer" not merely as those who buy the firm's products but whoever receives a product or service within the firm itself.

The "quality movement" at Pharmaco is seen as part of "World Class Business". Mimea's quality programme is geared towards problem-solving and consists of high-level management teams that run quality improvement programmes (QIPs). Their concept of Corporate Quality Cycle encompasses 'quality of work' and 'quality of organization', designed to offer more scope for a focused approach to the management of employees and is integrated with the other functions. As noted earlier, this relates mainly to a form of welfarism. At Chematox, "quality" is promoted under a "customer plus" approach, which is concerned to offer a better service than the customer expects within a "reasonable" cost regime. Similarly, at Automart, quality is related to customer service, but this firm has gone beyond "quality of service" to relate service to requisite employee characteristics.

Summary

The *prima facie* position of Quality is a prescriptive one, which accords with other stances organizations take in their quest for "superior performance", "dedication to continuous improvement", or "providing lasting solutions for the benefit of mankind". As argued above, however, Quality can be brought to a more *practical* level which is more in keeping with the logic of the functionalist paradigm. Quality can therefore serve to highlight management's perception of employees, eg in seeking to recruit "high-quality" employees and subsequently investing in staff welfare and development to sustain a high quality of expertise. It also means having high-quality management expertise, and aiming to provide superior goods/services by harnessing the high-quality expertise available within the organization.

Conclusions

This chapter has considered recruitment within the functionalist paradigm. As noted in the introductory remarks, this paradigm is underwritten by the assumption of purposive rationality and aims at the establishment of objective knowledge. It has been argued here that the functionalist paradigm is informed by a structural-functionalist ethos whereby human resource management is conceived of as a set of social relations whose "value" arises from the purpose they serve in sustaining continuity in the system. The significance of HRM from a normative theoretical point of view therefore is that the Personnel/HR function should cohere with other functions to maintain the functioning of the system. This biological analogy has been an important element in structural-functionalist thought.

Whereas the question of inter-functional or inter-departmental coherence was not specifically addressed, it is argued here that the managerial "core" received the greatest attention with regard to their role in "sustaining the system". This was even more prevalent in Mimea, Automart and Chematox. Companies like Autoco and Pharmaco with explicit HRM initiatives, coupled with Board-level representation and specific HR Committees, and so forth, will be better disposed to derive some measure of comparative advantage from HRM. Greater success in HRM initiatives will ultimately depend on the extent to which these practices pervade the organization, ie whether or not they encompass all the employees within a more meaningful "integrative structure". The existing multi-tier structure which is informed by the "core-periphery" dialectic currently prevents the achievement of this goal. This functional stratification also serves to institutionalize existing power relations.

The other important issue that arises in this chapter is the tenability of Guest's model of HRM with regard to recruitment. Within this paradigm, it is necessary to establish an integrative structure, which is what the dimension of Integration aims to achieve. Various institutional difficulties prevent the total achievement of integration, including weaknesses in strategy formulation, and the relatively low status of personnel/HR vis-a-vis other functions like finance, marketing and manufacturing. The Goal of Commitment has been found to be problematic on various counts, leading to the suggestion that while it may be desirable to foster employee commitment to organizational objectives, there is a need to give more attention to teamwork, welfare considerations and a commitment to individuals' opportunities to learn. Numerical flexibility accords well with functionalist rationality in so far as its quest for predictability in the use of labour through the manipulation of headcounts is underpinned by the cost rationale. However, the approaches that organizations use in the recruitment of the "peripheral staff" vis-a-vis the other tiers raise questions of equity and integration.

An attempt   was   also made to   illustrate how the dimension of Quality might be made more meaningful in the pursuit of HRM initiatives.

Notes

[1] A few years later, the HR Manager left the firm, (for undisclosed reasons), and the Personnel Manager advanced to the position of HR Manager. Reference will be made to these two in their respective capacities during the research.

[2] This echoes Onyemelukwe's (1973) observation of managers' fear of the erosion of authority through "over-familiarity" with subordinates.

[3] The law requires, however, that those on "continuous" temporary status must be confirmed as "permanent" staff after a period of ninety days.

6 An Analysis of Training within the Functionalist Paradigm

This chapter addresses the second element in our conceptual configuration of HRM: *training/development*. For the purposes of this discussion, training and development signify a concern with the following:

- orientation/induction
- performance appraisal
- the *actual* training, and job rotation, and
- job design

We begin by setting out the importance of training and development and then proceed to examine the practices in the five firms. The analysis, based on the key features of Guest's model, seeks to assess the ways in which training and development serves a structural-functionalist purpose

The Centrality of Training

Training and development are considered to be central tenets of the contemporary model of HRM (eg Keep, 1989; Storey, 1992). For example, Keep (1989, p111) wrote that:

> If a company has invested in training its workforce, it makes sense to develop policies that will help it to retain these employees and to motivate them in such a way as to put to best use their skills, thereby maximizing the return on investment.

This also illustrates how training serves the dual purpose of developing people and achieving organizational objectives in the face of changing technological and market imperatives. The extent to which an organization is prepared to *invest in* its employees by way of "developing" them is indicative of whether employees are seen as a cost to be rationalized, or a resource that has the potential to contribute meaningfully to the organization. There is a tendency to treat development as an avoidable cost in organizations in Kenya. Training itself is guided by the functional objective to equip employees with the requisite skills that will facilitate the attainment of organizational objectives mainly in the short run. The use of the term "development" aims to emphasize the centrality of training and development to strategy as well as the enhancement of the awareness of the need to increasingly view the employee as a "valued resource". In considering this aspect with regard to Kenyan companies, three issues come to the fore:

1. The need to link the elements of development in such a way as to facilitate the formulation of a processual, integrative broad policy. Such an approach would link recruitment and selection to training and development, with performance management playing a central role,
2. To signify the need to go beyond mere skill formation and instead focus on developing a systematic long-term policy to create a highly skilled national workforce, and
3. To emphasize the need to address effectively the contextual aspect that requires managers in developing countries to manage the "ambiguity" and "vagueness" immanent in all aspects of industry.

The third point refers to the lack of clarity in organizational goals, unpredictability in a panoramic socio-economic and political context, inadequate or non-existent infrastructural amenities and so forth. These factors often require managers to manage by improvisation, to be sensitive to individuals' personal circumstances, to interface with diverse stakeholders and to devise their own context-specific ways of problem-solving. Firms will have to take up the challenge not merely to *train* employees to do their job, but to contribute to the *development* of a broad national skill base.

The centrality of *performance* highlights the importance of having a well thought out appraisal system. An interpretation of this point within the functionalist paradigm highlights the importance of "employee productivity" and "organizational performance". The impact of effort on productivity is determined by evaluating performance against pre-set standards, which subsequently impacts on rewarding and training. Given this key role of appraisal, it is no wonder that so much controversy has come to surround this concept. Ever since McGregor's (1957) "uneasy look" at the subject, there has been a robust debate about the intricacies of the exercise and the numerous problems that prevent the formulation and effective use of appraisal systems, eg Long (1986); Townley (1989; 1990). The problems in appraisal include measurement imprecision, subjectivity and bias; trying to achieve too many objectives, some of which may be contradictory; defensiveness, suspicion and mistrust between the appraiser and appraisee; susceptibility to errors eg the "halo effect" and "central tendency". The interest in performance appraisal here focuses on the extent to which this exercise is contributing towards the formulation of an integrative structure of development.

A Thematic Analysis of Training

This part of the chapter looks at the actual practices in each of the five companies. The findings are summarised in Figure 6.1 Training expenditures were generally less than 1% of sales, which is very low, and is in part explained by a high reliance on on-the-job-training. At Chematox, the training budget was simply described as "very little". On a more encouraging note, Automart runs its own training school in which all the plant mechanics are trained. Mimea also runs a training centre which mainly offers courses on management training.

The Goal of Integration

This section considers the relevance of the dimension of Integration within the exercise of Development. Four sub-topics are considered: development strategy, coherence of policy, management support and employee integration.

Development strategy   Pharmaco comes closest to our normative model of HRM and best exemplifies the specific concern with the development of the human resource, in regard to its adoption of HRM/D. This represents what might be referred to as "emergent" HRM. According to the HR Manager, HRD was found necessary because the problem in managing people was found to lie in *development*, rather than in the "traditional administrative concerns". The new initiatives are coordinated by a HR Director. The company aims to ensure that they have the right calibre of staff, equipped with the skills that would enable the firm to remain competitive. The Mission Statement articulates that a sufficiently developed and committed team will contribute to the achievement of organizational objectives.

Figure 6.1 A summary of the case material on training and development

INTEGRATION   COMMITMENT   FLEXIBILITY

PHARMACO

INTEGRATION	COMMITMENT	FLEXIBILITY
- development aligned to departmental growth - comprehensive appraisal programme to realize employees' potential - appraisal for all permanent staff linked to training and on-the-spot rewarding - on-the-job training being curtailed - comprehensive tiers 1 and 2 appraisal	- concern with "right attitudes" - adherence to values sought and inculcated at appraisal	- some multi-skilling - skill diversity for higher tier staff - "corporate citizen" rhetoric rationalizes broad skill base - some employee involvement in job design

AUTOCO

INTEGRATION	COMMITMENT	FLEXIBILITY
- HR integrated with corporate strategy to develop "competent labour" - change-oriented training focused on departmental and company objectives - results-based appraisal of all permanent staff - absence of shopfloor multi-skilling due to cost and technology	- training supposed to inculcate "right attitudes" - control through appraisal	- specialization rationalized by nature of technology and product line - re-training based on model change - tier 1 routine rotation - some employee involvement in job design

MIMEA

INTEGRATION	COMMITMENT	FLEXIBILITY
- focus on management development - "differential appraisal" rationalized on cost and logistical grounds - lower cadre on-the-job training considered inevitable and on-going	- concern with "right attitudes" - focus on productivity and performance, hence control - integration of employees into the organization expected to enhance commitment	- specialization necessitated by nature of business - skill diversity for higher cadres - constraints on flexibility also imposed by union structure - "tailor-made" tier 1 training - no employee involvement in job design

Figure 6.1 (cont'd)

CHEMATOX

- development focus on higher tier management and technical expertise - focus on "induction/training" - differential appraisal - attention to quantifiable performance data - "unstructured" union appraisal due to cost	- quest for "right attitudes" - excessive use of the "stick syndrome" - appraisal thus strong tool of control to elicit compliance	- strict cost control in retraining - some cross-unit grading - skill diversity for tier 1 - "induction/training" precludes further training - no employee involvement in job design

AUTOMART

- development focus on management and technical expertise - traditional differential appraisal now mediated by new focus on production mechanics - attention to quantifiable performance data	- concern with "right attitudes" - control in conformity to requirements	- functional specialization justified on cost - skill diversity for tier 1 - job rotation experiment abandoned - re-training linked to technology change

The initial induction follows the standard format of orientation meetings and brief departmental attachments. Induction for unionisable staff lasts about a week; that of management trainees and supervisory staff takes up to a month. HRM/D in this company hinges upon the performance appraisal exercise which they refer to as the Performance Appraisal and Development Programme. The exercise is guided by the following policy:

> The overall objective of the Performance Appraisal and Development Programme is to realize the full potential of the company's most important asset - its employees. Providing guidance and opportunities for employees to develop their skills, their knowledge, and their careers for the benefit of both the individual and the company. These mutual benefits will only be achieved if employee development is approached in a systematic manner as part of a total company programme.

Source: Standard Appraisal documents

The first stage is the *self-appraisal*, which is thereafter followed by a "formal counselling interview" in which both the appraiser and the appraisee discuss the latter's performance and the views expressed in the self-appraisal form. The rigour of this exercise, and its future development orientation, rather than a simple concern with current results make it a viable exemplar in development. Pharmaco also appraises unionisable staff but the procedure is less rigorous and consists of one's supervisor and the foreman reviewing individual performance and discussing with the appraisee ways to enhance productivity, and necessary training needs. This has been designed as part of HRM/D policy, to serve the purpose of skill development, promotion and productivity rather than rewarding which is a matter for collective bargaining. The Personnel Manager reported, however, that pay increments based on individual merit are made where "it is felt that the union guideline is an inadequate measure of performance". Such increments are strictly discretionary and do not represent any formal performance-related-pay system.

The next stage of development is the actual training. This is now categorized into two parts:

- group-needs training which is mainly in-house (not necessarily on-the-job), and
- specific-needs training which is mainly external

The purpose of this distinction is to streamline the development exercise and expedite the process of identifying and addressing training needs. HRM/D also signifies a departure from on-the-job training which is now considered inadequate. This reflects the organization's desire to break out of this traditional mould which, as the HR Manager noted, has always seemed like an excuse for not training. Company-specific on-the-job training is ordinarily considered an economically rational approach to development across all the organizations. It is easy to see why this is the case: the potential for institutionalization justifies the investment. However, the introduction of HRM/D at Pharmaco constitutes a more focused consideration of the employees' development needs than before.

The other key objective of HRM/D in this company is multi-skilling. Workers were in the past calling for some form of multi-skilling because they were often required to perform tasks for which they were not qualified. The new HRM/D policy addresses this issue by carefully reviewing every requisition for recruitment, determining whether and how existing jobs can be re-designed or restructured, and seeking to accommodate multi-skilling. Job design has traditionally not gone beyond the preparation of job descriptions and delineation of duties and responsibilities. The reward system is essentially merit-based; they refer to it as an "on-the-spot" reward system with "check-points" throughout the year.

Management at Autoco seeks to integrate the HR dimension into the corporate strategy through the five-year manpower-development plan. The main objective at board level is to ensure that *there is competent labour over the long-term.* As noted in chapter five, the presence of the Personnel Manager on the HR Committee provides a useful link to the Board and ensures that development stays on the agenda. A four-half-day induction session for all new staff is the first stage in the development exercise. It prominently reflects the overriding unitarist perspective, illustrated by the sub-titles of the various sessions which are structured with the aim of emphasizing *the roles of the various departments in achieving company objectives.* Figure 6.2 presents the other items on the agenda.

Figure 6.2 The induction programme at Autoco

- the background information about the company,
     including the organizational structure
- the Mission Statement
- the operating philosophy
- the goals and objectives of the organization
- the "benefits programme" including the medical and training
     facilities, and
- Industrial Relations.

Appraisal assesses "performance" vis-a-vis pre-determined organizational objectives. This company has departed from the more common practice of self-appraisal; instead, they use a "results-oriented" MBO-like approach whereby the appraisee and appraiser discuss how specific tasks were accomplished vis-a-vis jointly predetermined goals. Seminars in performance appraisal for managers are held in order to harmonize the exercise and eliminate the scope for subjectivity and bias. It follows from the productivity-based appraisal that remuneration is strictly merit-based. This is the only other company (besides Pharmaco) which systematically appraises unionisable staff. The objective is to improve performance and thus raise productivity, and although the union Agreement supposedly imposes constraints on wage increments (by imposing a collective grade wage which, according to managers, hampers individual initiative) appraisal serves as a basis for promotion, productivity improvement and training.

Autoco has instituted a broad post-induction development programme which is guided by the rationale in Figure 6.3.

Figure 6.3 Autoco's training rationale

- the purpose of training is to improve the capabilities
of the personnel within the organization through imparting
positive changes in knowledge, skills and attitudes.

WHY?

- to increase employees' efficiency and effectiveness in
carrying out the job responsibilities assigned to them.
- Training should therefore be relevant to the needs of both
the organization as well as those of the individual employees.
Therefore, training must be focused on the organization's overall
and departmental objectives.

Source: Training policy documents.

The functionalist basis of training - to achieve organizational objectives - is repeated in the newsletters which reiterate the idea that all employees are "sufficiently trained in order to make them *more efficient and effective in their job performance*". It is worth noting the significance of the reference to "attitudes". This is further elaborated in a document which spells out the instances when training may be deemed necessary; it states, *inter alia*, that training is conducted, when "there is a desirable need *to change certain attitudes* either in an individual or across the organization". According to the Training Manager, there is no particular organizational preference for on-the-job training; the mode and location will depend on the specific need, but "in-house" programmes are preferred.

The manager also claimed that skill requirements in the case of shopfloor workers are fairly stable, thus limiting re-training needs. These views were echoed by a Production Manager who reported that the relatively unsophisticated nature of the technology makes shopfloor skill requirements standard and predictable. He also defended the absence of multi-skilling by arguing that the costs of re-training for re-deployment are unjustifiable on a single product assembly line.

After an initial induction, the linking of Development to corporate strategy at Mimea is limited to the very elaborate management development programme which begins with the appraisal of managers in Kenya and is coordinated at the head office in England. The induction of unionisable staff was described as "informal". The two-year management development programme is coordinated by the Group Personnel Manager (Training and Development) who liaises with the Production Director. Additionally, the board of directors ensures that the activity is conducted in accordance with laid-down policy. This programme relates only to the university graduates hired annually. A further five-year management development programme is prepared for all other "high flying" managers, which often involves various trips abroad. The scope of the second-tier intensive two-day induction course is summarised in Figure 6.4.

Figure 6.4 Second tier induction at Mimea

- course objectives/administrative information
- what the company expects of its new employees
- brief history of the company
- terms and conditions of service
- organizational structure
- personnel policies and procedures
- training and development
- factory visit

The brevity of this course contrasts sharply with the management trainee programme which aims to create the very heart of the core workforce. Third-tier workers are not appraised because the large numbers would make it too costly. Performance appraisal for the non-unionisable staff begins with a self-appraisal whereby employees are required to review their performance and comment on the following:

- their most important achievements vis-a-vis predetermined objectives
- their disappointments with respect to responsibilities

- what factors hindered the achievement of a better performance
- what new skills they learned and how these affected results
- what new skills they will require to improve performance and advance in their career
- what other skills and aptitudes they have which they feel are not being fully utilized

Evidently, this exercise is development-oriented and essentially addresses productivity, performance, skill development and career advancement. It also illustrates how performance appraisal helps to achieve integration through the control of behaviour by assessing results vis-a-vis predetermined goals.

Figure 6.5 The induction/training programme at Chematox

DAY ONE	- brief discussion of the role of the Internal Audit function
	- general introduction to Personnel matters
	- salary and wages system; office services; personnel and administrative instructions
DAY TWO	- Operations
DAY THREE	- Industrial gases department
DAY FOUR	- health care business
	- welding products business
	- factory tour
DAY FIVE	- visit to stores
	- credit control
	- data processing
DAYS SIX-NINE	- more detailed review of the operations of the department
	- review of the induction programme

Although "People" are depicted as one of the key aspects of the corporate plan at Chematox, development has not sufficiently been identified and treated as a central management concern: personnel/training is only a Section in the Administration Department. The initial induction programme for the majority of staff serves as the most important level of training, and is referred to as "induction/training". An example of an induction programme for an audit clerk is presented in Figure 6.5. This represents a standard approach for the second-tier staff. The management trainee system is more comprehensive; it involves various training courses, locally and abroad, and may cover several weeks. Despite the breadth of management training, there is a deficiency in what managers referred to as "man-management". According to the Operations Director, this has resulted in low "self-motivation" and a lack of spontaneity and initiative in idea-formulation amongst managers. An attempt to improve the management of human resources failed apparently because "managers were reluctant to discuss what they had learnt".

The programme is expected to be fairly comprehensive in order to cover as much as possible in terms of the actual tasks and the appreciation of the role of the individual's function in the various departments. Figure 6.6 depicts the tier 2 appraisal criteria.

Figure 6.6 Appraisal criteria at Chematox

- **Job knowledge:**   poor, fair, good, excellent
- **Dependability:**   unreliable, dependable, conscientious,
                           exceptionally reliable
- **Attitude towards
  the company:**   antagonistic; passive; loyal;
                           loyal and enthusiastic
- **Initiative:**   lacks self-reliance, follows precedence,
                           somewhat resourceful, exceptionally resourceful
- **Attendance:**   irregular, sometimes regular, usually regular,
                           very regular
- **Ability to learn:**   poor, fair, good, excellent
- **Accuracy:**   frequent errors, occasional errors, infrequent
                           errors, no error
- **Acceptance of
  responsibility:**   evades where possible, accepts as required,
                           accepts willingly, seeks eagerly
- **leadership:**   inadequate, below par, effective, exceptional
- **Appearance:**   shabby, tolerable, smart, very smart

The individual is rated on a point scale which ranks performance on an unsatisfactory-outstanding continuum. The system well illustrates the functionalist concern with "objectivity" and the need to represent information in a way which aids practical problem-solving. The appraisee participates by making his/her comments on "personal achievements and disappointments during the year and suggestions for general improvement". The appraisal forms are thereafter reviewed by the Company Secretary and the Business Management Committee; recommendations by line managers are therefore subject to top management scrutiny. It is through appraisal therefore that development receives top management attention, but this is mainly with regard to remuneration. Guidelines for salary increments are related to market rates. Appraisal for tier 3 unionisable staff was generally absent, and where it was done, it was described as "unstructured" and was related to evaluation of productivity. Similarly, training for the office and shopfloor staff is infrequent and fairly *ad hoc*.

It was noted earlier that the HR dimension at Automart has not been considered a key element in corporate planning, despite the Personnel Manager's efforts to introduce changes in recruitment and development. The Personnel Manager, however claimed that training is taken very seriously and that the organization sees itself as a "corporate citizen" highly committed to training. This is supported by their commitment to a company training institute and a three-year apprenticeship for mechanics. The Staff Relations Officer reported that insufficient *ad hoc* training for tiers 2 and 3 accounted for what he saw as a generally low level of morale and commitment.

The fostering of a "core" is a key feature of development at Automart. The entire comprehensive twenty two-month management development programme is designed to equip participants with the requisite skills for a diversified career in management. Some have a chance to attend training courses at assembly plants in Germany and Japan.

As in Mimea and Chematox, formal performance appraisal has traditionally only applied to tiers one and two. In 1989 management introduced a bonus payment system which opened the way for a more systematic appraisal of "production workers" (mechanics) based on "attendance", "work input" and "repeat jobs". The system represents a move towards performance-related-pay: the worker only earns the basic grade wage if he works the standard hours. They can earn more through efficient productivity.

The aspects of appraisal depicted in Figure 6.7 are graded on such continua as excellent - no hope, highly motivated - no initiative, and so forth. These measures are very subjective. Management tries to circumvent the arbitrariness that is potentially inherent in subjectivity through quantification, and by offering guidelines in terms of lower and upper limits, for example.

Figure 6.7 Tiers 1 & 2 appraisal criteria at Automart

1. Conduct
2. Ability
3. Progress
4. Motivation
5. Customer/Staff relations

6. Time/appointment keeping
7. Communication skills
8. Product knowledge
9. Physical appearance
10. General knowledge and potential to be trained

Coherence of policy Managers reported that they appraise performance primarily to improve productivity, which they hope to achieve by identifying training needs and then going on to provide the requisite skills. The primary purpose of training, therefore, is the functionalist equipping of employees with the skills necessary to discharge their organizational duties. At Autoco and Pharmaco, the notion of a stronger commitment to enabling the "human resource" to *realize* itself was also apparent. Both training and rewarding are based on performance evaluation. This is a plausible approach if there are unambiguous criteria for the evaluation of performance. It has been observed, however, that the imprecision of the criteria, coupled with a preponderance on a trait-based approach, raises doubt as to the "practical validity" of the exercise (see also Dawis, 1980). Such problems illustrate the lack of internal consistency which in the long run makes the goal of Integration illusory. In all the cases, grading and quantification were seen as important forms of objectivity, but some managers did admit that this was in itself not adequate. At Pharmaco, the aligning of appraisal to the "organizational values" helps to make the exercise more relevant and also explicitly seeks the "integration" of employees.

Managers are on the whole intent on discouraging the employee expectation that the acquisition of more skills should automatically be reflected in career advancement which is invariably interpreted in terms of a salary increment or promotion. At Mimea, for example, the company policy on training and rewarding is categorical on not wishing to directly link the two. According to the Personnel Manager, management does not want employees to develop the attitude that "they are going on courses to be promoted". While managers may sometimes be justified in efforts to water down the instrumentalism immanent in these employee expectations, this practice has implications on the reality of employee expectations as defined by contextual societal norms. We examine two issues related to this.

The first issue pertains to the generally low standards of living which have inevitably placed a high premium on monetary reward. This has resulted in *instrumental orientations* to work which are manifest in the great concern for material rewards and security of tenure. A policy that sidesteps this issue will be viewed with suspicion by employees. The second issue touches on meritocracy and the urge to concretize the effort-reward bargain, and relates more to non-unionisable staff.

Completion of a course for instance is seen to enhance one's career advancement prospects, and if the employer does not acknowledge and act on it, job search becomes a reality. Labour turnover among the better skilled, professional and managerial cadres is primarily accounted for by the search for "greener pastures". At Chematox, where the best data on labour turnover were maintained, over a five-year period, only 22% of the unionisable labour turnover is attributable to the quest for better prospects; in the case of the supervisory/managerial cadres, this figure rises to 61%. Similarly, at Automart, the corresponding figures over a two-year period are 17% and 28%.

The stratified approach to appraisal which has been identified to reflect the four-tier structure will be referred to here as "differential appraisal"; differential appraisal subsequently leads on to differential training, whereby only those with "promotion prospects" are appraised and trained. A merit-seniority reward distinction is also implicit in this schema, but given the gradual shift away from seniority altogether, this is not all that clear-cut. Figure 6.8 depicts the stratification in development. For all practical purposes, the management and senior professional cadres constitute the inner "core". It is not uncommon for the final stage of their appraisal to be carried out at the parent company, to be considered vis-a-vis other managers within their international network. They also attend a broad range of routine courses locally and abroad. The second tier staff undergo infrequent training strictly depending on skill deficiencies identified by line managers. The third tier are often only trained at initial induction; indeed at Chematox, this is referred to simply as induction/training. Managers reported that "on-the-job training" is the norm; but some did admit that this was ambiguous and even "troublesome". Subsequent training is supposedly restricted by technological

Figure 6.8 A four-tier development structure

Level	Constituents	Aspects of development
Tier 1	management trainees (and other managerial jobs)	very comprehensive induction (months) systematic results-based appraisal (final stage at parent company) "tailor-made" regular training "designer pay", plus perks and various forms of profit-sharing
Tier 2	supervisory office staff accountants technicians marketing staff	short induction programme (weeks or days) routine appraisal (for those with "promotion prospects") training rationalized by "need" and "cost" merit-based pay
Tier 3	salesmen skilled artisans mechanics craftsmen machine operators farm workers	induction at introductory meeting informal/unstructured appraisal in some cases on-the-job, company-specific training union agreement wage guideline
Tier 4	part-timers contractual casuals	no induction no appraisal no training contractual pay arrangements

requirements; this is best typified by Autoco and Automart where re-training only occurs when a new model is introduced, and even then, according to a production manager at Autoco, there rarely are any radical technological changes. Training at Chematox sometimes involves attaching workers to client sites to learn about their industrial needs in order to enhance the quality of service.

The purpose in appraising tier 3 unionisable staff was not remuneration as this follows stipulated collective agreement guidelines but productivity, hence control, and the identification of training needs. At Automart, the link to remuneration was more explicit, as it constituted a form of performance-related-pay. Mimea claimed that appraising unionisable workers is meaningless and logistically unfeasible, which is consistent with the functionalist rationale. The "logistical" rationale is evident in the large size of the organization, where the unionisable staff of almost 20,000 are spread over farms across the country. The cost rationale was the reason offered for the unstructured approach at Chematox, for the 180 unionisable staff.

The Personnel Director at Mimea noted that they try to "incentivize" rewarding so as to enhance motivation amongst workers despite the logistical problems of appraisal and the union agreement. In this regard, management sometimes gave increments to recognize "commendable performance" when the Agreement did not make such a provision. The two comments below, taken from employment files, illustrate this:

> In granting this increase, consideration has been given to the cooperative and cheerful manner in which you have carried out your duties, despite the situation whereby the Tripartite Agreement makes no provision for any increase for the next twelve months.

> The increment has been given under special circumstances in view of your good work

The other important consideration in differential appraisal and training is the stratification which defines the organizational status and power hierarchy. This point further helps to account for the inherent inconsistency in the development policy and is treated in more detail in chapter seven. We observe here, however, that within the functionalist paradigm, development is predicated on the *functional* importance the organization places on the different individuals' perceived contribution to organizational objectives, and hence to the maintenance of the system. Offe (1976) argues that society aims to determine the distribution of rewards on the basis of the *achievement principle*, which is supposedly based on merit. However, organizations often use various extra-functional criteria which negate the achievement principle. This, according to Offe, is due to such circumstances as technological restrictions of productive work ascribable to specific individuals and organizational limits on supervision of performance. As a result, the system which seeks to justify the distribution of rewards on the basis of achievement subsequently ends up legitimizing inequality. Our concern here is that development should be treated as a critical management activity, based on a processual approach, rather than a tool to legitimize inequality in organizations. Evidently, the existence of inequalities within the social hierarchy prevents the attainment of an integrative system and the functionalist paradigm is, in any case, ill-equipped to handle them.

It is also worth considering the choice between merit and seniority in appraisal and remuneration. There has been much controversy, both in the theory and the practice, about the appropriateness of the two approaches. The notion of cost rationalization is gradually phasing out the practice of seniority. Waweru (1984) cautions that seniority might result in the ritualistic devotion to duty in which perfection in trivialities, job-routines, and avoidance of taking initiative (so as not to antagonize the rewarding superior) prevail at the expense of imaginative and rigorous pursuit of challenging objectives. Onyemelukwe (1973) hints at some form of dual system by suggesting that rewarding individual effort may be acceptable to senior staff but not to the rank and file. These diverse possibilities demonstrate the difficulty of pursuing a "harmonized and integrative" policy in this regard. The dual approach Onyemelukwe talks about appears to have taken root (see also Kamoche 1992b). Meritocracy appears to be suited to the younger, better educated or highly skilled cadres particularly in the more professionally-run firms, ie mostly in MNCs. State corporations in particular are notorious for using tribal, party-affiliation and other such particularist factors to make reward and career management decisions. The older, lesser educated, semi- or unskilled workers understandably prefer seniority, and indeed companies have experienced resistance in phasing seniority out, as evidenced in letters of complaint at Mimea by older operatives who felt that they were being passed over for promotion in favour of new younger employees. The bonus system at Automart paves the way for individualized arrangements at the shopfloor. There was evidence in all the firms of some cases where workers earned bonuses of up to 5% of the Agreement wage. According to managers, this was not representative of a trend towards "individual remuneration arrangements", but simply a reflection of individual merit and "commendable performance" as noted above, which the non-company-specific Agreement might fail to address adequately. Wage increments over and above the Agreement are, however, at the discretion of management.

The case study findings indicate that even though seniority is no longer explicitly observed in appraisal, it is still implicitly recognized. Examples include policies like first-in last-out, preference in re-employment after redundancy and so forth. Long-service awards also fall into this category (at Autoco this is known as the Continuous Employee Recognition Programme).

Management support   The important issue in this section is the extent to which top management is giving its support to the development initiatives, and the involvement of line managers. The findings largely parallel those in chapter five, and this issue will not be given much attention here. Pharmaco exemplifies the situation whereby the development exercise is initiated by top management - HR Director and Manager. Most of the re-orientation towards HRM/D is handled by the HR Manager, and gradually, the role of line management has become more explicit. As in the other cases, however, managers felt that there was high involvement of line managers in such exercises as performance appraisal, determination of rewards and skill needs, as well as in actual training. At Mimea, for instance, one criterion for hiring and promoting managers is their ability to train.

Autoco represents a similar case though the focus is on human resource management in general while Pharmaco's interest is mainly development. At Autoco, the Training Manager liaises with the Personnel Manager to coordinate the training and development function. The former draws up a schedule of authorized and recommended courses which he circularizes to the various departments. On the basis of this schedule, line managers select relevant courses to meet training needs that would have been identified at appraisal. In the three firms, managers attend courses on how to appraise subordinates. At Chematox, the organizational structure affords little prominence to personnel/ training issues. However, top management review the final appraisal and proposed remuneration while departmental managers have to ratify proposed training. Staff reports on training courses attended are reviewed by departmental heads and Managing Directors. In addition to these practices, top management commitment to development at Automart is reflected in the management training programme and the establishment of a training school.

Employee integration   This section is concerned with the extent to which development may be employed toward the achievement of the goal of Integration. This is related to the quest for unitarist goal congruence in accordance with the functionalist paradigm. The normative proposition in this regard suggests that organizations will seek integration through the inculcation of company-specific skills in "on-the-job" training. This is, however, not all that clear-cut: on-the-job training which most closely fits the *company-specific* definition applies mainly to tiers 2 and 3. To the extent therefore, that the first tier goes through an elaborate development programme, the rationale of integration with regard to on-the-job and (firm-specific) training would seem to be restricted to the lower organizational cadres. It is also apparent that the integration of the higher-level cadres is sought through skill diversity such that the "core" can continue to fulfil their role as a "valued resource" in changing times. It is further suggested here that the inculcation of company-specific skills is motivated by the cost rationale just as much as by a strong desire to build a sense of belonging in the employees. This in effect amounts to *institutionalization* (Gowler and Legge, 1972) and may be interpreted in terms of the creation of circumstances that would make labour mobility unattractive and difficult because the employees' skills are not transferable.

Integration into the organization through development follows the usual *functional-hierarchical* structure. This is the norm in all the cases, but at Pharmaco, the HRM/D approach signals a departure, to the extent that certain activities like appraisal are now being extended to include all employees. Managers at Pharmaco believe that the new centrality of development will give employees more meaningful jobs where they can realize their potential and maintain organizational values. It is proposed, in the long run, to introduce multi-skilling across the board. To this extent, therefore, more diversified rather than a narrow range of specialist skills is expected to better meet the needs of employees and enhance a sense of belonging.

According to the Personnel Manager at Mimea, on-the-job training is preferred because it is "inevitable and on-going"; but he was also quick to emphasize that it was not meant to be "indoctrination". Although the quest for employee integration was not an explicit objective of development (except in the case of the management trainee induction programme), a review of reports written by employees upon the completion of training courses suggests that this was very much a mutually acknowledged arrangement. Some examples from training files are cited below.

An employee who was being prepared for a managerial appointment made the following comments after a training course:

> I learned the scope and contribution of my responsibilities and that the company is a continually developing organization. I came to understand how the various departments are inter-dependent. In the course I also learned how to conduct myself, and to appreciate the limits of the terms and conditions under which I work. I gained a sense of security, and learned to courageously make decisions. The course created a sense of belonging to the company and showed me how I can contribute towards making profits for the company through basic saving and

minimizing the costs of production. Finally, the course enabled the participants to see themselves as a larger family of employees.

The Head of the Department commented:

The individual seemed to benefit a great deal and looked more confident.

A secretary who attended a course on "The role of the secretary in management" made the following comments:

I was able to identify my past mistakes especially in human relations; I am now capable of working on my own, using my initiative and discretion without awaiting instructions. I have learned tact, confidentiality and diplomacy in handling inquiries, the phone, visitors, etc. I would like to see the course made longer, so that more can be taught.

The Managing Director commented:

The course was able to help her develop the right attitude.

The Head of the Department commented that:

The course has helped her to translate theory into practice for her own benefit and that of the company.

The foregoing demonstrates the way the organization uses the medium of training to achieve integration through an unitarist ideology. In addition to pinpointing the benefits of training, these comments also illustrate the employee-employer collusion - actual or potential - in the legitimation of the exercise.

The Goal of Commitment

It was noted that the pursuit of Commitment through development is not, generally speaking, an explicit organizational objective. The only exception was Pharmaco which evaluates performance on the basis of well-defined "organizational values". The practice of rating performance according to values that define the organizational ethos is designed to ensure the inculcation of these values in such a way as to achieve the integration of all employees into the organization and thus to enhance *commitment* to the firm.

The quest to identify and nurture some form of commitment to the organizational goals and objectives, particularly in the appraisal/counselling exercise, is prompted by the unitarist ethos in the functionalist paradigm. This emerges in the HR Manager's emphasis that HRM/D must strengthen organizational culture and reflect company profitability. The rationale of *company profitability* and *productivity* is evident in the views generally made by managers that training had to be "cost-effective". This is illustrated in Autoco's "Training Rationale" which emphasizes "efficiency and effectiveness", and also stresses that "training must be focused on the organization's overall and departmental objectives".

The view was generally expressed that by developing the "right attitudes" towards the organization management will create a labour force that will devote its skills and energies towards enhancing *productivity*. The Operations Director at Chematox for instance conceded that they had what he described as "an excessive use of the *stick syndrome*" whereby appraisal tended to be seen as a punitive measure rather than a motivational tool, for instance. This belief also found expression in managers' assertions that training would enable the employees *to apply themselves better to the job*. It follows from this functionalist analysis that the lack of a total commitment to training is self-defeating: management would be failing to effectively "tap" the potential contribution from the employees. This happens when the investment in training is very low, especially at Chematox.

The appraisal process which is often characterised by suspicion and mistrust offers an opportunity for the demonstration of conflict and tension. It also questions the managerial conception of unitarism and a congruence of interests within the functionalist paradigm. It becomes evident that the employer-employee interface is defined by divergent and possibly conflictual goals, which reflect similarly potentially conflictual commitments. The appraisal exercise plays an important role in mediating the employment relationship. The practice is characterised by two extremes: on the one hand, we find control of behaviour through appraisal, ie the "stick syndrome", and on the other, the inculcation of organizational values in order to *elicit* commitment. The latter is best typified by Pharmaco. Townley (1989) points out that one of the functions of appraisal is to communicate organizational norms or "culture" and to reinforce this process. Organizations are therefore concerned to identify "acceptable" traits and behaviour. Edwards (1979) illustrates this by identifying three key criteria: rules orientation, dependability and identification with the company; thus, this form of appraisal seeks compliance through regulatory and "extra-functional" rather than strictly bureaucratic norms.

While it is desirable from an organization's point of view to ensure that employees are "committed" to the attainment of organizational objectives, this may be impeded by *inter alia*, multiple and sometimes conflicting commitments, instrumental orientations to work and "meritocracy" which places a great premium on individual gain and advancement. The recommendation of the fostering of a team spirit as well as a commitment to creating learning opportunities is therefore reiterated here. This may be achieved for example through quality circles as in Autoco. Teamwork at Autoco can also be seen as having totemic qualities in the sense that it has been built into the organizational culture as a powerful integrative tool and source of identity (Kamoche, 1995). In his "kinship solidarity" thesis, Blunt (1980) stresses the importance of the psychological nurturance and companionship that migrant workers derive from groups at work. Although ethnic-based "solidarity" runs counter to non-particularist national imperatives, the notion of teamwork would appear to be compatible with the African socio-cultural ethos of a community spirit. A further illustration of this point is found in Onyemelukwe's (1973) *community concept of business*. This may, however, be more relevant at the shopfloor where an individualist ethos is less prevalent and individualized arrangements are mediated by collective bargaining.

A rather indirect and unusual mode of eliciting commitment is through labour relations training. Individuals are selected from time to time to attend courses on labour relations at a labour college. The suitable candidates are normally those who are involved in the organization of union activities. All shop stewards at Autoco are sent to the college. Managers in general consider labour relations training particularly vital given the often-cited "ignorance" of union leaders. Union leaders often accuse management of wanting to "co-opt" candidates by influencing the selection process; management in turn accuses union leaders of selecting only those who vote for them. This was particularly evident in Automart and Chematox. The selection process is often a matter of conflict and point-scoring. Managers in these two companies described with satisfaction incidents where "very vocal trouble-makers" came back "changed", or "singing a different song". Conformity to requirements cannot however be assumed to be a surrogate for commitment. Rather, it indicates the quest for unitarism and the elimination of deviance since this is expected to be dysfunctional from the organization's point of view.

The Goal of Functional Flexibility

Functional flexibility is sought so that employees can be re-deployed quickly and smoothly between activities and tasks (Atkinson, 1984). This may involve shifts between different types of jobs, eg mechanical and electrical, or a career change. This form of flexibility is designed to achieve maximum labour utilization and to ensure the sustenance of the system through the manipulation of skill and job demarcations. The institution of "flexible" work practices also highlights the effect that market and other pressures are having on the employment and development strategies. Managers in the case studies reported that they did not anticipate major changes in work practices to accommodate functional flexibility in the short-term. At Chematox they introduced a new grading system on the shopfloor for the hydrogen production and air separation units. This was feasible because of the apparent skills overlap across the two units. The purpose of this exercise was to identify ways in which these two departments could be harmonized. Production engineers were exploring the viability of extending this idea to other areas. In addition to reducing demarcation, this exercise aims to develop skill diversity and help attain some measure of adaptability in re-deployment. The only problem the engineers expected was resistance from the older operatives. They did not anticipate involving the union. This exercise was not expected to lead to any other substantial initiative toward multi-skilling.

It is reasonable to speculate that the second aspect of functional flexibility - career change and systematic retraining - seems improbable in these organizations. Managers in general justified this position on two counts: first, the high cost involved, with the likelihood of the highly skilled subsequently leaving the firm. With regard to the professional cadres, eg accountants, systems analysts, marketing staff and other skilled technicians, this fear was not altogether unfounded as noted in an earlier section. While noting that flexibility in skills enhances employees' opportunities in the external labour market, the Personnel Manager at Pharmaco was confident that this would not be a cause of concern because the company saw itself as a "corporate citizen", meeting the training needs of the country as a whole. This notion of *corporate citizenship* with respect to training was echoed by the Personnel Manager at Automart in his praise of their company training institute. This concept is important here because of its implications for a national skill-base which is particularly vital if the country is to achieve a meaningful degree of industrialization. This is targeted for the year 2020 but at the moment there seems to be little evidence of suitable educational and industrial policies to justify such a target.

The other reason offered for the unfeasibility of multi-skilling was *functional specialization*. According to this argument, there is a general preference for specialization rather than multi-skilling at all levels of the organization, which managers accounted for in the tradition of meritocracy. But this also reflects the tendency for the merit-based appraisal and reward system to be biased towards the possession of specialist rather than generalist skills. Specialization at the shopfloor at Autoco is explained in terms of the nature of the "unchanging" technology and single product-line. Another difficulty in the conception of the "core" with regard to "functional flexibility" is the categorization of the unionisable technician and other shopfloor workers, and office clerical staff.

These cadres are treated as "permanent" staff with a high level of job security vis-a-vis the temporary and casual staff, yet they are not provided with the diversity of skills that would facilitate effective redeployment in line with changing circumstances, especially those relating to market and technological changes. Rare opportunities to improve or broaden skills at the shopfloor are provided by new technology, or in the case of auto plants, the introduction of a new model, which may happen every few years. Autoco for instance uses a very labour intensive assembly line technology whereby the bodies are manually pushed down the line. Workers possess task-specific skills and although there is little formal attempt to provide variety, the workers get to pick up skills informally by observation, and from "experience", hence "on-the-job" training. Skills are alterable at short notice by running short-term training courses when a model change is being undertaken, reflecting the *ad hoc* nature of training.

The more traditional form of flexibility, job rotation, was also found to be virtually non-existent. This was accounted for by the importance attached to functional specialization. Routine job rotation was attempted at Automart in the late 1980s but found to be too costly because of the severity of the financial constraints imposed by import restrictions. The closest organizations come to using job rotation is in the case of the induction of tier 1 and some tier 2 staff who are rotated through various departments "learning the ropes". After the induction period they are normally expected to settle into an area of functional specialization. At Autoco, "high-flying" managers are also often rotated with the aim of preparing them for general-management senior appointments. At Mimea, "high-flying" managers are offered "tailor-made" training. This differential system is in keeping with the notion of functional stratification and the *achievement principle*.

The institution of HRM/D at Pharmaco and the regrading at Chematox offer some hope for multi-skilling. This has important implications for long-term skill-development. It also questions the orthodox logic which has come to legitimize functional specialisation and which in essence seeks integration through the institutionalization found in firm-specific on-the-job training. Managers at Mimea do not believe that functional flexibility is altogether desirable or even feasible. In the farms, for example, functional specialization is often dictated by the nature of business: the skills required for the delicate task of picking choice tea leaves may not be rapidly interchangeable with those required for tending carnations. The technical/chemical processing involved also varies accordingly. Similarly, farms are spaced out geographically, which introduces a logistical difficulty. Management also felt that a possible impediment to functional flexibility is their multi-union structure. In this company, managers prefer on-the-job training although they realize that it is "ambiguous" and difficult to organize. Ironically, they prefer this approach to training because "it is inevitable and on-going".

Quality in Training/Development

Following the comments made in previous chapters about the possible place of the dimension of quality, this issue will not be given much attention here. As regards the actual training, suitability is invariably seen from the organization's point of view in terms of justifying the cost, and organizations apply a strict measure of "approved" courses. This helps to ensure that *practical* solutions are found through the "right" type of training. Views expressed by employees and managers at Mimea were found to stress the inculcation of the "right attitudes", or how the experience helped the individuals to improve themselves and contribute to the organization's goals. It may be concluded that this was the way organizations would wish "quality" to be interpreted.

The other important issue here is the suitability of the performance evaluation parameters in use. The problematic nature of the conventional trait/personality approach has been discussed. In a detailed analysis of "performance management" in developing countries, Mendonca and Kanungo (1990) argue that the criteria for the choice of technique must obviously be its capacity to capture employee performance in terms of the predetermined job behaviours. They suggest that the use of personal traits to appraise performance should be avoided unless these are critical to the performance of the job, in which case the traits should form part of the performance standards.

Conclusions

This chapter has sought to illustrate the nature of training and development in the companies in question. It is evident that the practices in each of these organizations resemble the normative model of HRM with respect to development to differing degrees. Pharmaco and Autoco come closest to the model in so far as they have made the most decisive efforts to advance towards a "new" model of development. Development has also been found to contain a *structural-functionalist* purpose which aims to sustain the continuity of the system through the inculcation of skills necessary to achieve the organizations' goals. The tenability of the dimensions of training and development is mediated by a wide range of factors. Much of the discussion has focused on the dimension of Integration because this dimension enables us to examine analytically the actual practice and to tease out the policy aspects and policy implications. A strategic stance is considered vital to the institution of an integrative, future-oriented development programme. But this is restricted by, inter alia, the limited tradition of strategic management. This highlights the imperative to develop a broad skill-base at the national level, yet training is largely an *ad hoc* endeavour, except perhaps in management development. A problem of stratification also runs through the cases, except at Pharmaco and Automart, thus making the goal of an integrative approach illusory and encouraging a multi-tiered approach to development.

It was also found that the goal of commitment as defined by the normative propositions was not keenly pursued except at Pharmaco where the pivotal element of the development exercise was informed by *organizational values*. In the main, the quest to elicit commitment emerges as a subtle tool to exercise control. The four-tier structure of the "core-periphery" dialectic was also evident with respect to functional flexibility. Various factors were advanced to explain the observed absence of multi-skilling; family (dependency) pressures, instrumentalism and meritocracy are seen to legitimize functional specialization. Kenyan companies must demonstrate a greater commitment to the institution of development programmes that are designed to meet both the market-oriented needs of the organization as well as the personal and group development and reward requirements of the employees. This would be achieved through a more processual approach to development which places performance management at the heart of the exercise. The need for this is underpinned by the national development challenges, which are defined by a shortage of high skills and a failure of business and the State to treat training as a high-priority concern.

7 A Radical Critique of HRM

It is proposed in this chapter to set aside the assumption of purposive rationality and goal congruence in order to locate the HRM phenomenon within a societal context which acknowledges the central role of power and politics. This paradigm also recognizes the existence of actual or latent conflict amongst significant stakeholders. The discussion begins by introducing a rationale for a critique and then proceeds to examine HRM within the radical humanist and radical structuralist paradigms.

Toward a Critique of HRM

The critique of HRM is formulated in such a way as to illustrate the relevant issues that the perspective informed by the sociology of radical change problematizes, without necessarily merging the two paradigms. We make the assumption that there is a certain uniformity in Marx's concern to develop a radical social theory. While the "epistemological break" paves the way for a "paradigm journey", uniformity is provided by the theory of society pertinent to these two paradigms, ie the sociology of radical change, and it is this which permits us to advance a critique of the *status quo*. The proposed term "radical critique" is hereby used as a convenient device to articulate these objectives.

According to B/M the sociology of radical change has not been adequately explored by organization theorists, such that an intellectual tradition like the one found in the functionalist paradigm has not evolved here. In this regard, many of those who have defined their work as "radical" (eg human relations) are misusing the term. B/M (p325) state that:

> Their humanism represents a plea for reform rather than a well-founded and consistent theoretical perspective committed to an alternative view of society. For the most part, their perspective is grounded in a philosophy of social engineering and piecemeal reform within the problematic which defines the status quo.

The fact that the radical humanist paradigm is in contrast with the dominant functionalist paradigm on both dimensions of the sociological framework may explain the lack of a theory of organization within this paradigm. B/M point out that the radical structuralist critique of organizations has evolved in a reactive mould by setting itself against the functionalist tradition. According to this argument the critique has concentrated on accusing functionalist theorists of, inter alia, ignoring the historical dimensions of their subject, the works of Marx, class conflict and the role of the State.

There have been some attempts to analyse HRM from a radical critique point of view. Much of this critique currently draws more from the "post-modernism" of French philosophers such as Derrida and Foucault, than the Marxian writers Burrell and Morgan identify under their "sociology of radical change". Some writers resort to dismissing HRM as simply a case of "whistling in the dark" (Skinner, 1981); "the emperor's new clothes" (Armstrong, 1987), and so forth. Kamoche and Mueller (1998) identify the emergence of an increasingly fine-grained critique which focuses on ethical, rhetorical and ideological issues (eg Guest, 1990; Hart, 1993; Horwitz, 1990; Kamoche, 1994,1995; Keenoy, 1990; Legge, 1989, 1995; Townley, 1989, 1993). Kamoche and Mueller (1998) have proceeded to build upon this critique to explore the concept of appropriation: the underlying ethos as to why organizations seek to appropriate and retain for their own use the added value from utilizing the organizational stock of expertise.

The rest of this chapter undertakes a more trenchant critique at the level of the "totality".[1] The first part of our radical critique considers HRM within the radical humanist critique. This analysis draws from critical theory, in particular Gramsci's concept of *hegemony*. The second part locates the discussion within the radical structuralist critique, relating HRM specifically to the political economy of Kenya. Figure 7.1 illustrates how these different levels of analysis are interrelated.

A Radical Humanist Critique

In B/M's view, radical humanists are concerned with the "'pathology of consciousness', by which men come to see themselves trapped within a mode of social organisation which they both create and sustain in their everyday lives" (p 306). For radical humanists an understanding of this process must begin at the level of consciousness, ie, the human spirit must be set free in order that we can achieve change in the society. The radical structuralists on the other hand are more concerned with the fundamental contradictions in society, which for them, can only be resolved through revolutionary change.

Figure 7.1 Two levels of analysis in the radical critique

Level of analysis	Medium	Issues

TOTALITY [1]	Radical humanism
	Gramscian hegemony
		* moral and philosophical
		   leadership
		* active consent
		* ideological control
		* legitimacy
		* workplace commonsense
		* stratification and the
		   achievement principle
		   (Offe)
		* status ascription
		* power differentials

TOTALITY [2]	Radical structuralism *Politico-economy*	* crises and contradictions * class and class formation * capitalist structures * the labour process * periphery capitalism and the dependency theory * the State superstructure * international capitalism

Four major categories of social theory are identified in this paradigm: *Solipsism, French Existentialism, Anarchistic Individualism,* and *Critical Theory* (B/M p 283). The "paradigmatic lens" through which we propose to view HRM in this section draws from critical theory, the main social theory category within the current paradigm. Within this category, Gramsci's concept of hegemony (as developed in *Selections from Prison Notebooks,* {SPN} 1971) will be employed to assess the managerial initiatives to achieve a position of dominance within an organizational context characterized by power imbalances.

Gramsci's Concept of "Hegemony"

The concept of hegemony is arguably, Gramsci's most important contribution to social theory and philosophy. The concept was first formulated, however, by 19th Century Russian Marxists as a strategy to overthrow Tsarism. In this regard, Bocock (1986, p25) observes that:

> The term referred to the hegemonic leadership the proletariat, and its political representatives, should give in an alliance of other groups, including some bourgeois critics, peasants and intellectuals who were seeking an end to the Tsarist police state.

Gramsci's concern was how modern capitalist societies were organized or aimed to be organized and how hegemony is achievable in "civil society" Bocock (1986, p25). For Gramsci, hegemony is about how "moral and philosophical leadership" is acquired through a moral and intellectual route and the formation of alliances amongst major groups in a society. The hegemonic class "universalizes" its own interests, ensuring that "they can and must become the interests of the other subordinate groups" (SPN, p181).[2] The notion of "active consent" is at the heart of Gramscian hegemony; ie leadership must not be achieved by the use of force, nor is it imposed by a dominating class. Having initially drawn from Croce's pragmatic moral-ethical dimension, Gramsci subsequently treats Marxism as a moral philosophy in which people's collective action could define and shape their social reality as opposed to having it shaped by the "iron laws of history". This theoretical perspective enables us to explore the power/political dimension in social organization and to establish how, if at all, HRM represents management's attempts to "produce and reproduce" congruence of interests at the workplace and to seek consent for labour regulation strategies.

HRM and Workplace Hegemony

The analysis here begins with the observation that in societies characterized by unequal distribution of power, those who control the means of production, in this case management, would tend to invoke the "managerial prerogative to manage", as a way of legitimizing that control. By advancing the rhetoric that control is exercised for the good of, and while taking the interests of all the other relevant stakeholders, this perpetuates an unitarist ideology. This discussion demonstrates the value of the concept of hegemony in understanding the ideological underpinnings of the management of human resources. Two reasons make this concept appropriate for our analysis here: its relevance in the exercise of locating managerial activity within the "totality" of capitalist structures; and the fact that it constitutes an interesting *rapprochement* of philosophy and sociology, especially in enabling us to comprehend Gramsci's notion of free, rational consent.

It would thus appear appropriate to argue that HRM is (potentially) a new workplace hegemony which is being scripted by management in order to create workplace "common-sense". "Common sense", for Gramsci meant the general sense in which people perceive the world. This may include taken-for-granted assumptions, folklore and similar notions derived from everyday experience (see also Bocock, 1986). For our purposes, workplace "commonsense" refers the entire range of belief systems that describe the way people in organizations are managed. This includes the approaches to recruitment and development as well as the tacit and explicit manifestations of power in the social relations between groups. It is not claimed here that there is a well-articulated attempt by management to achieve Gramscian hegemonic leadership through the introduction of HRM. The concept of hegemony is employed here as a useful tool with which to critically examine the practice of HRM.

In contemplating the extent to which HRM constitutes "moral and philosophical leadership" that is based on the active consent of the *major groups* in the business community, it is noted here that the moral-philosophical dimension emerges in terms of managerial justification of the "right to manage", which is itself a statement about power relations. The radical humanist position holds that the claim about "consent" in fact creates a "false consciousness" amongst employees. Hegemony becomes a subtle way of achieving control while offering real compromises reinforced by actual consent, and avoiding the unpleasantness of outright manipulation.[3] This line of thought parallels the views expressed in previous chapters that Guest's dimension of "Commitment" and Walton's (1985) conception of HRM as a "Commitment model", are simply a more subtle form of control. Furthermore, Simon's (1982, p21) assertion that hegemony is "the organization of consent" echoes Buroway's (1979) notion of "manufacturing consent", which implies manipulation. "Consent" is sought within the unitarist framework and is demonstrated, for example, in the supposed shift from "control" to "compliance", which fosters a dependency syndrome and thus defines the power structure. It is expected that by offering better working conditions and more attractive remuneration, management will earn the faith and commitment of the employees. This scenario is typified by Pharmaco whereby managers reported that their introduction of HRM/D practices was making the union less attractive to the workers. The Personnel Manager claimed that workers were beginning to question the purpose of the union.

The feeling amongst managers in Kenya in general that unions were unnecessary and irrelevant, coupled with some managers' anticipation of the eventual withering away of unions is indicative of their desire for more pervasive control. Rather than forge an "alliance" with the trade unions as hegemony would suggest, the managerial class is more inclined to marginalize this group. The moral-philosophical impetus behind this form of leadership does not, evidently, accord with that of Gramscian hegemony. The reservations that we have expressed above about the hegemonic status of managerial leadership in Kenyan organizations lead us to consider HRM as a less-developed form of hegemony. It is a form of social control which appears to be moving towards a hegemonic status, but is hampered by its possession of a strong ideological strand that comprises two elements: the quest for legitimation, and the notion that what is being offered is in part false. This latter element in turn includes, *inter alia*, claims that:

- HRM is "different" from personnel management
- there is greater integration and harmonization in the formulation of recruitment and development policies and practices
- the selection and promotion of employees is based strictly on "rational" criteria
- organizations are now seeking to elicit "commitment" rather than to exercise "control"
- HRM is a source of competitive advantage
- SHRM, steered by top management "vision" and promoted via Mission Statements, is the new organizational philosophy

From a radical critique perspective, we are able to identify how these and other claims serve an "ideological" function.[4] Various writers have identified ideology as a set of beliefs about how the social world operates and how social actors decide what are the desirable outcomes of social actions (eg Beyer, 1981; Weiss and Miller, 1987; Simons and Ingram, 1997). For our purposes, HRM emerges not merely as a sophisticated form of labour regulation, but also as the legitimation of managerially-defined ideas and initiatives, hence social relations. These social relations constitute the "common-sense" that has evolved in various institutions in society, in this case, the "workplace". In chapter three these were traced back to the colonial era of brutality and forced labour, but which today still retain elements of managerial authoritarianism.

For Gramsci, however, ideology is not merely a system of ideas; he distinguishes between ideas forged by particular intellectuals and philosophers, and historically organic ideologies (SPN, p367). Hegemony thus becomes philosophical, and not merely ideological since for Gramsci, ideology connotes something false, or disguises other material interests (see also Bocock, 1986). In real life, evidence of genuine hegemonic leadership is scarce. Gramsci found no evidence of philosophical leadership in America because America "had no superstructure, no cultural self-consciousness, no self-criticism..." (Buci-Glucksman, 1982). Bocock attributes America's failure to lead hegemonically to the fact that the United States has not produced a world-view, a philosophy, which has moved beyond positivism and empiricism. The positivist-empiricist tradition within the functionalist paradigm clearly rings true for organization theory. From the foregoing, it is predicted here that HRM will develop as an *ideological phenomenon* - in particular the reformulation of an unitarist managerial ideology - rather than a *philosophical world-view* for the business community.

Horwitz (1990) offers a radical ideological view of HRM as "a sophisticated form of managerial control", whereby HRM developments reflect a determination to impose new forms of managerial control, facilitated by power imbalances created by political, technological and socioeconomic change". The political nature of management emerges, therefore, in the use of power, involving processes of persuasion, negotiation, manipulation and control. At a higher level of analysis, it becomes a way of seeking to confer legitimacy on and perpetuate managerial control (eg Hyman, 1981). Similarly, by creating and cultivating a corporate culture, promoting "common values" and seeking objectives on the basis of "congruence of interests", managerial initiative attempts to convey the notion of "consent" and *ipso facto* to confer legitimacy on its "leadership".

Recruitment, Training and Development

This section looks more closely at the case study material in an attempt to determine the extent to which the concept of hegemony helps us to fathom the nature of HRM. The exercise will pay close attention to our key dimensions of HRM without unduly duplicating the exercises undertaken within the functionalist paradigm.

The goal of integration It was observed earlier that integration aims, *inter alia*, to bind together the organizational entity and the members who comprise it into one harmonized system, with the underlying assumption of a unity of interests. Within the current paradigm it would be absurd to deny the existence of divergent interests; integration is therefore a vehicle for achieving "consent" within a politically-charged social milieu. The "ruling class" recognizes that it can effectively legitimize its dominance by, for example, hiring those whose values are consonant with the organizational ones, and by socializing the employees into this "integrative" culture and structure.

The practice of hiring the "right" person for the "right" job illustrates how the above is achieved. In addition to the more objective criteria of academic/skill qualifications and technical competence, selection is also guided by the notion of "acceptability" (Silverman and Jones, 1976), ie, someone whose face "fits". At Mimea, for instance, they specified such criteria as: communication skill, clarity of thought and creativity, ability to mature into management grade, the right personality for middle management, assertiveness, and so forth. Automart maintained up to 14% of its workforce on temporary status probably to facilitate easy de-selection of those whose faces do not "fit". Managers in general stressed the need to hire people who would "fit into the system", and help the organization to achieve its objectives. This point is even more relevant in socialization, a tool for integrating divergent interests. We observed in chapter five the existence of a multi-tiered socialization structure which prevented the attainment of the full benefits of socialization for certain groups. Socialization was seen simply as an orientational exercise through which employees were to be imbued with organizational values. Those managers who did admit that social inequality did exist simply hoped that solutions could be found in "changes of attitudes". The Personnel Manager at Automart hoped that the "us-and-them" attitudinal cleavages in the company could be resolved by workers getting to realize that "they were part of the organization", and that they were being misled by the union leaders who were described as "unenlightened".

The Personnel/Training Officer at Chematox, the only company that did not have sporting activities, asserted that the introduction of sports as a form of socialization would "break down social barriers". The Officer expressed satisfaction about the fact that they had one canteen for all the staff, and that there was no special menu for the managers. In this same company, the Operations Director reported that there was little social cohesion amongst the members; but he did not offer a definitive idea about how this issue might be resolved, especially amongst the employees. As for the managerial ranks, he reported that he had made efforts to "lighten" the atmosphere especially in meetings and thus eliminate the tensions that pointed to the existence of dysfunctional managerial conflicts. The idea of managing conflict was also expressed by the Personnel Managers in Automart and Mimea, who identified "ethnicity" as a possible source of conflict. Within this paradigm, ethnicity emerges as a potential source of the societal conflict which is defined by the complexity of the social structure, a complexity that is absent in the contemporary Western models of HRM. Ethnic tensions, which have generally remained latent, have on occasion flared into brutal "tribal clashes" which have threatened to plunge the country into civil war. "Taking care to mix tribes well" was therefore, according to these managers, an important challenge; it also symbolizes the complexity of the challenge to hegemonic leadership.

An interesting point that arises from the case studies was the duality in some of the practices, and the effect this has on the tenability of the dimension of Integration. The "core-peripheral" dialectic in HRM assumes the dimension of stratification which goes beyond the organizational hierarchy to the broader societal context. By emphasizing the "class" distinctions at the workplace through disparate employment practices, management compounds the task of legitimizing "consent", and HRM begins to look like something done only for some well-defined managerial "core". This is elaborated below by reference to Offe's (1976) *achievement principle.*

Stratification assumes prominence when we consider training and development. Only in two companies (Pharmaco and Autoco) was appraisal for all staff conducted; the other three cases maintained a system of "differential appraisal". The nature of and reasons for this were discussed in chapter six and will not be rehearsed here. The general practice was to appraise those who had "promotion prospects". A related issue is that of the formulation of staff development programmes. The most interesting contrast is found in Mimea: although the current management thinking takes into account the entire workforce of up to 23,000, the main thrust of HRM in this company seems to be the management development programme for "high flying" managers. The important point here is the hierarchical stratification that this engenders. As observed in chapter six, the critique of the achievement principle examines the way society seeks to legitimize privilege, and by a similar token, how it legitimize inequality. Offe describes the basis of the achieving society in terms of the following schema:

performance → status in organization → social status

According to Offe (1976, p42):

> The notion of the achieving society is based on the general rule that the social status of an individual is supposed to depend upon his status in the sphere of work and production, while in turn his status within the hierarchical organization is meant to depend on his individual performance.

Offe's model is elaborated here by introducing performance appraisal as the process through which performance translates into status in the organization. Figure 7.2 illustrates the two divergent routes to status ascription.

Figure 7.2 Dualism in status ascription

	Core	Peripheral
Appraisal	formal elaborate	very informal or non-existent
Rewarding	individual merit	collective bargaining
Training	diversified well-planned	ad hoc low cost on-the-job
Status	high	low

The existence of a system of "differential appraisal" is itself a statement of the manner in which "status" in organizations is determined. It will be recalled that the common usage of the terms "core" and "peripheral" only partially captures the complexity of the conceptual distinctions in our case studies. The multi-tier structure must be borne in mind while interpreting Figure 7.2.

Those with "promotion prospects" undergo an elaborate appraisal process which when compared with the informal or almost nonexistent appraisal for the other workers, clearly indicates their relatively higher status. This leads on to better training and career advancement. According to Offe's "achievement principle" these sorts of rewards accrue to these individuals because of the perceived relative importance of their tasks, hence the justification of higher status through the principle of "functional importance". It will be recalled that within the functionalist paradigm, stratification is justified in terms of structural-functionalism. The current paradigm illustrates the functionalist theory of stratification with regard to achievement as a criterion of status ascription in society.[5] As Offe points out, however, the concept of the achievement principle is a fiction; it has become an instrument of social control, rewarding loyalty to dominant, controlling interests and at the same time justifying social inequality on the basis of "scarcity of talent" and differential "functional importance" of tasks. This is facilitated in part by "functional appraisal" and the perpetuation of a "core-peripheral" distinction.

The goal of commitment This analysis begins by arguing that a group that is seeking hegemonic control would expect the subordinate groups to demonstrate active consent that is underwritten by a genuine commitment to its objectives. The objectives would have been appropriately defined and communicated to these parties. If all the parties understand and accept the objectives, and, more importantly, offer their consent voluntarily, it would be relatively easy for management (the dominant party), to realize an integrative ethos. However, the existence of multiple and often conflictual interests means that the reality is much more complex. Furthermore, it is argued in the current paradigm that the source of this diversity lies in the broader context of the "totality" of capitalist structures. To this extent, therefore, the key groups in organizations would be assumed to be committed to actual or potentially diametrically opposed objectives. The task for the "ruling class" would be to reconcile the diverse interests and thus cement the "commonsense" that defines the popular collective will. Management would have to persuade employees that the constituent goals of HRM indeed represent the interests of employees and management. As concerns recruitment, the theory predicts that management hires those whose value systems and beliefs are perceived to be compatible with those of the organization. But as observed in chapter five, the exercise of formally identifying and "matching" individual values with those of the organization is not common, mainly because organizations do not always spell out what the organizational values are, and the task of determining individual values is left to the more subjective approach of using "acceptability" criteria. The exceptions were Pharmaco and Autoco which have defined the kind of organizations they are in Mission/Value Statements. True to its function as a "service" company, Automart has defined its value orientation in terms of service to customers: the definition of what type of employer they are is effectively dictated by the market. In this company, the General Manager's attribution of workplace pilfering to a general lack of commitment to institutions in the country as a whole is noteworthy. With regard to Development, performance appraisal offers an opportunity for management and employees to reach some form of mutual understanding towards the establishment of goal congruence. In this respect, Townley (1989) considers appraisal as an important forum to communicate organizational norms or "culture". The best example of this was found in Pharmaco which appraises staff on the basis of "organizational values". According to managers in the other companies, appraisal was sometimes conducted in a strained atmosphere: employees' own perceptions about how appraisal should be conducted, what remuneration adjustments they expected, fears about unfair evaluation and so forth, all these and related anxieties come up against organizational rating systems and managers' subjectivity, as well as the financial pressures companies face. On a note that offers little hope for the reconciliation of these differences, the Personnel Manager at Autoco said that the contentious issue of "pay" impedes commitment to the organization, and that the question of commitment "can never be resolved because people will never feel they are being adequately paid". This statement must be understood with respect to tiers 2 and below. A manager at Chematox admitted that low pay accounted for employees' lack of a sense of belonging. The General Manager at Automart claimed that he would be prepared to take a salary cut if this would improve the company's financial fortunes; but lamented that most other managers in the country as a whole would not hear of it. He saw this as a sign of lack of commitment to organizations in general. The reader will recall that this same manager expressed concern about the general lack of commitment to institutions in the country as a whole.

Two issues need to be addressed before employees can be expected to offer their active consent to management's hegemonic leadership: attitudinal cleavages, and wage inequalities. Attitudinal changes are supposed to occur through the introduction of "more viable" approaches like HRM which will make employees identify more with the organization. Interestingly, the problem was invariably seen to lie with the employees, with two exceptions: the views expressed by the General Manager at Automart, who considered the problem of commitment to be much more pervasive; and the Operations Director at Chematox, who indicated the existence of dysfunctional managerial cleavages. Wage inequalities constitute an even more sensitive topic because they signify power inequalities. Managerial remuneration is considered very confidential; wide variations exist from company to company, and even between individuals within the same company.

According to House and Rempel (1976), labour market segmentation and the resultant glaring wage inequalities go back to the colonial days when the labour market was segmented by race: Europeans constituted the large-scale landowners, proprietors of industrial establishments and high-level civil servants; the Asians were the dominant traders and artisans while those Africans in wage employment laboured on European farms and were engaged in menial tasks in urban centres. The existence of power differentials raises doubt about the harmonization of interests. Whereas within the functionalist paradigm, wage differentials are explained in terms of the "functional importance" of tasks, within the radical critique, we must set aside the veil of "functional importance" and consider power cleavages which in turn reflect divergent interests in society. Management's failure to appreciate this dimension of conflict will prevent them from realizing why it is so difficult to achieve hegemonic leadership, ie leadership to which the subordinate groups are committed. We reiterate the suggestion made in the previous chapter that teamwork may be a more viable approach than commitment in securing employees' active consent, for the reason that meaningful teamwork affords them a chance to address their own interests in a way that is not in conflict with managers' interests.

The goal of flexibility The issue that is problematized here is what role flexibility plays in fostering the organizational "commonsense" in the first place, and secondly, in enabling management, if at all, to achieve effective leadership that the subordinate groups willingly comply with. Numerical flexibility both effectively derives from and in turn further perpetuates the "core-peripheral" dialectic. This is manifested in a dualistic hiring policy whereby the core group is "integrated" into the organization while the peripheral group(s) is (are) treated as more or less dispensable, depending on the changing needs of the organization or their status in the structural-functionalist hierarchy. Those who for the purposes of recruitment are defined as peripheral lack job security and are in many ways excluded from full membership of the organization. This approach runs counter to the logic of hegemony whereby the ruling class forms mutually beneficial alliances with the other subordinate groups with a view to securing their support and commitment.

Rather than combining the interests of the core with those of the peripheral groups, a dualistic approach actually polarises them. In this regard, the core-peripheral distinction is a reflection of the us-and-them dialectic that we find in Kenyan - and indeed any other - society. This dialectic is defined by market forces and the demands of capital and is well articulated in the maintaining of a casual and temporary group. Within a critical theoretical perspective, the distinction between core and peripheral staff is too deeply embedded within the capitalist structure to be treated merely as a convenient ploy to control headcounts. Managers find they can maintain a highly flexible peripheral workforce because of the high level of unemployment, which at the time of the research was about 16%. Economic considerations and the enduring demands of capital enable the creation of a workplace "commonsense" that allows for flexible hire/fire policies. Similar issues come to light when we consider functional flexibility, which relates mainly to the core staff. Training and development come to be seen as vital ideological tools to persuade employees to identify with the organization, especially where a preference for "in-house", on-the-job training results in the acquisition of company-specific skills. In a similar vein, Hassard (1985) employs the concept of hegemony to understand workplace ideology with regard to the use of management training as a medium of meritocracy serving as a mystification for the production of a business elite ideology.

Within the functionalist paradigm, the rationale for offering diverse skills to the group that constitutes the core staff is to enable them to respond, for example, to changing technology and to advance career-wise in line with the "achievement principle". The dualism immanent in functional flexibility therefore further enhances the core-peripheral dialectic. Those unionisable workers who would ordinarily not be classified as "peripheral" ultimately find themselves being left to acquire skills informally, whereas the managerial cadres have very detailed and comprehensive training programmes (see Figure 7.2).

Summary

The foregoing has attempted to illustrate that critical theory can yield useful insights in the study of organizational phenomena. From the perspective of Gramscian hegemony, the HRM goal of Integration is a potentially useful tool for achieving the "active consent" of the relevant groups in an organizational setting. It becomes apparent in this paradigm that the diverse interests among the different groups in an organization are a reflection of the conflicts embedded within capitalist structures. Similarly, an assessment of Commitment reveals that the interests that the different groups are committed to mask fundamentally divergent societal orientations that cannot be easily reconciled within a framework of goal congruence. Finally, Flexibility was found to accentuate these cleavages, and to thus reveal the extent of the internal contradictions within the framework. This analysis is concluded by observing that critical theory enables us to understand the way in which the "ruling class" ("management" for our purposes) strives to legitimize its power and control by seeking the consent of other stakeholders. In essence, this is an effort to forge order and stability, thus curtailing protest and the potential for radical change.

A Radical Structuralist Critique

The radical structuralist paradigm, according to Burrell and Morgan, is rooted in a materialist view of the natural and social world. As opposed to the radical humanists, radical structuralists do not merely provide a critique of the status quo; they actually seek to change it. The radical humanists locate their discourse within Marx's earlier development of Hegelian philosophy. The radical structuralists on the other hand locate theirs within Marx's later materialistic critique, as evidenced in works like *The German Ideology, Grundrisse* and *Capital*. In this paradigm, there is a greater concern with concepts like *totality, structural forces, contradiction* and *crisis*. B/M (p.328) argue that:

Society contains within it elements which stand in antagonistic relationships one to another, and which generate conflicts which eventually lead to the breakdown of the mode of production and its related social configurations... The notion of contradiction is central to Marx's explanation of social change and the way in which one form of society replaces another through crises produced by these contradictions. Marx saw these crises within a given mode of production as getting progressively worse and eventually leading to the cataclysmic crisis which would overthrow the society as a whole.

B/M identify three key schools of thought in this paradigm: *Russian social theory, contemporary Mediterranean Marxism* and *Conflict theory*. Russian social theory is located in the most objectivist region of the paradigm. B/M observe that the influence of Darwinism, and the intimate relationship which was seen to exist between man and nature, created variants of an evolutionary theory in which capitalism was regarded as a "genetic" monstrosity. Change would be achievable only by catastrophe and revolution. Contemporary Mediterranean Marxism lies somewhere between the extremist Russian social theory and the more subjectivist critical theory. According to B/M Conflict theory is the sociological expression of "radical Weberianism"; it focuses upon bureaucracy, authority and the corporatist role of the State, and is distinguished from the previous two by Weber's orientation to capitalism. Conflict theory and Mediterranean Marxism are said to come closest to radical organization theory. B/M (p.385) have identified some differences between Marxian structuralist and radical Weberian approaches to organization theory. For example, while the former emphasize the political economy, economic structures, monopoly capitalism, contradiction and catastrophe, the latter emphasize political science, political administrative structures, corporatism, power and factionalism.

The radical structuralist paradigm stresses the role of fundamental economic and political structures in the development of social relationships in society. In this regard B/M (p.368) treat organizations as "structural elements of a wider structure which they reflect and from which they derive their existence and true significance. The organization is, in this sense, a partial reflection of totality." This final part of the chapter seeks to locate HRM within the capitalist structures in Kenya through an examination of the political economy. The purpose is to illustrate the significance of the political economy in appreciating the emergence and relevance of HRM. It is noted here that the distinctions between Marxian structuralist and radical Weberian approaches should be treated with caution as they run the risk of masking the similarities between the problematics of the respective theorists working within them. For example, while it is proposed to focus on *political economy* and *contradiction*, other concepts like *monopoly capitalism* and *catastrophe* might only be of limited relevance. By a similar token, two aspects of the radical Weberian tradition, *corporatism* and *power*, are useful for our analysis. Therefore, a clear-cut distinction between the two strands will not be adhered to strictly in this discussion.

Kenya: The Political-Economic Context

In the Marxist analysis of Kenyan society, two main themes are evident in the literature: class formation, and the development of capitalist structures. The first theme tends to focus on the ambiguity of class formation in African societies, while the latter considers whether the Kenyan economy is a mere peripheral appendage to the broader "metropolitan" capitalism or whether it has indeed developed an autonomy of its own. The significance of these queries for our purposes, and the way in which they are interrelated, is demonstrated below.

Classes and Class Formation

Before contemplating the nature and magnitude of class conflict, we must first determine what form the relevant "classes" in Kenyan society take. It is necessary to clarify this point because the controversy about classes and class formation in African society has implications on the suitability of Marxian analysis in the African context. This takes us to the first theme above. It has often been argued that the colonial industrial policy of producing for the foreign market and failing to absorb the surplus labour led to the insufficient proletarianization of the African labour force, such that a working labour class in the Marxian mould did not develop (eg Siddique, 1989). The difficulties surrounding the study of "classes" in Africa are reflected in Kitching's attempts to provide a model. In an earlier paper Kitching (1972) proposes a model which argues that classes in Africa are *in the process of formation*. This model, whose structure concentrates on economic inequalities largely produced by income inequalities, identifies the following classes: the ruling class, a variegated middle class, urban manual workers and the rural peasantry. Kitching (1977) later revised his views and regretted his conception of "class" in Africa, on the grounds that he had fallen into the trap of bourgeois "methodological individualism" which is concerned with how accumulation facilitates "upward mobility".

According to this revised view, we need not apply Marx's class categories; instead, we should focus on the use of labour time, the use of money, surplus value/surplus labour and the accumulation of capital. Kitching claims that the group which benefits disproportionately from the process of exploitation, appropriation of surplus labour and accumulation is not a "capitalist class" but rather, a client group of the world capitalist class. By a similar token, a group which is simply a source of surplus labour and surplus value for others cannot be identified. This claim ignores the peripheral casual and temporary workers. This conception of classes in Kenya also seems to deny the potential indigenous capitalist-worker contradiction. Swainson (eg 1977), one of the commentators who acknowledge the potential of a local capitalist class, observes that the tendency of dependency theory (see below) to see the principal contradiction as an external imperialism leads to a failure to see the developing internal class contradictions.

The unresolved "class" debate points to the difficulty of specifying categorically the nature and momentum of class conflict with specific regard to the two key protagonists in industry: management and workers. These issues have important implications for HRM. As concerns class formation, we draw from the underlying logic of the radical paradigms that society is characterized by actual or latent conflict rather than stability and order. The two main groups in industrial society, management and workers, would be considered, within this paradigm, to be irrevocably pitted against each other. This class conflict (be it real or latent) defines power and exchange relationships which in turn reflect power inequalities.

This is something management would have to bear in mind when formulating management strategies. It implies for example that the "goal of Integration" is futile, because the divergent interests can never be reconciled. It further suggests that the diverse groups would be irrevocably committed to their own interests, thus leading to the entrenchment of factional interests. This implies that employees cannot develop a commitment to the organization because of extant property relations. Such a commitment can only arise if workers own the instruments of production, a point often reiterated by Waweru (1975; 1979; 1984). The crucial point here is that any form of labour regulation instituted by management is necessitated by an implicit acknowledgement of the polarisation of interests between those managing and those being managed.

Capitalist Development, the State and International Capitalism

The second theme in the study of the Kenyan political economy focuses more specifically on the capitalist structure and the role of the State. This discussion touches on whether the capitalist structure is autonomous or whether it is dependent on the "Western metropolis". This is the so-called "dependency theory" which owes much of its development to Gunder Frank, P Baran (cited in Swainson, 1977), and Samir Amin (cited in van Zwaneberg, 1974). This theory is related to the prominence of the multinational corporations in the Kenyan economy.[6] Without devoting too much attention to this question, it must be recalled that the capitalist structure in Kenya owes its origins to foreign capital; however, a local entrepreneurial group has developed in the country. Considering that our case studies relate to foreign owned firms, the issue of foreign control is inevitable, and it is argued below that this reveals another form of *contradiction*.

The radical Weberian analysis of the State superstructure in the Kenyan context is relevant to the extent that Weberian theorists allow for social change while retaining rather than overthrowing capitalism. It will be recalled that the State was considered in chapter three as a central contextual component in Kenya, and that capitalism (misleadingly referred to as "African Socialism") is the production ideology. The State's current central role in the Kenyan economy is traceable to the post-independence Keynesian development logic.[7] Over the years, the State has continued to forge wide-ranging alliances with foreign investors and the local entrepreneurs. Currie and Ray (1984, p562) explain these alliances in terms of symbiosis:

> Domestic and foreign capital need each other, and the State is an essential element in their relationship. The national bourgeoisie receives technology and management skills, while offering markets (amongst new high-income elites), and investment opportunities, with the guarantee of political protection and depressed wages.

The need for industrial peace and harmony has largely been fulfilled at the expense of the union movement. Kaniki (1981) observes that modern tropical African governments have retained the colonial legacy of autocratic and oppressive tendencies in the use of brute force and violence to control workers. This includes strong intimidation, banishment, imprisonment, detention without trial, and the deployment of police and other State militia against striking workers. Within the Kenyan context in particular, Chege (1988) has pointed out how the fear of retribution amongst the workers accounts for the apparent tranquillity in industrial relations.

In offering a historical perspective to the analysis of relationships between organizations and the State, McCullough and Shannon (1977) argue that organizations are offered protection by their nations such that they are organized in relation to a nation state and to a global balance of power involving competing nations. This allows multinational companies to exploit labour under the "protection" of the State. HRM then emerges as part of the scheme of controls available to MNCs. The control from foreign parent companies is particularly noteworthy in Pharmaco, Autoco and Mimea. This ranges from "high-level" controls through mission and policy statements to operational guidelines eg in performance appraisal procedures. Managers in the above three companies expressed pride about the fact that the appraisal of managerial cadres is conducted in accordance with international corporate guidelines. Similarly, the Manager in charge of Personnel at Chematox regarded highly the use of selection procedures developed in Britain. Within the current paradigm, these are seen as tools of control in the hands of "international capitalism".

The foregoing reveals that the management-worker "contradiction" must be seen within the broader international capitalist context. As regards the dependency theory, it is argued here that if indeed the capitalist structure in Kenya is subservient to international capitalism through multinational corporations, then the complexity of the managerial-labour problematic assumes a much broader dimension: the international arena. It is revealing that the "best" examples of HRM in our case studies, Pharmaco and Autoco, are both American companies, considering the American origins of contemporary HRM. By identifying the link between the Kenyan capitalist structure and the Euro-American one, the practice of western HRM begins to assume a neo-colonial complexion. As a tool of control, HRM seeks the intensification of labour for example through functional flexibility. Numerical flexibility represents the gradual rolling back of labour and the creation of an elite core. For Braverman (1974), this represents an extreme form of deskilling and degradation of labour within monopoly capitalism. A low commitment to training does not in itself indicate a tendency towards the degradation of labour. However, the dualistic approach to functional flexibility reveals something about the implicit reasons behind management's failure to train adequately the peripheral workers (this includes all those who are for the purposes of functional flexibility, treated as such).

Whereas in the radical humanist paradigm HRM emerged as a way of "manufacturing" consent, in the radical structuralist paradigm, the enduring concern is the extraction of surplus labour, accumulation and the entrenchment of managerial control in a way that deepens the already existing cleavages between the factional groups in society. Braverman's structuralist analysis sees organization theory as a tool in the hands of the bourgeoisie. Thus, the various approaches to the management of employees, such as scientific management, human relations, QWL and now HRM, are all manifestations of the labour process. The identification of the crucial role of foreign capital in this scenario reveals that the management-worker dialectic goes beyond the Kenyan geographical context. It is noted here, however, that historical experience offers little evidence of the inevitability of the classical Marxist prediction of revolutionary change in Kenya.[8] It is suggested here that this dialectic is unlikely to culminate in Marxian "catastrophe" that will see the overthrow of capitalism. There appears to be little revolutionary potential in the labour class, the State's commitment to the capitalist mode of production remains strong, and the owners of the means of production remain powerful, as they consolidate their position with international capitalists and the State machinery.

However, foreign investors are now being driven away by the breakdown in infrastructure, the climate of political uncertainty and institutionalized corruption. As a result, employment opportunities have lessened and more people are daily being driven into poverty. As these tensions intensify, and the gap between the rich and poor widens, the country is likely to see an unprecedented socio-political crisis.

Conclusions

This chapter witnesses a shift from the functionalist paradigm's concern to formulate a model of HRM based on purposive rationality to a critique of the same. In this regard we have attempted to fill a gap in the study of HRM by developing a radical critique perspective. The critique sought to relate the nature of HRM to the sociology of radical change, which, according to Burrell and Morgan comprises the radical humanist and the radical structuralist paradigms. Gramsci's concept of hegemony was adopted within the former, enabling us to unmask the ideology inherent in HRM and to explore the nature of the forces of control and domination that define this organizational phenomenon. Within the radical structuralist paradigm, these forces assume greater prominence: they define the fundamental contradictions within the totality of capitalist structures. HRM thus emerges as a "sophisticated" manifestation of the labour process and a tool of control in the hands of a powerful capitalist and managerial elite, acting in league with foreign interests, with the protection of the State.

Notes

[1] Marx perceived the concept of 'totality' as a process of social change. For Lukacs (1968), however, it is about grasping everything as a whole. This concept illustrates how, inter alia, the capitalist separation of the producer from the total process of production, the division of the process of labour and the atomisation of society "must all have a profound influence on the thought, the science and the philosophy of capitalism" (p 27).

[2] "Consent", for Gramsci is an important concept in creating hegemonic leadership. In an attempt to re-emphasize the significance of consent in Gramsci's hegemony, Buci-Glucksman (1982) argues that Gramsci's concept goes beyond both an economistic Marxist position which views consent as false ideology and the ideas of Talcott Parsons and Max Weber which define consent or consensus as legitimating a certain pre-existing social order.

[3] The supposed consensual leadership has invited debate about whether hegemony is not in fact a more subtle form of class dictatorship. Entwistle (1979) for instance, suggests that the term "hegemony" is a tactic for emptying the notion of class of the pejorative implications of dictatorship, such that the substitution of proletarian for bourgeois hegemony becomes merely a euphemism for dictatorship.

[4] Bendix (1970, p529) defines managerial ideologies as "all ideas which are espoused by or for those who exercise authority in economic enterprises, and which seek to explain and justify that authority".

[5] Offe offers Davis and Moore's (1967) conception of the theory, which is predicated on the notions of scarcity and perceived functional importance. These writers argue that if the duties associated with the various positions in society were all equally pleasant, equally important to societal survival and required equal ability or talent, it would make no difference who got what position. In this regard Offe asserts that "because of the basic *shortage* of talents, the *ability* to solve problems that are important for society commands a high price (equal to high status) on the labour market" (p 48).

[6]   Frank's model of political economy in Latin America, cited in Langdon, (1974), shows how metropolis-satellite relationships have created poverty through direct surplus appropriation and internal monopoly exchange structures. According to this theory, the change process on the periphery of the world capitalist system is not an endogenous path through stages, but a process subject to powerful exogenous factors. Less Developed Countries (LDCs) thus play a subordinate role in the "metropolis-satellite" exchange relationship: selling primary products and purchasing advanced industrial inputs. This situation arises when the industrial sector is dominated by multinational companies. The contrary view is that the endogenous dialectic retains significance, eg Langdon, (1974); van Zwaneberg, (1974); Swainson, 1977; Leys, (1978).

[7]   Corporatism in Kenya goes even farther back: Langdon (1974) observes that in the colonial days, the pattern of racial privilege and regulated exchange inevitably gave the State a central role, making Kenya an "administered exchange economy" through the use of monopolistic rules and discriminatory state expenditure and patterns, rather than market institutions. The State managed Kenya's exchange relationship with the metropolitan centre, "generating considerable prosperity for a few, and poverty and stagnation for many".

[8]   The question of the revolutionary potential of workers in general has generated an interesting debate. Kerr et al (1964) claimed that "worker protest" would be a diminishing force as the "evolution of industrialism" unfolds. They argued that class conflict involving workers was on the decline because the enlightened self-interest of employees made them amenable to compromise with trade unions and, more ominously, because the elites have gained more experience in controlling worker protest. In the African context, these views are largely associated with Franz Fanon (1967) who rejects the workers' revolutionary potential and considers rural peasantry as the genuine revolutionary force. According to Fanon, the urban working class in Africa enjoys privileges at the expense of the rural peasantry, giving rise to a "labour aristocracy". Arrighi and Saul (eg 1973) also subscribe to this view, while Sandbrook and Cohen (1973) reject it, on the grounds that the unionised "better-paid" are not socially or geographically separated from the peasantry; dependency interrelationships are created by extended family pressures. Furthermore, worker protest has often encountered state brutality, both in the colonial era and in post-independent Kenya.

8 An Interpretive Analysis of HRM

This chapter completes our paradigmatic journey. The aim of this chapter is to advance the case for an interpretive analysis of organizational phenomena and to examine HRM "at the level of meaning". We begin by positing the interpretive paradigm, and discuss its relevance to organization theory. We then develop a social-anthropological perspective in which we examine the construction of HRM in everyday organizational life through ritualistic and symbolic behaviour. The chapter concludes by drawing from language philosophy to examine the use of rhetoric in the "totemic" conception of teamwork. [1]

The Interpretive Perspective

The interpretive paradigm is defined by a concern to understand the world as it is, i.e to understand the fundamental nature of the social world at the level of subjective experience (B/M, p28). Thus, the social world is seen as an emergent social process which is created by the individuals participating in the social process. According to B/M (p260), the interpretive paradigm:

> emphasises that the social world is no more than the subjective construction of individual human beings who, through the development and use of common language and the interactions of everyday life, may create and sustain a social world of intersubjectively shared meaning. The social world is thus of an essentially intangible nature and is in a continuous process of reaffirmation or change.

B/M argue that by the end of the nineteenth century, the positivistic position came to be seen as increasingly unsatisfactory and problematic on two counts:

1. Within the natural sciences (*Naturwissenschaften*), it became clear that the process of scientific inquiry was ill-equipped to deal with human values; ie the scientific method was not value-free.

2. In the cultural sciences (*Geisteswissenschaften*), it emerged that man as an actor could not be studied through the methods of the natural sciences; the search for general laws was thus inappropriate to the essentially spiritual character of human consciousness.

The interpretive paradigm comprises four key categories (B/M, p235): *solipsism, phenomenology, phenomenological sociology,* and *hermeneutics.* Hermeneutics includes the role and influence of language. For solipsism nothing exists outside of the mind. B/M distinguish between the *transcendental phenomenology* of Husserl: the quest for "pure consciousness", and the *existential phenomenology* of Schutz. Phenomenological sociology incorporates phenomenology and language philosophy, for example as in the work of Wittgenstein. Social constructionism can be added to the above (eg Berger and Luckman, 1966). Schutz's (eg 1964; 1967) existential phenomenology is of particular relevance in laying the foundation for an interpretivist analysis in this chapter. For Schutz, meaning is dependent upon *reflexivity,* ie, attaching meaning to experience retrospectively. Thus, we understand "the other person" by conceptualizing his actions as being of such and such a type (eg Schutz, 1967). It emerges from this that we should endeavour to understand the social world from the point of view of the social actors, using methods that derive from our everyday stock of knowledge.

An Interpretive Approach in Organization Theory

Linguistic ethnomethodology helps us to understand the use of language to create social reality and how this is subsequently explained to others through an "accounting process. The process of constructing social reality through everyday interaction can be understood through phenomenological symbolic interactionism. These perspectives are important in developing an interpretivist analysis of HRM. In this regard, this chapter focuses on subjective social acts with a view to unearthing the meanings that are embedded within HRM. We examine the symbolic nature of HRM activities, drawing from socio-anthropological thought. The emergent research in this tradition has adopted a broad range of approaches; some of them relate to culture and organizational symbolism. The study of culture, especially its symbolic manifestations, is one attempt to characterize social phenomena from the point of view of social actors.

"Organizational symbolism" in particular has provided an opportunity to explore the subjective aspects of organizational reality. For example, Trice and Beyer (1985) urge managers to uncover the beliefs and values underlying their corporate cultures by treating activities as "rites". Bolman and Deal (1984) and Pondy et al (1983) also focus on how symbolic approaches can enhance our understanding of organizational action. Morgan et al (1983) argue that symbolism pervades every aspect of organizational life for it is through the medium of symbolic processes that humans engage and give form and meaning to their world. Gowler and Legge have adopted an interpretivist approach to a number of issues, eg the images of the future of work (1986a), images of employees in company reports (1986b) and the meaning of *management* (1983). Stevenson (1990) draws from the interpretive paradigm to analyse hype and rhetoric in Information Technology. Ahlstrand (1990) adopts a symbolic analysis of productivity bargaining which he suggests complements the structural and political approaches. Gambling (eg 1977; 1987) draws from socio-anthropology to argue that accounting performs the same function in modern society which witchcraft performed in earlier times. An earlier study is Cleverly's (1971) insightful and rather witty assessment of ritualism and magic in organizations. Wilson (1992) examines the role of metaphors in engendering the acceptance and justification of actions. Watson's (eg 1994;1995) interpretations of organizational practices/changes including HRM (and the use of rhetoric) are also instructive in this regard.

More specifically within HRM Armstrong (1987) applies the metaphor of "the emperor's new clothes" to understand the rhetoric of HRM. In a study of history, ritual and myth in HRM, Ulrich (1984) argues that HRM executives would be able to understand the challenges of HRM better if they were more sensitive to the traditions, myths and rituals that constitute organizational reality. She goes on to describe these "manifestations of culture" as keys that can be used to open the "cultural lock" and facilitate desired changes. Berg (1986) adopts a perspective that sees organizations as "shared frames of meanings", "cognitive maps" or as "symbolic fields of action". He argues that managers should provide organizational members with a set of unifying symbols that can be used for self-orientation.

The study of language provides potentially rich material for the analysis of organizational reality. An example is Silverman and Jones' (1976) analysis of conversations to understand, *inter alia*, how organizations verbally construct "acceptable" selection criteria. Gowler and Legge's (1983) socio-linguistic approach depicts how management as an oral tradition simultaneously accomplishes the meaning of management and the management of meaning by use of "plain speaking" and "rhetoric". These approaches demonstrate how man as *rhetorician* (eg Harre, 1980) uses language to create and communicate meanings.

The foregoing illustrates some of the approaches available in the analysis of social reality in the interpretive paradigm. It is within this paradigm that the issue of meaning at the level of subjective experience is problematized. *It is argued here that HRM must be seen, within this paradigm, as a manifestation of ritualistic and symbolic behaviour which essentially seeks to "communicate meaning".* Man as a social being is engaged in an on-going exercise to create and redefine "meaning" within his social reality and to communicate and share this with others.

Ritualistic and Symbolic Behaviour

The analysis here draws initially from Beattie's (1964) treatment of ritualistic behaviour. Organizational actors may not be aware of the ritualism inherent in the activities they engage in, but an analysis within the interpretive paradigm reveals that valuable comparisons can be drawn between organizational behaviour and ritual behaviour in "pre-literate" society. The enactment of rites is a particularly revealing form of meaning-construction. Beattie illustrates this notion by stating that the person who consults a rain-maker and the rain-maker himself are asserting symbolically the importance they attach to rain and their earnest desire that it shall fall when it is required. Rites thus enact the state of affairs which it is hoped to bring about. It follows from this argument that to the extent that it largely involves belief and faith, ritual behaviour can be regarded as *magico-religious*. Beattie suggests that magico-religious phenomena have three broad psychological and social consequences:

1. Beliefs are seen as providing acceptable explanations for events which would otherwise be inexplicable, and thus acting as an antidote to doubt.

2. Magico-religious behaviour may provide a way of coping with situations of misfortune or danger. Ritual procedures thus become very useful when

there is no real "body of empirical knowledge", or when such knowledge is inadequate.

3. The relevance of the social context: thus the implications are not merely for the individuals but for social institutions.

Ritual has two main characteristics: the *expressive* and the *instrumental* (Beattie, 1964; Cleverly, 1971; Trice and Beyer, 1985). The "expressive" aspect means that rites can be regarded as a kind of language; by enacting a rite, social actors are trying to communicate something. The "instrumental" aspect, on the other hand, suggests that when people carry out certain rites they are trying to bring about some favourable or desired state of affairs, or to prevent some unfavourable or undesired ones. Three aspects of HRM are considered below: selection, socialization and appraisal.[2]

Ritualism in HRM

The rite of selection involves bringing new members into the organization. As noted earlier, the decision to hire was based on two sets of criteria: technical or academic qualification, and the perceived subjective "suitability", which was likened to the notion of "acceptability" (Silverman and Jones 1976). In this latter regard, managers relied on their subjective perceptions of who was a desirable employee. The illustration of a selection process (at Mimea) in chapter five is a case in point. The articulation of "organizational values" at Pharmaco and "service related values" at Automart offered guidance as to the type of employees the firm considered "suitable". The selection process involves a sequence of rituals: the initial requisition form completed by the line manager and approved by departmental head, ratification by Personnel and vetting of applications by Personnel and recruiting department. Initial vetting of application forms seeks to establish suitability on the basis of the job specifications.

The second stage of the selection rites is conducted by the hiring department; this seeks to establish suitability and predict the viability of a "fit" mainly on technical qualifications. The final rite is the interview, where the interviewers and interviewees "size each other up". A vital part of this recruitment ritual is the requirement of references and a satisfactory medical report. Managers reported that they would typically make up their minds about the candidates but still go on with these two conditions "because this was the practice". There are two sides to this activity: first, its meaning must be sought in the symbolism of the activity rather than in some problem-solving ability. Secondly, it serves to confirm to the selectors that they have made the "right" choice, and allays whatever misgivings they may hold about the candidates. To this extent, it is in keeping with Beattie's condition of providing an antidote to doubt.

Closely related to selection are the rites of socialization. These specifically relate to imbuing employees with organizational values both at initial recruitment and subsequent ceremonies such as parties and sporting activities. It was noted in previous chapters that in the majority of cases, comprehensive initial socialization at recruitment was restricted to the management trainee "core". Socialization also constitutes organizational *rites of passage* (van Gennep, 1960). There are three stages: separation (pre-liminal), transition (liminal) and incorporation (post-liminal). The three stages aptly describe organizational socialization as illustrated in Figure 8.1.

Concerning the recruitment of potential managers, the first stage is purificatory, and entails the elimination of those who will be least acceptable to the managerial society (Cleverly, 1971). It involves the removal of the taints of allegiance to the ideals of the previous culture by an assessment of application forms and at interview. The second stage represents a state of limbo; full integration is achieved in the final stage.

Figure 8.1 Rites of passage in socialization

1.*Rites of separation*   *previous "community"*

Actual departure from   status   school
one's community   age-group   other company

2.*Rites of segregation*   *venue*

Segregation is physical   sacred forest   training institute
novitiates have no
real status

3.*Rites of integration*   *new status*

Acceptance into   warriorhood   management trainee
new community   adulthood   "new hires"

At Autoco, in addition to the usual job description, the new hires have to sign a "change of status" form, which symbolically serves as a certificate of acceptance into the new order. Other forms of ceremonial ritual include formal lunches or "beer busts" with warm welcoming speeches by senior management. This approach gives the HRM policy of "integration" a new complexion. In addition to its being a quest for congruence (functionalist paradigm), as a tool of control (radical critique), it emerges here as a series of initiation rites, an exercise of symbolic significance, whose meaning is constituted in the enactment of institutional stages.

In this paradigm, the function of socialization which engenders stratification serves the expressive purpose of communicating to the "core" staff that they constitute a "valued" resource. At the same time, those who do not undergo the elaborate socialization process are in effect being told that their full integration into the organization is not considered very vital. Following Schutz, it is argued here that these activities come to create the everyday stock of knowledge and the typifications that define social organization (ie the hierarchy of power relations). This has implications for the success of a company-wide "integrative" approach to the management of employees. If indeed the exercise is underpinned by a stratified view of the perceived "value" of the staff, then any claim to institute an "integrative" approach is false.

Certain post-induction rites (eg sports and office parties) attempt to redress (or indeed to mask) social inequalities. With the exception of Chematox, sporting activities were seen as an occasion for all the staff to interact "on an equal footing". This effectively creates the impression of "equality". Year-end office parties also provide an opportunity for the blurring of class demarcations. A notable symbolic gesture was found in Chematox in the form of *role reversal* where managers serve the drinks. To the managers this signified the assumption of an unusual humble role. Cynical employees might see it as an effort to control the consumption of alcoholic and by implication, behaviour. The concept of *symbolic reversal* is well-recognized in anthropology (see for example Babcock, 1978).[3] This activity serves as an antidote to the "status structure" described by the Operations Director. By organizing parties where day-to-day precepts, roles and hierarchical positions are reversed, ignored or discarded altogether, the organizational actors are saying "let us forget for a moment (to paraphrase Orwell) that some people are more equal than others".

Cleverly (1971) describes this scenario as "Saturnalia" - he argues that office parties are only of use if the normal taboos are not only ignored but broken. According to Gluckman (1963) ritualized rebellions actually preserve and defend the political systems within which they occur. As such, their cathartic expressiveness offers the arena for the enactment of a regularized and controlled form of protest. Gluckman indeed points out that the rituals ease tension and that their codification and institutionalization is testimony to the capacity of established order to contain and defuse disorder. But the parties also provide an arena where conflicts and tensions are played out as in the party at Automart described earlier.

Performance appraisal is another important rite. On paper, it is an opportunity to renegotiate the manager-employee interface and in particular to determine whether the initial "fit" is still tenable. This "fit" would have been impacted upon over time by such factors as effort, expectations, changes in attitudes and perceptions, skills, management style, the nature of the task itself and various external factors. Appraisal is also an opportunity to test the "acceptability" criteria, and to thus establish whether the appraisee meets the conditions for continued membership of the organization. Ordinarily, these criteria are described in fairly "objective" terms, eg productivity, sales quotas, and so forth, which relate to the more technical part of the job. Other criteria such as punctuality, personal appearance, acceptance of responsibility, leadership qualities and dependability reflect a more subjective conception of "suitability". The appraiser is seeking to communicate to the appraisee the rationale for determining membership; this is made more forceful by subsequently rewarding or penalizing (usually by withholding rewards).

Silverman and Jones (1976, p171) portray the exercises of selection and appraisal in terms of stratification. In an assessment of the use of language to affirm a market hierarchy and thus how speech becomes a commodity, they assert that:

> To evaluate is to collect (persons into groups) in order to differentiate (such persons from others). In this way, to evaluate is to stratify, for by producing and distinguishing two groups, the acceptable and unacceptable, evaluation operations do stratification.

The above observation is also related to the "differential appraisal" observed in chapter six. From the foregoing, it may be concluded that the expressive element in appraisal is to communicate both suitability for membership and the positioning or status ascription in the organizational structure. This becomes clearer when appraisal is linked to the "achievement principle". Similarly, appraisal communicates values and other such desired organizational attributes. A good example is Pharmaco where the appraisal criteria are based on "organizational values". By asking the appraisee to rate his performance vis-a-vis clearly-laid down values, the organization is asking him to demonstrate - and indeed *justify* - his suitability. The individual and the organization are therefore involved, to this extent, in the definition of their reality.[4]

This reality is renegotiated as an annual ritual. The ritualism as described by managers takes various forms: where both the appraisee and the appraiser *know* that the former's performance is such that the appraisal will probably result in a commendation, a salary increment or promotion, then the exercise merely confirms expectations. They nevertheless go through the motions as this is what is expected of appraisals. The standard exercise would consist of the appraiser clarifying points raised in the self-appraisal (where applicable), with the appraiser asking most of the questions. The appraiser also plays a counselling role by trying to resolve whatever other (personal) problems the appraisee might be facing that impinge on performance or affect his/her socialization.

There also exist cases with a high tension content: the Personnel Manager at Automart described cases where the employee is torn between expectations of reward or penalty. This involves cases where employees complained that they were evaluated unfairly, or where disagreements revealed mutual distrust and suspicion. Appraisals thus constitute an arena which enables the actors to enact their respective realities: the appraisee may be questioning the legitimacy of the appraisal as a tool for the ordering of a socio-functional hierarchy. The appraiser on the other hand may be trying to impose the firm's definition of this hierarchy on the appraisee. The General Manager at Automart reported that certain incompetent individuals had received favourable reports from senior benefactors, hence favouritism. In such cases, the appraiser line manager would be compelled to give an initial favourable report because the appraisee enjoyed "protection from the top"; significantly, the appraiser is bound by this tacit knowledge.

Following tacit rules and procedures, both actors in the appraisal activity play their respective roles according to their everyday knowledge of what the activity calls for. Whether the exercise serves to confirm expectations, or as an arena for the enactment of conflict, the ritualism at once draws from and reconfirms the stock of knowledge about what a "typical" appraisal should look like, and what the "typical" roles of the actors are. This illustrates the importance of Schutz's (eg 1967) concept of the typifications that define the social world.

Performance appraisal also embodies the second element in the nature of a ritual: instrumentalism. The organizational actors believe that the enacting of the ritual will bring about certain desired states of affairs: the appraisee expects a reward (wage increase, promotion or the acquisition of more skills) while the appraiser, acting on behalf of the organization, expects a change in the appraisee's attitude, productivity and performance. The organization might also be more interested in the symbolism of the act or process, while at the same time anticipating favourable outcomes. This would amount to *magical symbolism*. According to Beattie (1964, p206):

> Magic is the acting out of a situation, the expression of a desire in symbolic terms; it is not the application of empirically acquired knowledge about the properties of natural substances. For the intelligent magician and his subjects it is the whole procedure, the rite, that is thought to be effective, not just the substances by themselves.

According to this view, magic is not only a way of thinking about things but also a way of doing things. The manner in which the rituals are carried out is just as important as the rite itself. Rites involving activities like selection, appraisal, sports, training and induction, promotions, retirement, and so forth do not merely constitute part of the "corporate culture". They represent the real essence of organizational life, and their enactment fulfils a sense of organizational continuity. Bolman and Deal (1984) contend that even though they may produce no results, such activities are still important; they serve as rituals and ceremonies that provide settings for drama, opportunities for self-expression, forums for airing grievances, and arenas for negotiating new understandings and meanings. The performance appraisal is a good example of an arena where both the appraiser and appraisee enact their requirements and expectations.

Impression Management and the "Accounting Process"

"Impression management" comes about when the actual performance of a ritual becomes more important than the expected results. Goffman (1959) has described "the acts of impression management" as the way individuals offer their performance and put on their show "for the benefit of other people" in social situations. He goes on to offer the "dramaturgical" perspective as a way of "ordering facts" (in addition to the technical, political, structural and cultural). Morgan et al (1983, p20) argue that:

> It is often not sufficient for activities to be performed so that given ends are fulfilled; it is the nature of the way in which they are performed that is sometimes all important, for the manner of performance reinforces or contravenes a whole range of symbolic meanings associated with the event in question.

The *theatrical* or *dramaturgical* metaphor explains how human beings utilize symbols to dramatize the ritual and routine of everyday interaction. According to Morgan et al (1983) human action unfolds through theatrical modes of presentation to an audience of some kind either real or imaginary. This appears consistent with Mead's (eg 1934) interactionist view whereby through an interpretation of the acts of the "generalized other", man becomes aware of the reality around him. Organizations are, from this perspective, involved in the business of impression management, thus invoking the cliche "there's no business without showbusiness". This illustrates the theatrical or dramaturgical mataphor which involves the use of dramatization of everyday social interaction.

It is important to consider how man makes actions "accountable to others". In this regard HRM can be seen as the construction of reality which organizational actors are concerned to communicate and in the process account for their activities. The whole exercise of the management of employees (just like other managerial functions) is, within the interpretive paradigm, concerned with creating and enacting certain desired impressions which define the organizational members' social world. This may be viewed in terms of the concept of "enactment" which Weick (1982, p287) treats as follows:

> In the process of acting out and "real-izing" their ideas, (people) create their own realities ... (ie) people make real or turn into a reality, those ideas that they have in their heads.

By instituting changes to the treatment of employees, management is acting out their beliefs about the "proper" way to treat employees; ie, they are offering a performance (eg Goffman, 1959) whose purpose is principally expressive. The audience comprises the existing and potential employees, the parent companies abroad[5] and the public at large. The HR Manager at Pharmaco said, for example, that the company wished to be *seen* at the forefront of the "HRM Movement" in the country. Therefore, the "impression" or "performance" that defined their approach to the management of employees was for an audience loosely defined as "the country". The image of "HRM" would therefore be expected to explain why the company treated its employees in such and such a manner. The "accounting process" thus reveals another dimension of the *expressiveness* of ritualistic behaviour.

According to Bolman and Deal (1984), organizational structures, activities and events serve to signal to the outside world that all is well. This also applies to rituals such as reform, and the use of complex symbols to indicate decisiveness in action. Thus by introducing a "new" approach to the management of employees, the organization is communicating to some audience a supposed re-orientation to the treatment of labour. The setting up of "high-powered" HR Committees such as in Pharmaco and Autoco, the linking of the human resource dimension to corporate strategy, the introduction of company-wide changes in training and development (eg at Pharmaco) and so forth; all these are signals to significant others (and to the employees themselves) that the employees are a "valued resource". These signals also mask the less palatable realities that relate to stratification; hence a dual purpose in expressive ritualism.

The second characteristic of magico-religious behaviour that Beattie addresses is the idea of coping with insecurity and anxiety. According to this view, people usually resort to magic in situations of actual or potential danger; magic thus provides a way of coping with situations of misfortune, danger or uncertainty. Evans-Pritchard (1937) for example observes that Zande magic works towards its ends by preventing mystical interference. Thus, its main purpose is to combat other mystical powers rather than to produce favourable changes. Beattie (1964) suggests that one way to cope with the various hazards in society in the absence of an adequate body of empirical knowledge is to *spiritualize the universe*, hence expressive and instrumental ritualism. Man in contemporary society still searches for incantations, potions and spells to survive in the face of the threats he senses around him (Cleverley, 1971). Similarly, Gambling (1987) defines the practices of accountants as "the rituals of a secular religion". Deal and Kennedy (1982) see rituals as rules guiding behaviour in corporate life; by providing the place and script with which employees can experience meaning, *rituals actually bring order to chaos*. Similarly Bolman and Deal (1984) attribute the reliance on images, symbols, luck and the supernatural to managers' limited abilities to create organizational cohesion through power or rational design. Humans therefore resort to symbolism to reduce ambiguity, resolve confusion, increase predictability, and provide direction. The significance of this point is evident in the turbulence and uncertainty that characterize the organizational environment in developing countries in general. Business-related uncertainties today echo those found in "traditional settings". It is believed that only certain unique individuals possess mystical powers that enable them to practice magic successfully - *sorcerers*.[6]

An example of sorcery in HRM is found in Pharmaco where an HRM consultant was recruited to set up and coordinate the new HRM/D function. He was made the HR Manager: a resident sorcerer. The Personnel Manager who was instrumental in articulating the HRM initiatives was left to deal with the more mundane, "traditional personnel" issues. This accords with anthropological observations that the magic of outsiders, especially those from distant lands, was considered more potent than that of local sorcerers.

Practices relating to HR/personnel assume an added dimension. Aptitude tests, reference letters and interviews become ways to establish a firm "fit" in order to circumvent the anxieties and potential conflicts that might arise from an ambiguous "psychological contract". This scenario is re-enacted during performance appraisal. Routine tests and appraisals are expected to yield some measure of "objectivity", thus achieving order and predictability in the face of uncertainty and doubt. Similarly, training/development may offer the requisite technical expertise as well as psychological assurance of being able to handle increasing responsibilities or more complex technology.

At the general level of planning, the notions of "luck" and "hope" were identified in Chematox and Automart. This was seen as complementary to the more rationalistic element in planning. The managers in these firms reported that the uncertainties noted above make the day-to-day managerial work very challenging indeed. This helps to account for the *ad hoc* way in which personnel issues have tended to be handled. The notions of *Management by Deciding* and *juggling with policy* are under the circumstances, appropriate approaches to create order out of the chaos of organizational anxieties.

Language and Rhetoric

Language has an important role to play in creating and sharing meanings, as typified by linguistic ethnomethodology. This is particularly the case in impression management and when individuals make activities accountable to significant others as noted above. Burrell and Morgan argue that within the hermeneutic tradition, language comes to represent an objectification of the human mind; hermeneutics thus aims to intepret the products of the human mind which characterize the social world. To this extent, we suggest that it is what is claimed about HRM that constitutes its essence: HRM becomes manifest through the claims made about it, through the forms of language and rhetoric used to describe it and in the day-to-day activities that involve managing people. Philosophers like Wittgenstein (eg 1963) have highlighted the importance of the meaning of language and its role in making sense of the world. This can be illustrated in Wittgenstein's (1963, #23) concept of "language games":

> the term 'language-game' is meant to bring into prominence the fact that the "speaking" of language is part of an activity, or a form of life.

This concept links the use of language closely with human interaction and the realization of human experience.

This perspective is developed further by Berger and Luckman (1966) who argue that language originates in and has its primary reference to everyday life. For our purposes, this indicates how the activities that comprise HRM may be seen to be constituted in the usage of language. The language used by organizational actors to describe HRM initiatives reveals to us the stock of knowledge that constitutes HRM. This section considers the verbal and non-verbal methods used to create and sustain certain notions of the reality of HRM either in the statements made in the interviews or in the ideas expressed in newsletters and other literature. To the extent that the purpose of such activities is both to shape and to communicate certain conceptions of the phenomenon, the language metaphor reveals HRM as an expressive verbal (or non-verbal) construct.

An interesting starting point is the view expressed by some sceptics that HRM is *merely* a rhetoric, by which they mean it is simply a verbal construct which does not accord with the actual practice.[7] In postulating HRM as rhetoric, Keenoy (1991) argues that in the absence of evidence of a "convincing practice" of HRM, this rhetoric reveals that HRM is more a consequence of normative appeal and ideological support. When the "practice" of HRM does not accord with prior notions of what constitutes the phenomenon, this leads some observers to perceive a gap between such "reality" and the "rhetoric". Within the interpretive paradigm, the analysis of social phenomena begins with the subjective experience of individual actors.

Thus, we treat the rhetoric as reality if we begin by examining the verbal claims made about it, without the handicap of prior conceptions as to what it comprises. Keenoy's assessment is perhaps helpful in that he sees the rhetoric as a means of "manufacturing meaning" to create a particular image or to sustain commitment and motivation in difficult times; the rhetoric may also serve both to motivate action and obscure undesirable realities. However, as Watson (eg 1995) has shown, those who write about and those who "practice" HRM are involved in a "double hermeneutic" in which they influence each other as they deploy language to construct social phenomena.

The sceptical view of HRM as mere rhetoric is also found in Guest's (1990) contention that HRM is yet another manifestation of the American Dream. Similarly, Armstrong's (1987) reference to "the emperor's new clothes" could be taken further to explore this metaphor. If it can be shown that extravagant claims are being made about the novelty of HRM, then Andersen's (The Emperor's New Clothes) metaphor is an apt description of HRM. The position adopted here is that there is a lot of diversity in the approaches adopted in the case studies. However, the appropriateness of this metaphor is retained even where it can be shown that a distinct HRM approach is being pursued, eg at Autoco and Pharmaco. Within the interpretive paradigm, the emphasis is on the meanings that people attach to the activities rather than on the activities themselves. Goffman (1959, p29) sees this as an illusion, though, and says that a performer can come "to be fully taken in" by his own act - he can be sincerely convinced of the concreteness of the impression of reality he is staging. Thus it is conceivable that the emperor and his subjects really believe he is wearing new clothes. For them, that constitutes a *reality*, rather than a mere false impression.

The notion of "rhetoric" is hereby linked to the earlier discussion of ritualism in Parkin's (1975, p119) observation that:

> Rhetoric, like ritual, may be more than a symbolic reaffirmation of social relations. Through rhetoric people have licence, so to speak, to explain and evaluate the causes and consequences of social relations, sometimes to the point of distortion.

Parkin describes rhetoric as a form of word-delivery, a type of ritual which says something about the speaker, the spoken-to, and the situation, and which goes beyond what is contained in the surface message. These views relate to Parkin's study of bureaucratic communication in a cooperative movement in Kenya. The study found that ideology involves rhetoric since it is "lavish in symbolism", and contains the following three elements: it is emotive; it contains multiple possible meanings or connotations, and offers scope for verbal and ideational creativity. Parkin represents plain speaking and rhetoric as two ends of a continuum; as symbolic content increases, one moves from "plain speaking" to "rhetoric". Gowler and Legge (1983) have developed this continuum to show how by constantly shifting from flowery speech to stark statement, managers use the ambiguity of rhetoric to arouse emotion and the clarity of plain speaking to direct behaviour. Kamoche's (1995) examination of the construction of meaning through rhetoric and ritualistic behaviour at Autoco also draws from Parkin's continuum to demonstrate the creation of the totem of teamwork through verbal and symbolic assertions. Some of this analysis is reported here.

The section below discusses a number of statements made mainly by the managers of Pharmaco, Mimea and Autoco. These statements illustrate how HRM activities are constructed by the everyday use of language.

Selected Statements Relating to HR Activities

1. We now consider employees as our most valuable resource (Managers in the three firms).

Various versions of this view were expressed in the three firms in particular and to a certain extent in Chematox and Automart. In its world-wide use, this statement is increasingly being seen as a cliché. The rhetoric creates an image of the employee as a valued resource, who possesses technical competence and scarce skills which the firm is committed to fostering (eg Gowler and Legge, 1986b). Interestingly, this rhetoric was not restricted to management. The following statement, taken from a newsletter at Autoco, indicates the extent to which management had succeeded in fostering this belief amongst the workers.

2. We believe we are the organization's greatest strength. Through our dedication and commitment to excellence, we are the key to achieving customer satisfaction goals (Worker, Trim Line).

The next 5 statements were made by the HR Manager at Pharmaco.

3. The introduction of HRD was necessitated by our recognition that problems of employee relations, motivation and morale lay in inadequate training, rather than in personnel administration work.

The supposed failures of the "traditional" personnel approach are the justification for the trying out of a new form of "magic". This new magic is designed to generate motivation and act as the impetus for organizational renewal, as in statements 4 and 5 below – illustrating the use of plain speaking to clarify organizational intentions:

4. HRD is expected to instil a sense of direction in the management of employees henceforth.

5. In order to meet our goal of creating a team of talented, highly motivated and skilled workforce, employee issues are now receiving much more attention at board level.

6. Our HRD approach begins from company specifics and goes on to individual specifics.

It is interesting that the use of the term "specifics" in fact masks the specificity of the approach the manager is describing. This is quite in keeping with the tendency for managers to adopt a type of speech that is highly ambiguous and flowery (Gowler and Legge, 1983). This form of word delivery is also found in the use of jargon and symbolism as in the statement below. The use of jargon reminiscent of the military or car-racing is expected to galvanize resolute action:

7. Rewarding in HRD means an "on-the-spot" rewarding system with "check-points" all through the year.

The above was explained as offering feedback on a continuous basis rather than simply at the annual appraisal, and systematically noting commendable performance which would be rewarded accordingly. In the statement below, jargon is employed to both obscure reality and create the impression of "positive" action despite the difficulty.

8. The appraisal of unionisable staff is almost unfeasible given the size of the workforce but we propose to "incentivize" remuneration (Personnel Director, Mimea).

The above statement effectively sought to mask the crucial point that the Personnel Manager had made to the effect that the appraisal of unionisable staff was "pointless".

Parkin (1975) has observed how the excessive use of symbolism in rhetoric captures attention and generates emotion. The statement below, for example, illustrates the use of flowery speech to achieve just such objectives. This statement was made by a marketing representative at Autoco upon receiving a trophy for the firm's performance in a product exhibition. The remarks were reported in a newsletter:

9. It is Autoco's tenacity for hard work, quality and excellence, a source of vast and shifting energies that manifests itself in business and engineering expertise that makes us a giant of substance, sprawl and splendour incarnate.

10. We are proud of our "corporate citizenship" image which we have cultivated through our community and charity activities; we do not therefore mind very much if people train with us and then leave the firm (Personnel Manager, Pharmaco).

From one point of view, this statement reveals how the firm is meeting the national developmental challenge. In another sense, however, it serves to reduce the organizational cognitive dissonance that arises from labour turnover. "Corporate citizenship" is offered to rationalize the unavoidable use of financial resources in a way that is ordinarily non-viable.

11. We identify "high flyers" at appraisal and design specific training for them (Personnel Manager, Mimea).

12. Although we still have faith in the machinery of collective bargaining, we expect that by offering workers better terms than the union can negotiate for, workers can have a stronger sense of commitment to the firm (Personnel Manager, Pharmaco).

Statements 11 and 12 reveal a power/political dimension to rhetoric. Statement 11 illustrates the use of rhetoric to justify the "achievement principle" (Offe, 1976), and the fostering of a managerial "core". Statement 12 demonstrates that the enhanced unitarism (reflected in a diminishing role for traditional collective bargaining) is also designed to achieve a shift in power balance: commitment to the firm is expected to rise, and by a similar token, commitment to the union is expected to decrease because workers' faith in collective bargaining will have decreased. Gowler and Legge (1981) see rhetoric in language as "political" in three ways: it serves to legitimize real or latent power and exchange relationships; it eliminates real or potential challenges to existing power and exchange relationships, and finally, it expresses those contradictions in power and exchange relationships that are otherwise difficult to admit or resolve. The rhetoric of achievement thus legitimizes the power structure in the organizational hierarchy, while the rhetoric of implied unitarism seeks legitimation from the workers by "offering more".

Rhetoric can also serve to express belief about social relations and desired social consequences, as illustrated by the two statements below:

13. Our staff welfare is fairly extensive, and this certainly creates a sense of loyalty and commitment. We therefore do have some Mimea people here, people who certainly belong (Personnel Director, Mimea)

14. It is true, and unfortunate that we have an excessive use of the stick syndrome here, and more could be done for us to be more together, but we do have some Chematox people here (Operations Director, Chematox).

Rhetoric Creates the Totem of the "Team" at Autoco

Following the argument advanced in preceding chapters about the viability of "teamwork", an attempt is made here to illustrate the role of rhetoric in realizing the concept of teamwork in Autoco, where the concept was most highly developed. We argue here that *the rhetoric of teamwork is a totemic approach to the reformulation of the unitarist ideology*. The term *totem* is taken from a North American Indian language. It symbolizes relationships between individuals in a clan or other social group (Levi-Strauss, 1964). According to Beattie (1964), a totem can be little more than a clan symbol or emblem, or something that signifies ritual avoidance.

As a magico-religious institution, it symbolizes the unity and solidarity of a group (Beattie, 1964). For the purposes of this discussion, "team" represents an organizational totem which both symbolizes the unification of diverse interests in the organization, and defines a common identity. Like a flag, a totem is held up to symbolize unified interests. At Autoco, the rhetoric of teamwork is repeated over and over again in such a way as to ensure that this totem is a constant reminder to all that it symbolizes and embodies their joint aspirations.

The organization members of Autoco see themselves pitted against hostile forces and uncertainties (especially market competition). Their totem is expected to generate the hope, conviction and strength to meet these challenges and achieve profitability and customer satisfaction. In his conception of symbolic management, Berg (1986) illustrates the notion of creating a sense of cohesion through organizational symbols in terms of such views as "we belong to the same tribe", or "we have the same totem". Berg (1986) recommends that management should create unifying symbols that give meaning to the organization and help them to take appropriate action.

The images of teamwork described below were taken from Autoco newsletters. The American Managing Director (MD) was described as making great efforts to foster a sense of "teamwork" and a team spirit in the firm. It was considered necessary that if such organizational themes as teamwork and customer satisfaction were to succeed, then the impetus had to be generated right from the top.

The MD's perspective The MD used language very effectively to direct action and offer a vision through a mix of plain speaking and rhetoric. Plain speaking gives specific guidelines for decisive action, thus directing and controlling behaviour.

1. As we pursue a strategy of growth, we must work as a team to achieve our objectives.

On concluding an emotive exhortation to the employees to re-dedicate their energies to serving the firm, the MD details out the challenges and observes that:

2. ...it is only through effective teamwork that we will succeed.

3. All of us on the Autoco team must now commit ourselves to doing the best in our respective areas to contribute to a strong finish in Calendar year 1990 ... We have the vision; we have the tools.

Statement 3 effectively captures the twin elements of the symbolic (ie the vision), and the more tangible (the technology and structure to achieve this).

On the parent company's vision for Africa, the MD said:

4. Several members of Autoco's staff and I attended an Autoco Inc. meeting in Cairo. The objective of this meeting was to review Autoco Inc's performance in Africa and to discuss its future in Africa... Autoco Inc is recommitting to growing its business in Africa.

This visionary picture which includes important major players assures employees that they are partners in a grand programme of action. It serves to impress them and capture their attention so that they can digest the strategic scenario that follows:

5. So what does the above mean for Autoco? ... We must now actively pursue a strategy of growth – that it, we must increase our factory output. We must increase from our recent average of 2400 units per year to our one-shift production capacity of 3500 units per year... As we pursue a strategy of growth, we must work as a team to achieve our objectives.

The MD then turns to symbolic language:

6. Success in the initial stages will bring about success in subsequent projects. So, although the early stages may be difficult as we plough new ground, we must pursue our plans doggedly to succeed from the start.

His exhortation ends with action-directed plain-speaking that reinforces the totem of the team:

7. If you need more details on how we plan to grow, and especially what is expected of you, talk with your immediate supervisor. Because only through effective teamwork will we succeed.

There can be no room for ambiguity where the situation calls for the accomplishment of the core structure of the totem. Rhetoric in turn furnishes the impressionistic embellishments on the surface as well as the underlying socio-psychological impulses that account for the existence of the totem. The role of ideology in rhetoric is clearly evident in these assertions. Ideology is generally regarded as the coherent and integrative sets of beliefs about the social world and how it is supposed to work (eg Apter, 1964; Beyer, 1981; Simons and Ingram, 1997). The notion that ideology links belief to action (eg Apter, 1964; Wilson, 1973) is an important device for helping us to appreciate how management at Autoco seek to create a desired pattern of social relations through the concept of a team. It is expected that once the organizational members *accept* the rationale for the team, including its integrative nature, organizational strategies become tenable. The wide use of teamwork across Autoco showed the extent to which the ideology was accepted. The term "team" was used fairly often in ordinary conversation, whereby people referred to the company in general or parts of it (eg a group, or department) as a "team". The statements below illustrate this:

A visiting executive director's comments on the "Quality of Working Life philosophy":

1. Autoco's enabling environment has enabled all employees to realize their capacities for growth and team performance.

2. We are trying to create a culture where we can all see ourselves as members of a team (Training Manager).

Upon the receipt of another superior product prize in a matter of months, the newsletter reported:

3. The Autoco team has received another first prize from the President (of the Republic)... within a space of a couple of months in style and glory.

On the same issue, a Sales/Marketing Officer reported, in typical flowery language:

4. Employees are feeling good about their power, their destiny and achievement and the brilliant performance has become a spectacular dramatization of the great Autoco's entrepreneurial energy and optimism.

After the firm had been selected by an international health body for a study, the Head Nurse reported:

5. The fact that our government, various companies and other organizations have used Autoco's clinic as their model should be cherished by all of us. It is yet another example of how teamwork can be effective in our day-to-day operations.

The totem of the "Autoco team" is held up for all to admire, envy and even emulate. The Head Nurse also said:

6. The Nursing team's main objective is that of promoting and maintaining the health of all Autoco employees. This stems from our belief that healthy employees are valuable assets to our organization.

The notion of teamwork is particularly relevant on the shopfloor where quality circles exist. Circles are referred to as "quality teams" and the workers as "quality makers". The "quality teams" meet every morning for 10-15 minutes to review the previous day's performance and set targets for the day. Their other major concern was described as "welfare concerns", or more specifically, personal problems. According to one Production Manager, these teams serve a useful purpose because "African workers have too many personal problems". When the circles were first started they received only lukewarm support from the workers until workers were allowed to introduce personal/family welfare issues on the agenda. This demonstrates the importance of teamwork vis a vis "organizational commitment" in a developing country context. The following statements were reported in a section for workers' in the newsletters:

1. We perform in friendly rivalry divided into small teams that define our jobs and monitor quality output. We conduct our own quality (Body shop).

2. It's the responsibility of everyone of us to be a leader. In Autoco we believe in leadership by example and in sharing the leadership task. And the test of leadership is the extent to which we contribute and work effectively as a team (Body Shop).

3. Mutual trust binds the Autoco team and prevails throughout the organization. Trust creates an openness in problem solving relationships and for this to flourish there must be openness, honesty and respect (Body Shop).

Trust, openness, honesty, and respect constitute the rule structure that governs social relations in the clan. The three statements below illustrate the acceptance of the MD's two enduring themes: teamwork and customer satisfaction, and the way in which the latter acts as a rationale for the former.

4. Total customer satisfaction is the master plan for us. To achieve the goals of the plan we are committed to the improvement of every aspect of the business. The foundations of this commitment are employees working together for the customer (Chassis line).

5. We know that technology is applied knowledge. We believe that through teamwork and technology we multiply our power to offer superior products to customers and to maintain leadership in the industry (Trim line).

6. Joined as a team in a spirit of cooperation, we are working to achieve a common goal ... total customer satisfaction (Chassis line).

Evidently, the team emerges as a totemic unifying device and a subtle way to re-confirm the unitarist organizational ideology. By giving employees a chance to address their personal welfare concerns and making the notion of teamwork real through quality-orientated activities, the team offers employees an opportunity for participation and a sense of identity. Managers are thus able to achieve organizational objectives, control of behaviour and to legitimize the desired structure of social relations through the use of language games.

Conclusions

This chapter has presented an interpretive approach to the analysis of human resource management. Within this paradigm, we have sought to understand the social phenomena by examining how social actors define and create their reality from subjective experience. This entails understanding HRM at the level of *meaning*, ie the meaning that individuals attach to their activities and how they explain these activities to others. In this regard, it has been necessary to preclude prior "objective" conceptions of the nature of the subject and to examine how the "meaning" of HRM actually comes to be constructed through language and social interaction. It becomes evident that HRM constitutes a form of ritualistic and magico-religious behaviour. Individuals as social actors make sense of the world around them and conduct various rites whose significance is in part found in the enactment itself. They undertake social activities to communicate the nature of their social reality to "significant others". They use language and rhetoric to express the desired states of affairs, to direct action and arouse emotion, and to relay as well as obscure certain realities. They also develop totems to foster kinship and a shared identity, and to achieve political and ideological ends.

Notes

[1] Much of this chapter is derived from Kamoche (1995), reprinted with permission from Plenum Publishing.

[2] It is suggested here that structuring the discussion on the basis of the three key dimensions of HRM as in the previous chapters may mask vital interrelationships between the dimensions here; furthermore, retaining that approach runs the risk of monotony without further elucidating the issues.

[3] Gluckman's (1963) "rituals of rebellion" yield further insights about the social function of acts of symbolic reversal. The rituals of rebellion involve reversals of "normal" gender behaviour and convention, whereby women in an African tribe "assert licence and dominance" as against their formal subordination to men. Other cases include princes behaving to the king as though they covet the throne, and subjects openly expressing their resentment to authority.

[4] It must be noted, though, that there is a power differential to the extent that the organizational requirements are formulated from the organization's point of view, yet the interpretive often ignores the power dimension.

[5] This mainly refers to Pharmaco, Autoco and Mimea, where parent company prompting played a big role in HRM initiatives.

[6] Cleverly (1971) suggests that management consultants, who possess systematically acquired knowledge or special skills have become the organizational sorcerers.

[7] The view that HRM is merely a "rhetoric" which is separate from the "reality" is not tenable in this paradigm. Here, the rhetoric is the reality; what the rhetorician says represents his understanding of the phenomenon, and what language does for him, therefore, is to objectify his subjective experience. The concern of the current perspective, therefore, is to examine how the reality of HRM is constructed through the expressiveness of language, ie through rhetoric.

9 Conclusion

This final chapter serves several purposes; first, it brings together the different themes and paradigms in order to present an overall picture of the analytical schema. Secondly, it recapitulates the diverse arguments that have been pursued in this book to indicate how they have enhanced our appreciation of the subject matter. Related to this is the spelling out of the key contributions that this discussion has sought to make. This chapter also indicates how the analyses have helped us to gain a greater awareness of the type of approach that is suitable in the management of employees in an African context. Conclusions are also drawn about Guest's model and multi-paradigm analysis. Finally a possible agenda for further research will be suggested.

A Summary

In seeking to characterize and critically examine the management of people, it was found expedient to conceive of employment practices in terms of "human resource management" (HRM). However, HRM was itself found to be problematic both in terms of its theoretical construction and practical application. This problematic nature of the concept has resulted in some confusion about what HRM really *is*. In order to attain clarity in both the theoretical and substantive issues, it was found necessary to undertake a trenchant analysis into the nature, origins and aims of HRM.

HRM thus emerges in many forms. In the first instance, it is an elaboration of the personnel function, with distinctiveness emerging only in so far as it offers "something new". Our historical perspective into the evolution of the *human side of enterprise* identified certain aspects that have captured the attention and imagination of theorists and practitioners, creating different patterns, styles and approaches in the management of people. In this regard, we can identify a number of sub-themes which help to account for the emergence of the HR phenomenon. These include the quest for status, power and legitimacy on the part of Personnel/HR practitioners, and no doubt, HR academics and consultants; the reformulation of managerial prerogative; the drive to offer some form of fairness in "equitable" practices; and the discovery that HR could be a source of competitive advantage.

These objectives are not necessarily mutually compatible, and in fact it could be argued that it is their very contradictory nature that has generated so much controversy. It becomes difficult, therefore to conceive of HRM as an internally consistent set of practices, especially when HRM is analysed in an international context characterized by cultural, economic and political diversity. This leads us to the next two central themes: how is the context for HRM in Kenya defined; and, how does a multi-paradigmatic analysis contribute towards an understanding of the issues and their implications for the adoption of HRM? The context was characterized in terms of those elements of the Kenyan business environment which are expected to impinge on the chosen approach to the management of employees.

The multi-paradigmatic scheme sought to reach beneath the surface level of the epistemological status of social phenomena. In addition to demonstrating that *our appreciation of the concept of HRM depends on the way we look at it*, it becomes readily apparent that the different *paradigmatic lenses* have different things to offer in helping us to determine how best to formulate an appropriate approach to the management of people. It is not proposed here to synthesize the paradigms into a "whole"; such an approach is untenable if we wish to permit each of the paradigms to develop in its own right. However, there is a case for inter-paradigm dialogue and paradigm elaboration because there is nothing particularly sacrosanct about Burrell and Morgan's conceptual axes and boundaries. These borders reflect a particular patterning of underlying assumptions; therefore, both the assumptions and borders can change. However, we need to guard against extreme relativism in going down that route. Therefore, the paradigmatic framework is for the sake of argument, taken as it is. The prospect of inter-paradigm debate permits the supposition that if the social theorist can learn the language and learn to use the tools of analysis of another paradigm, then it is possible to address the next important question: how is "progress" signalled in the formulation of knowledge?

The question of "progress" here derives from Hassard's (1987) doubts about the possibility of achieving progress and setting standards in the event of absolute hermetic isolationism. Two issues are relevant in this scenario: first, absolute hermeticism is rejected in favour of inter-paradigm debate while retaining paradigm incommensurability in the initial stages of conducting research. This allows each paradigm to mature and acquire legitimacy on its own terms. It should be recalled that the paradigm debate (and the search for knowledge) is not necessarily the quest for *truth*. There is no reason for us to believe that there is a paradigm out there that holds all the answers, and that we are engaging in inter-paradigm debate in order to discover the most useful paradigm. Multi-paradigmatic enquiry is first and foremost the quest for different forms of knowledge, and not exclusively a problem-solving exercise. It is also noted here that "progress" is not an end in itself.

For our purposes, "progress" is seen in two respects: first, in terms of enhancing our understanding of phenomena, and secondly, in terms of the "perceived value" of the form of knowledge. This perceived value refers to the importance that a community of scholars attaches to the outcomes of social enquiry, and therefore, how they "measure" such value on the basis of their need to understand and/experience the phenomenon, or how the paradigm helps them solve their problems. This has important implications for things like the transfer of management techniques, technology and so forth. The real "value" of such initiatives depends on how the community defines its needs and expectations.

A Final Look at the HRM Model

This section takes each of the dimensions of HRM, examines their tenability in the Kenyan context, and considers how the insights from the multi-paradigmatic enquiry might enable us to identify what factors hinder or foster the cultivation of HRM in the country.

The first strand in Integration is strategy. It was argued that long-term strategy has not been a central feature of management in Kenyan organizations. A strategic conception of HRM has, subsequently, not fully developed. Management has therefore tended to use an opportunistic and pragmatic approach in the management of labour. This permits the making of a categorical statement about the definition and relevance of the strategic dimension, given the popular view that a salient distinctive feature of HRM is the strategic dimension. If strategic HRM is taken to mean that the decisions relating to the management of employees flow from the strategic business plan, then the empirical evidence does not wholly show HRM in the case studies to be strategic. It is only at Autoco and Pharmaco that a strategic stance exists with respect to the management of employees in general, and in Mimea with regard to management development.

In Autoco and Pharmaco, this is facilitated by the HR Committees where

Personnel Managers (and a Personnel Director in Pharmaco) are able to represent HR issues at senior management level. The mission statements further help to shape the underlying ethos. In these three cases, however, the strategic dimension was seen from one point of view: how strategic decisions in finance, marketing and production affected personnel/HR and not vice versa. Through human resource development, Pharmaco aims to address the other side of the issue - a long-term, consistent strategy of developing employees is expected eventually to be a source of competitive advantage. The above derives from the definition of strategy as a deliberate, rational, and long-term consistent set of decisions (eg Andrews, 1987; Porter, 1985). An alternative view holds that strategy is emergent, political and incremental (eg Quinn, 1980; Mintzberg, 1985). In this latter regard, decisions are strategic to the extent that they commit the organization to a certain course of action for the foreseeable future, involving the commitment of resources (eg Purcell and Ahlstrand, 1989). This approach to strategy was evident in Automart - "Management By Deciding" - and at Chematox - "juggling". Too broad a description of "strategic HRM" therefore risks masking the complex circumstances found in specific cases.

The existing approach was necessitated by environmental uncertainty and institutional and structural weaknesses, and these factors in turn account for the problems of lack of coherence and consistency in the chosen approaches to HRM. All the firms were subject to these uncertainties, especially those relating to foreign exchange availability and exchange rate fluctuations, the political risk, consumer demand and labour market pressures. However, it was those firms (Pharmaco and Autoco) that had clearly defined a long-term strategic approach to HRM that appeared to operate with more certainty and less opportunism. Mimea operated a dual approach: a rational strategic approach for the "core" managerial staff, and an opportunistic one for the vast majority of the farm manual labour. The problems at Mimea were exacerbated by fluctuating foreign demand, which largely accounted for their high magnitude of casual and temporary labour; this best typifies the impact of market forces on numerical flexibility. Autoco and Pharmaco were also relatively small (as compared, for instance to Mimea and Automart) and maintained a small union labour force. Managers saw the advantage of small size in terms of feasibility and cost-effectiveness in administration and record-keeping, hence more rational strategic planning in recruitment and training, etc; closer inter-personal relations which facilitated teamwork; and performance appraisal. Size in itself is not a sufficient condition: witness the case of Chematox.

Financial position determines the firm's *ability* to invest in the human resource. Chematox maintained a relatively small training budget and poor records on training practices. This was also the smallest firm, both in terms of total workforce and sales. Autoco's and Automart's training investments were high; the latter's was accounted for by the training institute. Mimea's training budget per employee is held down by the low investment in the large size of farm labour force. The effect of technology and product-market factors is readily evident in Autoco in the form of one-model one-assembly line production. The relatively unchanging and supposedly unsophisticated nature of the technology permitted more systematic planning and the standardization of work practices and evaluation. Similarly, with this kind of production, it was relatively easier to form quality circles and operate on a team basis. Managers argued that they saw little need for any major re-orientation towards more line management involvement. If anything, there was an emphasis on strengthening the Personnel/HR function seemingly in line with the proposition made here that HRM seeks an enhanced status for the personnel/HR practitioners. An interesting case was Pharmaco where the Personnel and HR departments were being run in parallel. While Personnel was to retain the "administrative" personnel activities, including interfacing with trade unions, the HR department not only took over the functions of the training department, it also undertook a restructuring of the entire function of the management of employees. This constituted a centralization of HR practices, whereby line managers were "offered guidance" (in effect instructed) on how to streamline their HR activities. At the same time, line managers were expected to gradually assume a bigger role in HR issues.

Top management involvement is also argued to be a central feature of HRM and indeed a prerequisite to the success of HRM initiatives. This is borne out in the case studies and it further supports the aspect of power/status at Pharmaco, Autoco and Mimea. The other two organizations which had not embraced contemporary HRM had little personnel representation at top management level. The processual system in development which hinged on performance appraisal was suggested in chapter six as an appropriate way to conduct the exercise in that it enables the organization to both reward and develop on the basis of individual characteristics and needs identified at appraisal. Various difficulties in this system are identifiable, eg *differential appraisal*. This was justified on cost and structural-functionalist grounds and was reflected in the "core-peripheral" distinction which in turn was found to be underpinned by the *achievement principle*. Differential appraisal leads on to differential training.

Managers at Autoco and Pharmaco reported that the exercise is still limited by the union agreement which sets out the wage per grade. This also means that the typical shift towards more "individualized" rewarding arrangements in HRM is less evident in these cases, and is likely to remain so within the existing structure of industrial relations. The use of bonuses at Automart - the other company which has a thorough appraisal of a section of the unionisable staff - indicates a possible way in which organizations might institute individualized arrangements. However, this system exists at management's discretion and is a potential area of IR contention. This offers a good opportunity for union involvement, but part of the reason for management's reluctance to involve the union was because it might be opposed by other employers.

A link between training and rewarding was observed in terms of employee expectations. This was attributed to the pressures borne of low standards of living and instrumental orientations to work. It is essential to take these pressures into account without necessarily allowing them to dictate policy. There is scope for further research into this link. It was noted that the appraisal exercise itself deviated from the normative rational model, and was found to contain elements of subjectivity. It must be observed, however, that where a subjective approach is used either in selection or in appraisal, this reflects two things: the dual existence of technical and non-technical (social) aspects of work (eg Wood, 1986), and the inappropriateness of an overly rational approach. This latter point echoes the dual approach to strategy made above, and the relevance of "logical incrementalism"; a suitable integrative approach must be cognizant of these issues.

The *differential* approach observed above is related to a more profound stratification which is reflected in a complex variant of the "core-peripheral" distinction. This exists in the very first stages of the employment relationship: induction and socialization. Stratification on the basis of structural-functionalism, ie "utility", reveals the underlying rationale of the maintenance of a non-integrative approach, yet HRM is supposed to foster a harmonization of interests. The diverse interests amongst the constituents of Kenyan society make it difficult to achieve this harmonized, integrative picture. The radical critique facilitated an exploration of the meaning and implications of this reality. So, whereas on the one hand, the assumption of purposive rationality and the existence of "objective" knowledge within the functionalist paradigm permit the formulation of a rational model that seeks to attain certain ends, the functionalist paradigm is ill-equipped to handle the contradictions within the HRM model.

The concept of Commitment constitutes a further attempt to achieve congruence by matching the interests of the employees with those of the firm in the form of a viable "fit". Pharmaco is a good example of the way a "fit" is achievable by specifying "organizational values" and using these as criteria to determine acceptability. These values sought to spell out the "kind" of employees the organization wished to retain. An attempt to achieve a "fit" ought also to identify the perceived values of the individuals. This would enable managers to identify the employees' expectations and orientations to work, and thus make more informed decisions about how to manage the "fit". The definition of "organizational commitment" itself is highly problematic, particularly in view of the diversity of interests at the workplace.

It was therefore suggested that organizations might consider fostering a spirit of teamwork as pursued in Autoco. Teamwork helped to link group and organizational objectives and at the same time offer members a sense of identity which is a starting point in fostering a sense of belonging. The integrated team structure at Autoco ensures that group and organizational interests do not clash. In addition to the organizational objective to maximize customer satisfaction, which has been built into the organizational culture, the shopfloor teams in particular serve a useful social-welfare function. The concept of welfarism was found to be an imperative in the country generally. This is most highly developed at Mimea. Managers conceded that us-and-them attitudes are common in the country, and these introduce the spectre of managerial authoritarianism.

Welfarism without the price of authoritarianism would be an appropriate dimension to the practice of HRM. It must be noted that HRM as conceived in the West seems to assume that the welfare question has already been addressed adequately, especially at the level of the State, not merely in more obvious areas like unemployment benefits and health/medical schemes but in other seemingly unrelated but nevertheless important issues like education, infrastructure, consumer protection and good governance. The provision of schools and hospitals by Mimea is a case in point. There is clearly a constructive and developmental role for business in the community.

Various aspects of flexibility as formulated in our model were identified in the case studies. The general conclusion that numerical flexibility relates to the peripheral staff while functional flexibility relates to the core staff accords in general with the "flexible firm" model. However, the distinctions were not all that clear-cut. The overall picture was that of an implicit strategy based on the needs of the organizations, which subsequently translated into short-term responses to market changes in the case of the selection of casual and part-time workers. Similarly, the general lack of an adequate commitment to train employees raised doubt about the extent to which they can be regarded as "core" staff.

The focus on management development especially at Mimea and Chematox was a statement about what cadre was expected to contribute most to organizational effectiveness. This practice results in the sidelining of the majority of the workforce for the purposes of development. The distinction between "core" and "peripheral" staff was therefore found to be too simplistic to capture effectively the complex nature of the workforce structure. Similarly, the workforce structure itself varied from company to company, such that it is unrealistic to define a generalized picture. The existence of a multi-tiered development structure also poses a challenge to the achievement of a processual integrative approach in recruitment and development, ie to the dimension of Integration. Once again this was seen to reflect the underlying ethos of structural-functionalism.

There was some doubt about the centrality of Guest's dimension of Quality to HRM. A prescriptive stance would suggest that the recruitment and development practices should address specific policy objectives. This would require specifying how the organization intends to achieve integration through well thought out strategies that feed into procedural activities; the establishment of a thoroughgoing teamwork system; and the creation of selection and development practices that address the existing stratified approaches. A possible link to TQM was also proposed. On the whole, therefore, Guest's model is useful to the extent that it enables us to focus on specific aspects of HRM. However, its tenability in the Kenyan is mediated by contextual and conceptual considerations.

Final Thoughts on Multi-Paradigm Analysis

This section summarizes the concept of multi-paradigm analysis and considers the future of this kind of research in general. The purposes and benefits of multi-paradigm research are also considered. The challenge of bringing together the different paradigms potentially invites the charge of attempting a synthesis. The problem assumes a further dimension when we consider the impact of professional and institutional expectations. Hassard (1985) identifies various problems in this regard: pressures against paradigm diversity can be created by the nature of access agreements; the pressure to produce generalizable and publishable results; the lack of adequate training that would allow scholars to "transpect" between paradigms; a lack of adventurousness, and so forth. The key point Hassard's observations raise is that barriers result in orientation towards the more orthodox, positivist, and predominantly managerialist positions. We now consider how the implications of the multi-paradigm analysis can best be grasped.

The significance of the radical critique is evident in the first instance in the inability of the functionalist paradigm to deal effectively with controversies and contradictions in HRM. Drawing from critical theory and radical structuralism enabled us to address the forces of control and domination that emanate directly from the way society is constituted. The issue arose as to whether HRM is a "new" workplace hegemony, and if so, what does this mean to managers, especially in the formulation of HRM? The adoption of Gramsci's concept of hegemony revealed that the dimension of integration offers scope for the achievement of "active consent", which means that the managerial "class" would have recognized that diverse interests *do* exist, and would subsequently have to legitimize its position by seeking consent. This position differs from the practice in so far as managers in the case studies seemed, on the whole, to want to ignore the existence of the other major interest group: unions. This unitarist ethos is central to HRM thinking. An assessment of the dimension of commitment similarly reveals that the commitments of the different groups are deep-seated and perhaps irreconcilable.

The concept of hegemony enables us to draw from critical theory to link an organizational phenomenon to the broader societal reality - ie the totality of capitalism. The pursuit of an integrative approach would therefore be interpreted either as an attempt to mask the seemingly irreconcilable differences or to actually come to terms with them and seek ways to reconcile them. The ways in which this might be achieved is beyond the scope of this analysis; our concern here is to highlight the fundamental challenge to managers when they come to accept that the management of people essentially deals with exchange and power relations. The existing capitalist structure defines a certain hierarchy which places management high above employees. Managers therefore need to appreciate the implications of structure of privelege and status of which "core-peripheral" distinction is but one part. Additionally, it is worth contemplating whether by pursuing integration and commitment or even teamwork, managers are merely cultivating belief systems and ideologies that simply create the impression of integration.

The interpretivist paradigm sought to understand *meaning* from the point of view of individuals, ie *from the level of subjective experience*. The importance of this is that it enables us to examine action and relate that to what *is* going on in the minds of organizational actors. According to this paradigm, the world as we know it is created through consciousness, and it becomes "real" through such manifestations of behaviour as enactment, ritual and language. If we therefore accept that *reality* is constructed through what we say and what we do, it becomes clear that meaning must be sought in actions and in language. This also implies that both actions and language provide the medium through which certain *forms of meaning can be communicated*.

It becomes apparent from this that those who devise HRM policies and procedures are trying to communicate something to "significant others". The aspect of communicating meaning and offering accounts (or explanations) for chosen approaches and forms of behaviour helps us to unearth the "hidden meanings". A stratified form of socialization, differential appraisal and differential training send messages to significant others about the way the organization views them and their potential contribution to organizational effectiveness. Those cadres who receive regular, systematic training obtain the message that they are a valued resource while those at the "periphery" are in effect being told that their place in the organizational pecking order is lower and less significant. Generalizing about people being "the most important asset" is thus shown to be at best misleading.

Appreciating this interpretation may help managers to form more informed judgements about the effect implicit messages have on the perceived audience. Language is an even more direct form of communication. Conceiving of Wittgenstein's language games as "forms of life" enables us to ponder what reality particular language games might constitute and how therefore it is possible to structure and restructure social relations through the use of language. Rhetoric reveals various practical implications which are seen in terms of its purpose and the audience. As for its purpose, it was argued, following Parkin (1975) that rhetoric is emotive, ambiguous and rich in verbal and ideational creativity. By promulgating particular approaches to managing, or promoting certain procedures, management can draw from these aspects of rhetoric. The analysis of the constitution of a "team" through rhetoric revealed that this was indeed what Autoco was doing. The audience is also important, because communication requires that messages are sent from a particular source to a recipient, ie the "significant other(s)" who may well be specified or not. Thus, projecting the desired image to potential employees is particularly crucial to a firm's recruitment strategy. Through its ambiguous character, rhetoric also serves to obscure certain undesirable realities.

The view from social anthropology offered very useful insights in unearthing the meaning of acts and procedures which are interpreted as forms of ritual behaviour. The enactment of ritual therefore acts, *inter alia*, as a way of coping with imponderables and misfortune. Also, ritual emerges as both expressive and instrumental. In this regard, it is helpful for us to seek the meaning of an activity in the act itself. The enactment of appraisal might thus reveal to us that the appraiser is seeking to imbue the appraisee with certain organizational values (expressive), or that both the appraisee and appraiser are seeking to redefine their social relationship and bring about some desired change in behaviour (instrumental).

Similarly, viewing a team as a totem helps us to discover what purposes the team serves: is it just a term for some form of organizational structure or does it symbolize unified interests? The interpretivist paradigm therefore offers managers another way to understand the meanings of their actions and claims. They can therefore become aware of the hidden meanings in the chosen approach to manage employees, meanings which are otherwise lost or disregarded because managers are not aware of this analytical perspective.

Looking to the Future

Finally, although this chapter recognizes that the time frame of contemporary HRM in Kenya is relatively short, it has still been possible to identify some noteworthy trends. Thus we can propose provisional suggestions both about the direction of HRM in an African context. One important aspect of HRM is that it facilitates a re-focusing of managerial initiative on the question of the management of people. It is apparent, for example, that those companies which have adopted HRM or some variant of HRM have been able to highlight the management challenges as well as the needs of employees. The companies are however, in different circumstances, and it is apparent that the conditions identified in chapter three will have an impact on the approach specific firms choose.

There is scope for further research in this subject. It is hoped that the multi-paradigmatic scheme has opened the possibilities for research in the diversity of ways of conceptualizing organizational phenomena, including HRM. The post-modernist critique of HRM (eg Legge, 1995; Townley, 1993) is consistent with this view (see also Keenoy and Anthony, 1992). It may be possible, for example to pursue specific questions within the paradigms that have been considered as alternatives to the orthodoxy, in order to give attention to specific aspects of HRM, for example examining the incidence and role of totemism in various HR initiatives. It is also hoped that researchers might explore the prospects of paradigm dialogue. This might require researchers to be more sympathetic to alternative ways of "seeing", and to be more conversant with the *language and tools of analysis* in different paradigms.

There is also a need to determine what are the relevant quintessential worldviews in Africa and how these can be constituted in such a way as to inform the study of organizational phenomena. There clearly is a need to develop a critical perspective and to draw from disciplines like anthropology. Further research on management in Africa is also needed, so that we can fill the existing gaps in this field and gain a clearer picture of the challenges and problems of managing. It is hoped, finally, that this study will generate interest in other organizational forms, particularly indigenous small and medium-sized enterprises, whose lesser economic status presents them with a more acute set of challenges in the way they manage people.

Bibliography

Abudu, F. (1986) 'Work Attitudes of Africans, With Special Reference to Nigeria', *International Studies of Management and Organization*, vol. 16, pp.17-36.

Adler, N.J. (1986), *International Dimensions of Organizational Behaviour*, Kent, Boston, MA.

Ahiazu, A. I. (1986), 'The African Thought-System and the Work Behaviour of the African Industrial Man', *International Studies of Management and Organization*, vol. 16, pp.37-58.

Ahlstrand, B. (1990), *Productivity Bargaining*, Cambridge University Press, Cambridge.

Akinnusi, D.M. (1991), 'Personnel Management in Africa: A Comparative Analysis of Ghana, Kenya and Nigeria', in C.Brewster, and S.Tyson, (eds) *International Comparisons in Human Resource Management*, Pitman, London, pp.159-172.

Andrews, K.R. (1987), The Concept of Corporate Strategy, Irwin, Homewood, IL.

Angle, H.L. and Perry, J.L. (1986), 'Dual Commitment and Labour-Management Relationship Climates', *Academy of Management Review*, vol.29, pp. 31-50.

Apter, D.E. (1964), *Ideology and Discontent*, Free Press, New York.

Armstrong, M. (1987), 'HRM: A Case of the Emperor's new Clothes?' *Personnel Management*, August, pp.30-35.

Arrighi, G. and Saul, J. (1973*), Essays on the Political Economy of Africa*, Monthly Review Press, New York.

Atkinson, J. (1984), 'Manpower Strategies for Flexible Organizations', *Personnel Management*, August, pp.28-31.

Atkinson, J. and Meager N., (1986), 'Is Flexibility Just a Flash in the Pan?' *Personnel Management*, September, pp.26-29.

Babcock, B.A. (1978) *The Reversible World: Symbolic Reversal in Art and Society*, Cornell University Press, London.

Bamberger, P. Bacharach, S. and Dyer, L. (1990), 'Human Resource Management and Organizational Effectiveness: High Technology Entrepreneurial Start-up Firms in Israel,' *Human Resource Management*, vol. 28, pp.349-366.

Barley, S.R. (1980), 'Review of Burrell and Morgan (1979)', *Sloan Management Review*, Summer, vol.2, pp. 92-4.

Barney, J.B. (1991), 'Firm Resources and Sustained Competitive Advantage', *Journal of Management*, vol. 17, pp. 99-120.

Beattie, J. (1964), *Other Cultures*, Cohen and West, London.

Beer M., Spector B., Lawrence P., Mills D. and Walton R., (1985), *Human Resource Management: A General Manager's Perspective*, Free Press, London.

Bendix, R. 1970. *Work and Authority in Industry: Ideologies of Management in the Course of Industrialization*, Harper and Row, New York.

Berg, PO, (1986), 'Symbolic Management of Human Resource Management', *Human Resource Management*, Winter, vol.4, pp.557-79.

Berger, P. and Luckmann, T. (1966), *The Social Construction of Reality*, Penguin, Harmondsworth.

Beyer, J.M. (1981) 'Ideologies, Values and Decision Making in Organizations', in P.C. Nystrom and W.H. Starbuck (eds) *Handbook of Organizational Design*, Oxford University Press, New York, pp. 166-202.

Bhushan, K. (1988), *Kenya Uhuru Factbook*, Nairobi.

Blunt, P. (1980), 'Bureaucracy and Ethnicity in Kenya: Some Conjectures for the Eighties', *Journal of Applied Behavioural Science*, vol.16, pp.336-353.

Blunt, P. (1982), 'Worker Alienation and Adaptation in Sub-Saharan Africa: Some Evidence from Kenya', *Journal of Contemporary African Studies*, vol.2, pp.59-79.

Blunt, P. (1983), *Organizational Theory and Behaviour: An African Perspective*, Longman, London.

Blunt, P. (1990a), 'Recent Developments in Human Resource Management: The Good, the Bad and the Ugly', *International Journal of Human Resource Management*, vol.1,pp. 45-59.

Blunt, P. (1990b), 'Strategies for Enhancing Organizational Effectiveness in the Third World', *Public Administration and Development*, vol.10, pp.299-313.

Blunt , P and Jones, M (1992) *Managing Organizations in Africa*, Walter de Gruyter, Berlin.

Blyton, P. and Morris, J. (1992), 'HRM and the Limits of Flexibility', in P.Blyton, and P. Turnbull (eds), *Reassessing Human Resource Management*, Sage, London, pp. 116-130.

Bocock, R. (1986), *Hegemony*, Ellis Horwood, Tavistock.

Bolman, L.G. and Deal, T.E., (1984), *Modern Approaches to Understanding Organizations*, Jossey-Bass, San Francisco.

Boxall, P.F. (1992) 'Strategic Human Resource Management: Beginnings of a New Theoretical Sophistication?' *Human Resource Management Journal*, vol.1, pp.60-79.

Braverman, H. (1974), *Labour and Monopoly Capitalism*, Monthly Review Press, New York.

Bryman, A. (1988), *Doing Research in Organizations*, Routledge, New York.

Buchanan, B. (1974), 'Building Organizational Commitment: The Socialization of Managers in Work Organizations', *Administrative Science Quarterly*, vol.19, pp.533-46.

Buci-Glucksman, C. (1982), in A.S. Sassoon, *Approaches to Gramsci*, Writers and Readers, New York.

Bulmer, M. (ed) (1977), *Sociological Research Methods* Macmillan, London.

Burawoy, M. (1979), *Manufacturing Consent*, Chicago University Press, Chicago.

Burns, T. and Stalker, E. (eds) (1961), *The Management of Innovation*, Tavistock, London.

Burrell G. and Morgan G. (1979), *Sociological Paradigms and Organizational Analysis*, Heinemann, London.

Cappelli, P. and Singh, H. (1992), 'Integrating Strategic Human Resources and Strategic Management', in D. Levin, O. Mitchell and P. Scheller (eds), *Research Frontiers in Industrial Relations,* Industrial Relations Research Association, Madison, WI.

Castaneda, A, (1971) *A Separate Reality*, Penguin, Harmondsworth.

Chandler, A.D. (1962), *Strategy and Structure: Chapters in the History of Industrial Enterprise*, MIT Press, Chicago.

Chege, P.M. (1988), 'The State and Labour: Industrial Relations in Independent Kenya,' in P. Coughlin and G.K. Ikiara (eds), *Industrialization in Kenya*, Heinemann, Nairobi, and James Currey, London.

Child, J. (1981), 'Culture, Contingency and Capitalism in the Cross-National Study of Organizations', in L.L. Cummings and B.M. Staw, (eds) *Research in Organizational Behaviour*, JAI Press, Greenwich, CT, vol. 3, pp.303-356.

Clegg, S. (1982), 'Review of Burrell and Morgan, (1979)', *Organization Studies*, vol. 3, pp.380-1.

Cleverly, G. (1971), *Managers and Magic*, Longman, London.

Coopey, J. and Hartley, J. (1991), 'Reconsidering the Case for Organizational Commitment', *Human Resource Management Journal*, vol. 1., pp.18-32.

Currie, K. and Ray, L. (1984) 'State and Class in Kenya: Notes on the Cohesion of the Ruling Class', *Journal of Modern African Studies*, vol. 22, pp.559-93.

Dahrendorf, R. (1959), *Class and Class Conflict in Industrial Society*, Routledge and Kegan Paul, London:

Damachi, U.G. (1978), *Theories of Management and the Executive in the Developing World*, Macmillan, London.

Davies, L.E. and Cherns, A.B. (eds) (1975) *The Quality of Working Life*, Vols I and II, Free Press, New York.

Davis K. and Moore W.E. (1967), 'Some Principles of Stratification', in R. Bendix and S.M. Lipset (eds), *Class, Status and Power*, Routledge and Kegan Paul, London.

Deal, T.E. and Kennedy, A.A. (1982), *Corporate Cultures*, Addison-Wesley, Reading, Mass.

Dierickx, I. and Cool, K. (1989), 'Asset Stock Accumulation and Sustainability of Competitive Advantage,' *Management Science*, vol.35, pp. 1504-1511.

Edwards, R. (1979), *Contested Terrain*, Heinemann, London.

Entwistle, H. (1979) *Antonio Gramsci, Conservative School for Radical Politics*, Routledge and Kegan Paul, London.

Evans, P. A.L. (1986) 'The Strategic Outcomes of Human Resource Management,' *Human Resource Management*, vol. 25, pp.149-167.

Evans-Pritchard, E.E. (1937) *Witchcraft, Oracles & Magic Among the Azande*, Oxford University Press, Oxford.

Fanon, F. (1967). *The Wretched of the Earth*, Penguin, Harmondsworth.

Feyerabend, P. (1975), *Against Method*, New Left Review, London.

Flamholtz, E. (1985), *Human Resource Accounting*, Jossey-Bass, San Francisco

Fombrun, C., Tichy, N.M. and Devanna, M.A. (1984), *Strategic Human Resource Management*, Wiley, Chichester.

Fox, S. and McLeay, S. (1992), 'An Approach to Researching Managerial Labour Markets: HRM, Corporate Strategy and Financial Performance in UK Manufacturing,' *International Journal of Human Resource Management*, vol. 3, pp. 523-554.

Freire, P. (1972), *Pedagogy of the Oppressed*, Penguin, London.

Gambling, T.E. (1977), 'Magic, Accounting and Morale', *Accounting, Organizations and Society*, vol. 2, pp.141-51.

Gambling, T.E. (1987), 'Accounting for Rituals', *Accounting, Organizations and Society*, vol.12, pp.319-329.

Giddens, A. (1976), *New Rules for Sociological Method*, Hutchinson, London .

Glaser, B.G. and Strauss, A.L. (1967), *The Discovery of Grounded Theory*, Weidenfeld & Nicholson, London.

Gluckman, M. (1963), *Order and Rebellion in Tribal Africa*, Cohen and West, London.

Goffman, E. (1959), *The Presentation of Self in Everyday Life*, Doubleday, New York.

Gowler, D. and Legge, K. (1972), 'Occupational Role Development: Part 1', *Personnel Review*, Spring, vol. 1, pp.12-27; and Part 2', *Personnel Review*, Summer, vol.1, pp.58-73.

Gowler, D. and Legge, K. (1981), 'Negation, Sythesis and Abomination in Rhetoric', in C. Antaki, *The Psychology of Ordinary Explanations of Social Behaviour*, Academic Press, London.

Gowler, D. and Legge K. (1983), 'The Meaning of Management and the Management of Meaning', in M. Earl (ed), *Perspectives in Management*, Oxford University Press, Oxford.

Gowler, D. and Legge, K. (1986a). 'Personnel and Paradigms: Four Perspectives on the Future of Work', *Industrial Relations Journal*, Autumn, vol.17, pp225-235.

Gowler, D. and Legge, K. (1986b). 'Images of Employees in Company Reports: Do Company Chairmen View their Most Valuable Asset as Valuable?', *Personnel Review*, vol.15, pp.9-18.

Gramsci, A. (1971) *Selections from the Prison Notebooks of Antonio Gramsci*, edited by Q. Hoare, and G. Nowell-Smith (eds), Lawrence and Wishart, London.

Grant, R.M. (1991) 'The Resource-Based Theory of Competitive Advantage: Implications for Strategy Formulation', *California Management Review*, vol. 33, pp114-135.

Guest, D. (1987), 'Human Resource Management and Industrial Relations', *Journal of Management Studies*, September, vol. 24, pp.503-521.

Guest, D. (1989), 'Human Resource Management: its Implications for Industrial Relations and Trade Unions', in J. Storey, *New Perspectives on Human Resource Management*, Routledge, London.

Guest, D. (1990), 'Human Resource Management and the American Dream', *Journal of Management Studies*, July, vol.27, pp.377-397.

Habermas, J. (1972), *Knowledge and Human Interests*, Heineman, London.

Hart, T.J. (1993) 'Human Resource Management: Time to Exercise the Militant Tendency', *Employee Relations*, vol.15, pp.29-36.

Harre, R. (1980), 'Man as Rhetorician', in A.J. Chapman and D.M. Jones (eds), *Models of Man*, The British Psychological Society, Leicester.

Hassard, J.S. (1985), *Multiple Paradigms and Organizational Research: An Analysis of Work Behaviour in the Fire Service*, PhD Thesis, University of Aston.

Hassard, J.S. (1987), 'Multiple Paradigms in Organizations', *Graduate Management Research*, Autumn, vol.3, pp.4-34.

Hassard, J.S. and Pym, D. (eds) (1990) *The Theory and Philosophy of Organization*, Routledge, London.

Hendry, C. and Pettigrew A., (1986), 'The Practice of Strategic Human Resource Management', *Personnel Review*, vol.15, pp.3-8.

Hendry, C. and Pettigrew, A. (1990), 'Human Resource Management: An Agenda for the 1990s', *International Journal of Human Resource Management*, June, vol.1, pp.17-43.

Henley, J.S. (1977), 'The Personnel Professionals of Kenya', *Personnel Management*, 9.2, 10-14.

Henley, J.S. (1989), 'African Employment Relationships and the Future of Trade Unions', *British Journal of Industrial Relations*, vol.27.

Hofstede, G. (1980), *Culture's Consequences*, Sage, Beverly Hills, CA.

Hopper, T. and Powell, A. (1985), 'Making Sense of Research into the Organizational and Social Aspects of Management Accounting', *Journal of Management Studies*, vol. 22, pp.429-465.

Horton, R. (1967), 'African Traditional Thought and Western Science', *Africa*, Part 1 & 2, pp.50-71, pp.155-187.

Horton, R. (1982) in Hollis and Lukes, eds, *Rationality and Relativism*, Basil Blackwell, Oxford.

Horwitz, F.M. (1990), 'HRM: An Ideological Perspective', *Personnel Review*, vol.19, pp.10-15.

House, W.J. and Rempel, H. (1976), 'Labour Market segmentation in Kenya', *Eastern Africa Economic Review*, vol.8, pp.35-54.

Hyman, R. (1981), *Strikes*, Macmillan, Basingstoke.

Jackson, N. and Carter, P. (1991), 'In Defence of Paradigm Incommensurability', *Organization Studies*, vol.12, pp.109-127.

Jaeger, AM. and Kanungo, RN. (eds) (1990), *Management in Developing Countries*, Routledge, London.

Kamoche, K. (1990), *The Applicability of the Japanese Human Resource Management Model to Kenya*, MPhil Thesis, Oxford University.

Kamoche, K. (1992a) *A Multi-Paradigmatic Analysis of Human Resource Management in Kenya*, DPhil Thesis, Oxford University.

Kamoche, K. (1992b) 'Human Resource Management: An Assessment of the Kenyan Case', *International Journal of Human Resource Management*, vol.3, pp.497-521.

Kamoche, K. (1993) 'Toward a Model of HRM in Africa', in J.B. Shaw, P.S. Kirkbride, K.M. Rowland and G.R. Ferris (eds) *Research in Personnel and Human Resource Management*, JAI Press, Greenwich, CT., Suppl. 3, pp.259-278.

Kamoche, K. (1994), 'A Critique and a Proposed Reformulation of Strategic Human Resource Management', *Human Resource Management Journal*, vol.4, pp29-43.

Kamoche, K. (1995), 'Rhetoric, Ritualism and Totemism in Human Resource Management', *Human Relations*, vol. 48, pp.367-385.

Kamoche, K. (1996), 'Strategic Human Resource Management within a Resource-Capability View of the Firm,' *Journal of Management Studies,* vol. 33, pp213-233.

Kamoche, K. (1997), 'Managing Human Resources in Africa: Strategic, Organizational and Epistemological Issues', *International Business Review*, vol. 6, pp.537-558.

Kamoche, K. (2000) 'From Boom to Bust: The Challenges of Managing People in Thailand', *International Journal of Human Resource Management* (forthcoming)

Kamoche, K. and Mueller, F. (1998) 'Human Resource Management and the Appropriation-Learning Perspective', *Human Relations*, vol.51, pp. 1033-1060.

Kaniki, M.H.Y. (1981), 'Wage Labour and the Political Economy of Colonial Violence', *African Social Research*, June, vol.3, pp.1-26.

Keenoy, T. (1990), 'Human resource management: rhetoric, reality and contradiction', *International Journal of Human Resource Management*, vol. 1, pp.363-384.

Keenoy, T. and Anthony, P. (1992) 'HRM, Metaphor, Meaning and Morality', in P. Blyton and P.Turnbull (eds), *Reassessing Human Resource Management,* Sage, London, pp.233-255.

Keep, E. (1989), 'Corporate Training Strategies: The Vital Component?' in J. Storey, *New Perspectives on Human Resource Management*, Routledge, London.

Kerr, C., Dunlop, J.T.. Harbison, F.H. and Myers, C.A. (1964), *Industrialism and Industrial Man*, Oxford University Press, London.

Keto, T. (1989), *The African-Centred Perspective in History*, K.A., Blackwood, N.J.

Kiggundu, M.N. (1989) *Managing Organizations in Developing Countries*, Kumarian Press, Connecticut.

Kim, C.A. (1986) *Africanization and the Rise of a Managerial Class in Kenya*, DPhil Thesis, Oxford University.

Kitching, G.N. (1972), 'The Concept of Class and the Study of Africa', *The African Review,* vol.2, pp.327-350.

Kitching, G.N. (1977) 'Modes of Production and Kenyan Dependency', *Review of African Political Economy,* vol. 8, pp.56-74.

Kochan, T.A., Katz, H. and McKersie, R.B., (1986), *The Transformation of American Industrial Relations,* Basic Books, New York.

Kuhn, T.S. (1962; 1970a), *The Structure of Scientific Revolutions,* University of Chicago Press, Chicago.

Kuhn, T.S. (1970b), 'Reflections on my Critics', in I. Lakatos and A. Musgrave, (eds) *Criticism and the Growth of Knowledge,* Cambridge University Press, Cambridge.

Langdon, S. (1974), 'The Political Economy of Dependence: Note Toward Analysis of Multinational Companies in Kenya', *Journal of Eastern African Research and Development,* vol.4, pp.123-159.

Langdon, S. (1981), *The Multinational Corporation in the Kenyan Political Economy,* Macmillan, London.

Langdon S., (1987), 'Industry and Capitalism in Kenya: contribution to the debate', in P.M. Lubeck, *The African Bourgeoisie: Capitalist Development in Nigeria, Kenya and the Ivory Coast,* Lynne Rienner.

Laurent, A. (1986), 'The Cross-Cultural Puzzle in International Human Resource Management', *Human Resource Management,* vol. 25, pp. 91-102.

Lawler, E.L., Mohrman, A.M. and Resnick, S.M. (1984), 'Performance apraisal revisited', *Organizational Dynamics,* Summer, pp.20-35.

Legge K., (1978), *Power, Innovation and Problem-Solving in Personnel Management,* McGraw-Hill, London.

Legge K., (1989), 'Human Resource Management: A Critical Analysis', in J. Storey, (ed) *New Perspectives on Human Resource Management,* Routledge, London, pp.19-40.

Legge, K. (1995), *Human Resource Management: Rhetorics and Realities,* Macmillan, Houndsmills.

Leonard, D.K. (1977), *Reaching the Peasant Farmer in Kenya: Organization Theory and Practice in Kenya,* University of Chicago Press, Chicago.

Levi-Strauss, C (1962), *Totemism,* (Trans, Needham, R), Beacon Press, Boston.

Leys, C. (1975), *Underdevelopment in Kenya: The Political Economy of Neo-Colonialism, 1964-1971,* Heinemann, London.

Leys, C. (1978) 'Capital Accumulation, Class Formation and Dependency: The Significance of the Kenyan case', *Socialist Register,* pp.241-266.

Lockwood, D. (1956), 'Some Remarks on "The Social System"', *British Journal of Sociology,* vol.7, pp.134-43.

Long, P. (1986), *Personnel Appraisal Revisited,* IPM, London.

Louis, M.R. (1980), 'Surprise and Sensemaking', *Administrative Science Quarterly,* vol. 25, pp.226-251.

204 *Sociological Paradigms and Human Resources*

Lukacs, G. (1971), *History and Class Consciousness*, Merlin, London.
McCullough, A. and Shannon, M. (1977), 'Organization and Protection', in S. Clegg, and D. Dunkerley, (eds), *Critical Issues in Organizations*, Routledge and Kegan Paul, London.
McGregor, D. (1957), 'An Uneasy Look at Performance Appraisal', *Harvard Business Review*, vol.35, pp.89-94.
MacInnes, J. (1988), 'The Question of Flexibility', *Personnel Review*, vol.17, pp.12-15.
Mabey, C. and Salaman, G. (1995), *Strategic Human Resource Management*, Blackwell, Oxford.
Manning, K. (1983), 'The Rise and Fall of Personnel Management', *Management Today*, March, pp.74-77.
Marcuse, H. (1964), *One-Dimensional Man*, Routledge and Kegan Paul, London.
Marginson, P, Edwards, P.K., Martin, R., Purcell, J. and Sisson, K. (1988), *Beyond the Workplace, Managing Industrial Relations in Multi-Plant Enterprises*, Basil Blackwell, Oxford.
Marris, P. and Somerset, A. (1971), *The African Businessman: A Study of Entrepreneurship and Development in Kenya*, Routledge and Kegan Paul, London.
Maruyama, M. (1974), 'Paradigms and Communication', *Technological Forecasting and Social Change*, vol.6, pp.3-32.
Masterman, M. (1970), 'The Nature of a Paradigm', in I. Lakatos and A. Musgrave, (eds) *Criticism and the Growth of Knowledge*, Cambridge University Press, Cambridge.
Mead, GH, (1934), *Mind, Self and Society*, Chicago University Press, Chicago.
Means, R. (1988) 'Fighting Words on the Future of the Earth', in J. Zerzan, and A. Carnes (eds), *Questioning Technology*, Freedom Press, New York.
Mendonca M. and Kanungo R.N. (1990), 'Performance Management in Developing Countries', in A.M. Jaeger and R.N. Kanungo, *Management in Developing Countries*, pp.223-251.
Meyer, J.P. and Allen, N.J. (1988), 'Links Between Work Experiences and Organizational Commitment During the First Year of Employment: A Longitudinal Analysis', *Journal of Applied Psychology*, vol. 61, pp.195-209.
Miles, R., (1965), 'Human Relations or Human resources?' *Harvard Business Review*, July-August, vol.43, pp.148-63.
Miles, R. and Snow, C. (1984), 'Designing Strategic Human Resource Systems', *Organizational Dynamics*, Summer, pp.36-53.
Miller, D. (1987), 'The Genesis of Configuration', *Academy of Management Review*, vol.12, pp.686-701.
Miller N.M. (1984), *Kenya: the Quest for Prosperity*, Gower, London.
Miller, P. (1987), 'Strategic Industrial Relations and Human Resource Management - Distinction, Definition and Recognition', *Journal of Management Studies*, July, vol.24, pp.347-361.

Mintzberg, H. (1985), 'Of Strategies, Deliberate and Emergent', *Strategic Management Journal*, vol. 6, p.257-272.

Mobana, M. (1960), 'Towards an African Philosophy,' *Presence Africaine*, vol. 2, pp.73-85.

Morgan G., Frost P.J. and Pondy L.R. (1983), 'Organizational Symbolism', in L.R. Pondy, P.J. Frost, G. Morgan and T.C. Dandridge, (eds), *Organizational Symbolism*, JAI Press, Greenwich, CT.

Morgan, G. and Smircich, L. (1980), 'The Case for Qualitative Research', *Academy of Management Review*, vol.5, pp.491-500.

Mowday R., Porter L. and Steers R., (1982), *Employee-Organization Linkages: The Psychology of Commitment, Absenteeism and Turnover*, Academic Press, San Diego, CA.

Mueller, F. (1996) 'Human Resources as Strategic Assets: An Evolutionary Resource-Based Theory', *Journal of Management Studies*, vol. 33, pp757-786.

Munene, J.C. (1991), 'Organizational Environment in Africa', *Human Relations*, vol.44, pp.439-458.

Nelson, R.R. and Winter, S.G. (1982) *An Evolutionary Theory of Economic Change,* Belknap Press, Cambridge, MA.

Noon, M. (1989), 'Human Resource Management in Practice: a case study at Company Level", *Personnel Review*, vol.18, pp.15-23.

Nzelibe, L.O. (1986) 'The Evolution of African Management Thought', *International Studies of Management and Organization,* vol. 16, pp. 6-16.

Offe, C. (1976), *Industry and Inequality*, Edward Arnold, London.

Ogolla-Bondi, D. (1980) *The State and Trade Unions: A Study in State Control and Regulation of Union Power in Kenya.* LLM Thesis, Nairobi University.

Onah, JO. (1981), *Management Practice in Developing Countries*, Cassell. London.

Onyemelukwe C.C., (1973), *Men and Management in Contemporary Africa*, Longman, London.

Otite, O. (1978) *Themes in African Social and Political Thought*, Fourth Dimension, Enugu.

Parkin, D (1975), 'The Rhetoric of Responsibility: Bureaucratic Communication in a Kenyan Farming Area', in M. Bloch, (ed), *Political Language and Oratory in Traditional Society*, Academic Press, San Diego.

Penrose, E. T. (1959) *The Theory of the Growth of the Firm*, Wiley, New York.

Peters, T. and Waterman, R. (1982), *In Search of Excellence*, Harper and Row, New York.

Pinder, C.C. and Bourgeoise, V.W. (1982), 'Borrowing and the Effectiveness of Administrative Science' *Working Paper No. 848*, University of British Columbia, cited in J. Hassard, (1987).

Pondy, L.R., Frost, P.J., Morgan, G. and Dandridge, T.C. eds, (1983), *Organizational Symbolism*, JAI Press, Greenwich, CT.

Poole, MJ (1982), 'Personnel Management in Third World Countries', *Personnel Review*, vol.11, pp.37-43.

Popper, K.R. (1970), 'Normal Science and its Dangers', in I. Lakatos and A. Musgrave, (eds) *Criticism and the Growth of Knowledge*, Cambridge University Press, Cambridge.

Porter, L.R., Steers, R., Mowday, R. and Boulian, P. (1974), 'Organizational Commitment, Job Satisfaction and Turnover Among Psychiatrist Technicians', *Journal of Applied Psychology*, vol.59, pp.603-609.

Porter, M. E. (1985), *Competitive Advantage*, Free Press, New York.

Prahalad, C.K. and Hamel, G. (1990), 'The Core Competence of the Corporation', *Harvard Business Review*, vol. 90, pp.79-91.

Purcell, J. and Ahlstrand, B. (1989), 'Corporate Strategies and the Management of Employee Relations in the Multi-Divisional Company', *British Journal of Industrial Relations*, November, pp.396-417.

Quinn, J.B. (1980), *Strategies for Change: Logical Incrementalism*, R.D Irwin, Homewood, IL.

Radcliffe-Brown, R.A. (1952), *Structure and Function in Primitive Society*, Cohen and West, London.

Redding, S.G. (1994) 'Comparative Management Theory: Jungle, Zoo or Fossil Bed?' *Organization Studies*, vol. 15, pp.323-359.

Reed, M. (1985). *Redirections in Organizational Analysis*, Tavistock, London.

Salaman, G. and Thompson, K. (eds) (1973), *People and Organisations*, Longman, London.

Salancik G., (1977), Commitment and Control of Organizational Behaviour, in Staw, B. and Salancik, G., (eds), *New Directions in Organizational Behaviour*, St. Clair Press, Chicago.

Sandbrook R., (1975), *Proletarians and African Capitalism, The Kenyan Case*, 1960-1972, Cambridge University Press, Cambridge.

Sandbrook,R. and Cohen, R. (eds) 1973. *The Development of an African Working Class; Studies in Class Formation and Action*, Longman, London.

Schein, E.H. (1978). Career Dynamics, Addison Wesley, Reading, MA.

Schein, E.H. (1988) *Organizational Psychology*, Prentice-Hall, Englewood Cliffs, New Jersey.

Schuler, R.S. (1989), 'Strategic Human Resource Management and Industrial Relations', *Human Relations*, vol.42, pp.57-84.

Schutz, A. (1964), *Collected Papers, Studies in Social Theory*, Martinus Nijhoff, The Hague.

Schutz, A. (1967), *The Phenomenology of the Social World*, Northwestern University, Evanston.

Seddon, JW. (1985), 'The Development and Indigenisation of Third World Business', in V. Hammond, (ed), *Current Research in Management*, Francis Pinter, London.

Selznick, P. (1948), 'Foundations of the Theory of Organizations', *American Sociological Review*, vol. 13, pp.25-35.

Shweder, R.A. (1991), *Thinking Through Cultures: Expeditions in Cultural Psychology*, Harvard University Press, Cambridge, Mass.

Siddique, SA (1989), 'Industrial Relations in a Third World Setting: A Possible Model', *Journal of Industrial Relations*, September, vol.31, pp.385-401.

Silverman, D. (1970), *The Theory of Organizations*. Heinemann, London.

Silverman, D. and Jones, J. (1976), *Organisational Work: The Language of Grading/The Grading of Language*, Collier/Macmillan, London.

Simon, H.A. (1957), *Administrative Behaviour: A Study of Decision Making Processes in Administrative Organizations*, Collier/Macmillan, New York.

Simon R. (1982), *Gramsci's Political Thought*, Lawrence and Wishart, London.

Simons, T. and Ingram, P. (1997), 'Organization and Ideology: Kibbutzim and Hired Labour', *Administrative Science Quarterly*, vol. 42, pp.784-813.

Singh, M. (1969), *History of Kenya's Trade Union Movement to 1952*, East African Publishing House, Nairobi.

Singh, M (1980), *1952-56: Crucial Years of Kenya's Trade Unions*, edited by B.A. Ogot, Uzima Press, Nairobi.

Skinner W., (1981), 'Big Hat, No Cattle: Managing Human Resources', *Harvard Business Review*, September-October, vol.59, pp.106-114.

Stalk, G. Evans, P. and Shulman, L.E. (1992), 'Competing on Capabilities: The New Rules of Corporate Strategy', *Harvard Business Review*, vol. 70, pp. 57-69.

Stevenson, H. (1989), *Expert Systems, Hype and the Social Construction of Reality*, DPhil Thesis, Oxford University.

Storey, J. (ed) (1992) *Human Resource Management: A Critical Text*, Routledge, London.

Swainson, N. (1977), 'The Rise of a National Bourgeoisie in Kenya', *Review of African Political Economy*, January-April, pp.39-55.

Swainson, N, (1980), *The Development of Corporate Capitalism in Kenya, 1918-1977*, Heinemann, London.

Swainson, N (1987), in P.M Lubeck, (ed), *The African Bourgeoisie, Capitalist Development in Nigeria, Kenya and The Ivory Coast*, Lynne Rienner, London.

Tayeb, M. (1988), *Organizations and National Culture: A Comparative Analysis*, Sage, London.

Tayeb, M. (1995) 'The Competitive Advantage of Nations: The Role of HRM and its Socio-Cultural Context', *International Journal of Human Resource Management*, vol. 6, pp.588.605.

Thurley, K. (1981), 'Personnel Management in the UK: a case for Urgent Treatment', *Personnel Management*, vol. 13, pp.24-29.

Tichy, N.M., Fombrun C.J. and Devanna, M.A. (1982), 'Strategic Human Resource Management', *Sloan Management Review*, Winter, pp.47-61.

Torrington, D. (1988), 'How Does Human Resource Management Change the Personnel Function?' *Personnel Review*, vol.17, pp.3-9.
Townley, B. (1989), 'Selection and Appraisal; reconstructing social relations?' in J. Storey, (ed), *New Perspectives on Human resource Management*, Routledge, London.
Townley, B. (1990), 'A Discriminant Approach to Appraisal', *Personnel Management*, December, pp.34-37.
Townley, B. (1993), 'Foucault, Power/Knowledge, and its Relevance for Human Resource Management', *Academy of Management Review*, vol.18, pp.518-545.
Trice H.M. and Beyer J.M. (1985), 'Using Six Organizational Rites to change Culture', in Kilmann et al, (eds), *Gaining control of the Corporate Culture*, Jossey-Bass, San Francisco.
Trist, E.L. and Bamforth, K.W. (1951), 'Some Social and Psychological Consequences of the Longwall Method of Coal Getting', *Human Relations*, vol.4, pp.3-38.
Tyson, S. (1995), *Human Resource Strategy*, Pitman, London.
Tyson, S. and Fell, A. (1986), *Evaluating the Personnel Function*, Hutchinson, London.
Ulrich, WL (1984), 'HRM and Culture: History, Ritual and Myth', *Human Resource Management*, Summer, pp.23.2.
van Gennep, A. (1960), *The Rites of Passage*, (English trans), Routledge, London.
van Maanen, J. (1977), *Organizational Careers*, John Wiley, New York.
van Zwaneberg, R. (1974), 'Neocolonialism and the Origin of the National Bourgeoisie in Kenya Between 1940-1973', *Journal of Eastern African Research and Development*, vol.4, pp.161-188.
Walton, R.E. (1985), 'From Control to Commitment in the Workplace', *Harvard Business Review*, March-April, pp.77-84.
Walton, R.E. (1987), *Innovating to Compete*, Jossey-Bass, San Francisco.
Walton, R.E. and Lawrence, PR. (eds) (1985), *Human Resource Management: Trends and Challenges*, Harvard University Press, Cambridge, Mass.
Watson, T. J. (1977), *The Personnel Managers: A Study in the Sociology of Work and Industry*, Routledge and Kegan Paul, London.
Watson, T. J. (1986), *Management, Organization and Employment Strategy: New Directions in Theory and Practice*. Routledge and Kegan Paul, London.
Watson, T.J. (1994) *In Search of Management*, Routledge, London.
Watson, T.J. (1995), 'In Search of HRM: Beyond the Rhetoric and Reality Distinction or the case of the dog that didn't bark', *Personnel Review*, vol. 24, pp.6-16.
Waweru, E.M. (1975), *The Development of Personnel and Industrial Relations in Kenya*, MBA Thesis, Nairobi University.

Waweru, E.M. (1979), 'Capital Accumulation and Alienation at the Shopfloor Level: the Kenyan Situation', *Journal of Eastern African Research and Development*, vol.19.

Waweru, E.M., (1984), *Management of Human Resources in Kenya*, Kenya Literature Bureau, Nairobi.

Weick, K.E. (1982), 'Enactment Processes in Organizations', in B.M. Staw and G.R. Salancik, (eds) *New Directions in Organizational Behaviour*, R.E. Krieger, Malabar, Fl.

Weiss, R.M. and Miller, L.E. (1987) 'The Concept of Ideology in Organizational Analysis: The Sociology of Knowledge or the Social Psychology of beliefs?' *Academy of Management Review*, vol. 12, pp.104.116.

Wernerfelt, B. (1984) 'A Resource-Based View of the Firm', *Strategic Management Journal*, vol. 5, pp171-180.

Whipp, R. (1992), 'Human Resource Management, Competition and Strategy: Some Productive Tensions', in P. Blyton, and P. Turnbull (eds), *Reassessing Human resource Management*, Sage, London, pp. 33-55.

Wilkinson A. (1991), 'TQM and the Management of Labour', Employee Relations, vol.13, pp.24-31.

Willmott, H.C. (1990), 'Beyond Paradigmatic Closure in Organizational Enquiry", in Hassard and Pym, pp.44-60.

Wilson, F. (1992), 'Language, Technology, Gender and Power', *Human Relations*, vol.45, pp. 883-904.

Wilson, J. (1973) *Introduction to Social Movements*, Basic Books, New York.

Wittgenstein, L (1963), *Philosophical Investigations*, Basil Blackwell, Oxford.

Wood, S. (1986), 'Personnel Management and Recruitment', Personnel Review, vol.15.

Wright, P.M., McMahan, G.C. and McWillams, A. (1994) 'Human Resources and Sustained Competitive Advantage', *International Journal of Human Resource Management*, vol. 5, pp301-326.